Ethics, the Heart of Leadership

Ethics, the Heart of Leadership

Third Edition

Joanne B. Ciulla, Editor

Foreword by James MacGregor Burns

 PRAEGER

AN IMPRINT OF ABC-CLIO, LLC
Santa Barbara, California • Denver, Colorado • Oxford, England

Copyright 2014 by ABC-CLIO, LLC

All rights reserved. No part of this publication may be reproduced, stored in a retrieval system, or transmitted, in any form or by any means, electronic, mechanical, photocopying, recording, or otherwise, except for the inclusion of brief quotations in a review, without prior permission in writing from the publisher.

Library of Congress Cataloging-in-Publication Data

Ethics, the heart of leadership / Joanne B. Ciulla, editor ; foreword by James MacGregor Burns. — Third Edition.
    pages cm
Includes bibliographical references and index.
ISBN 978–1–4408–3067–9 (hardcover : alk. paper) — ISBN 978–1–4408–3065–5 (pbk. : alk. paper) — ISBN 978–1–4408–3066–2 (ebook) 1. Business ethics. 2. Leadership—Moral and ethical aspects. I. Ciulla, Joanne B.
HF5387.E875   2014
174'.4—dc23   2014015665

ISBN: 978–1–4408–3067–9 (hardcover)
ISBN: 978–1–4408–3065–5 (paperback)
EISBN: 978–1–4408–3066–2

18 17 16 15 14   1 2 3 4 5

This book is also available on the World Wide Web as an eBook.
Visit www.abc-clio.com for details.

Praeger
An Imprint of ABC-CLIO, LLC

ABC-CLIO, LLC
130 Cremona Drive, P.O. Box 1911
Santa Barbara, California 93116-1911

This book is printed on acid-free paper ∞

Manufactured in the United States of America

In memory of James MacGregor Burns
(1918–2014)

Contents

Foreword

James MacGregor Burns

Welcome to the new edition of *Ethics, the Heart of Leadership*—a brilliant and indispensable work that goes to the heart of both leadership and ethics, a crucial combination. If you are teaching a class in leadership and wish to start up a lively discussion, try posing that old chestnut of a question—"Was Adolf Hitler a leader?" The last time I tried this, in an honors course at the University of Maryland, a student vehemently answered, "Yes"—bad as he was, she said, he mirrored the hopes and hates of the German people, he won elections, and he fulfilled his promises by changing Germany along the lines his followers wanted—how could he not be called a leader? She had the class all but convinced and almost me. Almost.

It was not, of course, that she was in any way pro-Hitler, who stands as the most universally detested man in history. The problem was not confusion about Hitler but about the true nature of leadership. One of the many virtues of this excellent collection is Joanne Ciulla's confrontation at the outset of the question, What constitutes a good leader? This central question raises further questions about ethical and moral leadership. The problem is that in this book, and in many others on leadership, the richness and heterogeneity of the field of leadership have led to great confusion about the difference between ethical and moral leadership; some use the terms interchangeably in this volume and elsewhere.

I discern three types of leadership values: *ethical* virtues, old-fashioned character tests such as sobriety, chastity, abstention, kindness, altruism, and other "Ten Commandments" rules of personal conduct; *ethical* values, such as honesty, integrity, trustworthiness, reliability, reciprocity, accountability; and *moral* values, such as order (or security), liberty, equality, justice, and community (meaning brotherhood and sisterhood, replacing the traditional term *fraternity*).

Each of these types of leadership values has implications for styles and strategies of leadership itself. *Status-quo* leaders, presiding over relatively stable communities, are dependent on ethical virtues, rules of personal behavior, such as kindness and altruism, that make for harmonious communal relationships. *Ethical values* are crucially important to transactional leaders, whether in politics or education or other fields, who must depend on partners, competitors, clients, and others to live up to promises and understandings, as they must themselves. Responsibility and accountability are the tests here. *Moral values* lie at the heart of transforming leadership, which seeks fundamental changes in society, such as the enhancement of individual liberty and the expansion of justice and of equality of opportunity.

Wouldn't it be lovely, in this fragmented world, if all these three sets of values, and hence all these forms of leadership, could exist in happy harmony? Alas, it cannot be. The more that a community embraces *ethical* virtues of mutual helpfulness, the more it is likely to come into conflict with the ethical virtues of other communities—for example, in business practices, or in religious dogma and behavior. *Ethical* values too tend to be culture based and hence diverse. One society's honesty is another society's incivility; one society's reciprocity is another society's corruption.

Consider the question of manipulation—*managing* other persons' motives—which is so crucial to transactional leadership. Decades ago, in the April 1965 issue of the *Journal of Social Issues*, Herbert Kelman, recognizing increasing concern over ethical problems in the study of behavioral change, saw a basic dilemma: "On the one hand, for those of us who hold the enhancement of man's freedom of choice to be a fundamental value, any manipulations of the behavior of other constitutes a violation of their essential humanity. ... On the other hand, effective behavior change inevitably involves some degree of manipulation and control, and at least an implicit imposition of the change agent's values on the client or the person he is influencing." In short, a dilemma.

Of my three sets of values, I would guess that ethical values are most diverse from culture to culture. While ethical virtues have had far more relevance to modern market societies than to Third or Fourth World *traditional* cultures, transactional leadership values may become more universal as markets and privatization become more global. What about *moral* values? One might assume, in this ideologically torn world, with its fierce religious and secular conflicts, that moral values might be the most multifarious of all.

I believe, however, that the people of the world, even under diverse leaders, have been—slowly, gropingly, tortuously—shaping and rank-ordering sets of supreme principles. I believe the Enlightenment values of liberty, equality, and fraternity (community) are still evocative and controlling for vast numbers of people in the Western world at least. I believe that life, liberty, and the pursuit of happiness dominate not only the American *mass mind* but that of most other societies in the West. Despite numerous violations of its terms, the UN Universal Declaration of Human Rights continues as a moral standard for most nations of the world.

Moral values are not only standards by which we measure our character, our transactions, our policies and programs. They may also contain enormously evocative and revitalizing ideas, for which men and women fight and die. Hence, they can serve as transforming forces. But much depends on a crucial step—to translate ideals into action, promises into outcomes, "to walk the talk." Joanne Ciulla wrote me: "You have to make a lot of assumptions to make a value *do* something. You have to assume that because people value something they act accordingly, but we know this isn't the case. Value articulations of ethics often leave the door open for hypocrisy. Many people sincerely value truth, but often lie. People can also tell the truth, but not value it" (correspondence, March 1997). The test lies in *outcomes*—real, intended, and durable change.

And what is the relationship of all these values to *vision*? We think of vision as an overarching, evocative, energizing, moralizing force, ranging from broad, almost architectural plans for a new industry, say, to an inspirational, spiritual, perhaps morally righteous evocation of future hopes and expectations for a new political movement. Visions are often projected by charismatic leaders, calling for mass mobilization and action over the long run on many fronts, perhaps even for a revolution. To the extent that vision is transformational—that is, calls for real change—must it not embody supreme values in some kind of hierarchy? Otherwise would not vision be a kind of loose cannon, lurching back and forth as the visionary leaders follow their own guiding stars?

Another question posed by visionary leadership is the balance of cognitive and affective forces in change decisions. The proponents of visionary leadership do not deny that it embraces much that is spiritual and even emotional—they assert it. They like to point to Thomas Jefferson's famed dialogue between "the Head and the Heart" as proof that even a great Enlightenment rationalist understood the place of sentiment in the affairs of state as well as the affairs of people.

So, was Adolf Hitler a leader, measured by those three levels of values? He was a terrible mis-leader: personally cruel and vindictive, politically duplicitous and treacherous, ideologically vicious and annihilative in his aims. A leader of change? Yes, he left Germany a smoking devastated land. My student may have Hitler—I'll take Gandhi, Mandela, and King.

Acknowledgments

This book was originally published in 1998 and then in a second edition in 2004. Since the first edition, there has been a tremendous growth in work on ethics and leadership in general and the field of leadership ethics in particular. The most exciting thing about this is that there is more interest in leadership ethics by philosophers and scholars from a variety of disciplines outside of leadership studies.

Three chapters have been added in this new edition. Terry L. Price's "Why Leaders Need Not Be Moral Saints," Nannerl O. Keohane's "Democratic Leadership and Dirty Hands," and Joseph Nye's "What Is Ethical Foreign Policy Leadership?" Edwin P. Hollander's contribution, while on the same topic, is also new. With the exception of Michael Keeley's historical chapter, "The Trouble with Transformational Leadership," the rest of the chapters are so extensively updated and rewritten that they are virtually new as well.

Writing chapters for a collection like this is an act of generosity. I want to express my gratitude to the contributors for their willingness to take part in this project. I send my thanks to my editor, Hilary Claggett, who had worked on the second edition of this book and came back for the third. I'd also like to acknowledge Tammy Tripp from the Jepson School for her editorial assistance. Lastly, I am indebted to my friend and former colleague James MacGregor Burns, who wrote the foreword and to whom the book is dedicated. In the year of his 95th birthday, I asked him if he would revise the preface. He declined—at 95 he deserved a rest—but he sent me his good wishes in a sentence that he added to the foreword. I am also grateful to Burns for the many years of conversation and correspondence that we have had on the subject of ethics and leadership. While we don't always agree with each other, we both share the passionate belief that ethics are at the heart of leadership.

Introduction

Joanne B. Ciulla

Some people become leaders because they develop or possess certain talents and dispositions, charisma, or passions, or because of their wealth, military might, job title, or family name. Others lead because they possess great minds and ideas or they tell compelling stories. And then there are those who stumble into leadership because of the times they live in or the circumstances in which they find themselves. No matter how people become leaders, no one is a leader without willing followers. Managers, coaches, generals, and others may act like playground bullies and use their power and rank to force their will on people, but this is coercion, not leadership. Leadership is not a person or a position. It is a complex moral relationship between people, based on trust, obligation, commitment, emotion, and a shared vision of the good. Ethics is about how we distinguish between right and wrong, or good and evil in relation to the actions, volitions, and characters of human beings. Ethics lie at the heart of all human relationships and hence at the heart of the relationship between leaders and followers. The chapters in this volume explore the ethical complexities of leadership.

I dedicate this book to James MacGregor Burns because his theory of transforming leadership rests on the ongoing moral relationship

of leaders and followers. In his book, *Leadership*, Burns describes transforming leadership as a relationship in which leaders and followers
morally elevate each other. Leadership for Burns is about change and
sharing common purposes and values. The transforming leader helps
people change for the better and empowers them to improve their
lives and the lives of others.

In the foreword to this book, Burns laments that the authors in this
volume do not make a crisp distinction between ethical and moral
leadership and that they fail to consistently use the terms. If you look
the words up, you will see that ethics is defined as morals and morals
as ethics. In ancient times, the Romans translated the Greek word *ethi-
kos* into the Latin word *morale*. In the foreword Burns's definitions of
ethical virtues, *ethical values*, and *moral values* may be different from
the way other writers in this book define them, but rather than quibble
over terms, let us look at what he means. For Burns, the values of
moral leadership are those of the enlightenment, liberty, equality, and
community. This is a big-picture view of the ultimate ends of leadership. Most authors in this book probably believe in these ideals, just
as they would agree that leaders should be honest, fair, and just.
Nevertheless, in ethics, as with many things, the devil is in the details.
The chapters in this book probe the details of the many aspects of
ethics and leadership.

In the beginning I said no one is a leader without willing followers.
Most people agree that coercion is not leadership, but what is coercion
and what is a willing follower? How do we draw the moral line
between free will and subtle forms of manipulation, deception, and
the pressure that group norms place on the individual? Similarly, few
would argue with Burns's idea that the leadership relationship should
be one that morally elevates both parties, but here again, the details
matter. Elevate from what to what? Who determines which moral values are better and what are the criteria for better values? What if people don't want to be elevated? What if they incorrectly understand
the common good? Authors in this collection treat questions like this
in different ways.

The chapters in this book touch on three very general facets of
leadership ethics.

1. The ethics of the means: How do leaders motivate followers
   to obtain their goals? What is the moral relationship between
   leaders and followers?
2. The ethics of the person: Do leaders have to be saints?

3. The ethics of the ends: What is the ethical value of a leader's accomplishments? Did his/her actions serve the greatest good? What is the greatest good? Who is and isn't part of the greatest good?

These may all seem like obvious questions until you consider cases where a leader is ethical in some of these areas but not in others. For example, some leaders may be personally ethical but use unethical means to achieve ethical ends; other leaders may be personally unethical, but use ethical means, to achieve ethical ends, and so forth. This raises the question, Do leaders have to be ethical in all three areas to be ethical? Some might argue the only thing that matters is what the leader accomplishes. Others might argue that the means and ends are ethically important, but the personal morality of a leader is not.

The chapters in this collection examine the ethical challenges of leadership. The first section of the book provides two overviews of ethics and leadership, one from the perspective of leadership studies and one from business ethics perspective. In the first chapter, I extensively revised and updated my original article, written in 1995, called "Leadership Ethics: Mapping the Territory." I still argue that a greater understanding of ethics will improve our understanding of leadership and discuss why questions about the definition of leadership are really about what constitutes good leadership, where the word *good* refers to both ethics and effectiveness. There is much more research on ethics in leadership studies since I wrote the original article. I critically discuss this literature and to make the case for why leadership studies need research from the humanities as well as leadership ethics. Al Gini and Ronald M. Green have extensively rewritten and updated the chapter on the intersection of business ethics and leadership studies (Chapter 2). They offer an excellent profile of the issues and literature in both fields. They emphasize the role that "the witness of moral leadership" plays in improving the standards of business, organizations, and everyday life.

The second section of the book is about the relationship between leaders and followers. Distinguished leadership scholar Edwin P. Hollander examines the ethical challenges of authority and power in the leader-follower relationship. He argues that we need an inclusive leadership, which he describes as "[d]oing things *with* people, rather than *to* people." Hollander's chapter is about organizations, but it also has implications for the increasing disparities of wealth and power in many societies today. My chapter on "bogus empowerment" is about

honesty and the distribution of power in the leader-follower relationship. I examine the failure of empowerment schemes in the workplace
and argue that empowerment aimed at making people feel good, but
not at giving them resources and real discretion, is bogus. Real
empowerment requires honesty and a full understanding of how the
redistribution of power changes the leader-follower relationship.
Robert C. Solomon's chapter analyzes the role of emotions in the
leader-follower relationship. He begins by exploding what he calls
the myth of charisma. According to Solomon, charisma is not a quality
of a leader's character nor is it an essential element of leadership.
He believes it is a general and "vacuous" way of talking about the
complex emotional relationship of leaders to followers that is empty
of moral content. He argues that trust is the emotional core of the
leader-follower relationship and that we can better understand this
relationship by looking at how the leaders and the led give trust to
others.

The third section on the morality of leaders is new. Both authors
look at this issue in terms of ethics and what it takes for a leader to
effectively lead. Terry L. Price explores the provocative question about
"whether leaders ought to be moral saints." So much of the leadership
literature talks about leaders as role models and moral exemplars.
Price offers practical and moral reasons for why leaders do not have
to be saints and concludes that "We can expect leaders to work within
the bounds of morality, but we cannot expect them to do all that is
within their power never to approach morality's limits." In a similar
vein, Nannerl O. Keohane raises the question, "Must a political leader
who wants to govern effectively be prepared to behave immorally?"
The answer, she says, is not a simple yes or no. In it she discusses what
philosophers call "the dirty hands problem." This is when a leader
faces an ethical dilemma and is forced to pick one among several unsa-
vory options. Keohane uses Max Weber's "ethic of responsibility" to
examine the situations in which leaders should be held responsible
or allowed to have dirty hands in a democracy.

The final section of the book is about the ethical influence of leaders.
Popular media, communitarian writers, and recent management literature suggest that communities and organizations are rife with social
interest groups who pursue their own selfish interests without regard
for the common good. Burns, along with other scholars, believes transformational leadership offers a solution to this problem because it
refocuses people's attention on higher goals and collective interests.

Michael Keeley thinks this is a dangerous solution, one that James Madison and the Constitutional Convention of 1787 sought to thwart. Using examples from the organizational literature as well as history, Keeley argues that it is better to accommodate factions and individual interests by building them into the leader-follower relationship. For Keeley, a system of checks and balances is morally better than transforming people so that they share the same higher collective goals. In foreign policy the problems of factions take on new meaning because of the competing interests of nations and groups within them. In another new addition to the book, Joseph S. Nye, Jr., examines how leaders develop ethical and unethical foreign policies. In a chapter rich with examples of leaders and the ways they pursue foreign policy, Nye argues that there is little evidence that leaders with transformational objectives or inspirational styles are more effective or ethical. He argues that because the context of foreign policy is highly complex, it is sometimes better to have a leader who is not a visionary but a "careful gardener."

What is clear from all of these chapters is that the morality of leadership depends on the particulars of the relationship between people. It matters who the leaders and followers are, how well they understand and feel about themselves and each other, and the context of their relationship. It depends on whether leaders and followers are honest and trustworthy, and most importantly, what they do and what they value. Behind all of these things are broad philosophic questions such as: What is the common good? Do people have free will? How should we treat one another? What should be like? Who deserves what? These are eternal questions that have kept generations of leaders and thinkers up late at night. The chapters in this book probe what the answers to these questions mean for today's leaders. They offer the reader hands-on insights into the ethical dynamics that make the heart of leadership tick.

Part I

The Scope of the Issues

Leadership Ethics: Expanding the Territory

Joanne B. Ciulla

We live in a world where leaders frquently disappoint us. Meticulous biographers sometimes diminish the image of great leaders, such as Martin Luther King, Jr., and George Washington, by probing their moral shortcomings. It's difficult to have heroes in a world where every wart and wrinkle of a person's life is public. Ironically, the increase in information that we have about leaders has increased the confusion over the ethics of leadership. The more defective our leaders are, the greater our longing for highly ethical leaders. The ethical issues of leadership are found not only in public debates but lie simmering below the surface of the existing leadership literature.

I wrote this chapter soon after I began doing research on leadership ethics in 1992. In earlier editions of this book, it was called "Leadership Ethics: Mapping the Territory." Then and now most scholars and practitioners who write about leadership genuflect at the altar of ethics and speak with hushed reverence about its importance to leadership. Somewhere in almost any book or article devoted to the subject, you would find a few sentences, paragraphs, pages, or perhaps a chapter on how integrity and strong ethical values are crucial to leadership. Yet given the central role of ethics in the practice of leadership, it seemed remarkable the paucity of sustained and systematic treatment of the subject by scholars. In 1993, I did literature search of 1,800 article abstracts from psychology, business, religion, philosophy, anthropology, sociology, and political science that yielded only a handful of articles that offered any in depth discussion of ethics and leadership. Articles on ethics and leadership tend to be either about a particular kind of leadership (i.e., business leadership or political leadership), or a particular problem or aspect of leadership, or they are laudatory articles about the importance of honesty and integrity in leadership. For the most part, the discussion of ethics in the leadership literature has grown substantially. While a large portion of this literature is calcified around a few theories that mostly focus on management, there are more scholars from the humanities writing about ethics in leadership. In the first rendition of this chapter, I mapped the place of ethics in the study of leadership and argued that ethics should be at the heart of leadership studies. This chapter builds on that map to examine and critique some of the new territories of research. My goal is to help readers understand where we are and the importance of leadership ethics for getting us to where we need to go in leadership studies.

Throughout the chapter, I use the term *leadership ethics* to refer to the study of ethical issues related to leaders, followers, and leadership. Leadership ethics has emerged as a new and growing field of applied ethics. The study of ethics generally consists of examining questions about right, wrong, good, evil, virtue, duty, obligation, rights, justice, fairness, and responsibility in human relationships with each other and other living things. Leadership entails a distinctive kind of human relationship with distinctive sets of moral problems. Leadership studies, either directly or indirectly, aims to understand what leadership is and how and why the leader-follower relationship works. It looks at questions such as "What is a leader and what does it mean to exercise leadership?" "How do leaders lead?" "What do leaders do?" "Why do people follow?" and "What makes leadership work?" Recently, scholars have taken to calling the subject of ethics in leadership "ethical leadership." This is an unfortunate choice of words first, because sometimes this expression is refers to a very narrow construct, which I will discuss later, and second, because leadership ethics encompasses much more than descriptions of ethical and unethical leaders.

The goal of establishing a field called leadership ethics is to put it on equal footing with other interdisciplinary areas of applied ethics. So, for example, business ethics encompasses more than the study of ethical businesses and business people. In the first reference set on leadership ethics my coeditors Mary Uhl-Bien, Patricia Werhane and I describe leadership ethics this way: "Leadership ethics is the study of ethical problems and challenges that are distinctive to and inherent in the processes, practices, and outcomes of leading and following. In short, it examines the successes, failures, and struggles of the imperfect human beings who lead, aspire to lead, or follow."[1] The other function of leadership ethics is to offer a critical perspective on research in the field of leadership studies, which is where I turn next.

ETHICS WITHOUT EFFORT: ETHICS IN LEADERSHIP STUDIES

Ethics is one of those subjects that people rightfully feel they know about from experience. Most people think of ethics as practical knowledge, not theoretical knowledge. One problem in applied ethics is that scholars from other discipline sometimes feel that their practical knowledge and common sense (and exemplary moral character) are adequate for a discussion of ethics in their area of research. The resulting research is sometimes good, sometimes awful, but without some background in ethics, it is often not very informative. Philosophic writings on ethics are frequently ignored or rejected because the writing is obtuse or tedious and the content appears irrelevant to people writing about ethics in their own area of research or practice. Researchers often assume that philosophic ethics is simply a handful of theories, when in fact it also includes literature on metaethics, which focuses on the nature of moral reality and the logic and meaning of moral language.[2] This literature would be very useful for designing survey studies about ethics.

What continues to be striking about the literature in leadership studies is not the absence of philosophic work on ethics, but the fact that authors expend so little energy understanding the nature of ethics from any discipline whatsoever. For example, this is true of Joseph Rost's book, *Leadership in the Twenty-First Century*, which, when it was published, offered one of the better critiques of the field of leadership studies. The book is extensively researched and contains a terrific 24-page bibliography. However, the chapter on ethics stands out because there are relatively few references. After a very quick run through utilitarian, deontic, relativistic, and contractarian ethics, Rost concludes that "None of the ethical systems is particularly valuable in helping leaders and followers make decisions about the ethics of the changes they intend for an organization or society."[3] He then complains, "The first thing that I want to emphasize is that the ethics of what is intended by leaders and followers in proposing changes may not be the same as the ethics of those changes once they have been implemented. This troubling distinction is not often developed in books on professional ethics, but it does turn up time and time again in real life."[4] He not only condemns all ethical theories as useless, using only two citations, James Rachels's *The Elements of Moral Philosophy* and Mark Pastin's *The Hard Problems of Management*.[5] But he does not seem to understand ethical theories and how they might be used.

Scholars who reject or ignore writings on ethics, usually end up either reinventing fairly standard philosophic distinctions and ethical theories, or doing without them and proceeding higgledy-piggledy with their discussion. Rost concludes his chapter on ethics by saying, "Clearly, the systems of ethical thought people have used in the past and that are still in use are inadequate to the task of making moral judgments about the content of leadership."[6] Citing the work of Robert Bellah et al., William Sullivan, and Alasdair MacIntyre, Rost proposes "a new language of civic virtue to discuss and make moral evaluations of the changes they [leaders] intend."[7] Rost seems to miss the point that all of these books are reapplications of older traditions of ethics. Bellah et al. and Sullivan make this point clear in their books. Rost does not discuss virtue ethics in this chapter, so it is not clear whether he means to discard this too when he rejects "ethical theory." After dismissing ethical theory, Rost goes on to say that out of this new language there will "evolve a new ethical framework of leadership content, a system of ethical thought applied to the content of leadership, that actually works."[8] Rost does not really tell us what will take the place of all the theories that he has dismissed, but rather he assures us that a new system of ethics will emerge. At least Rost pays some attention to the literature in ethics—even if he spends most of his time throwing it out. Then he runs out of steam when it comes to offering anything concrete in regard to leadership, except for some form of communitarianism. Moreover, he never really tells us what is so distinctive about moral judgments in leadership that renders thousands of years of ethical theories useless.

Another more significant example of the paucity of research energy expended on ethics is *Bass & Stogdill's Handbook of Leadership*

(3rd edition), hailed by reviewers as "the most complete work on leadership" and "encyclopedic."[9] In the 1990s, this was considered the source book on the study of leadership. The book is 914 pages long and contains a 162-page bibliography. There are 37 chapters in this book, none of which treat the question of ethics in leadership. If you look ethics up in the index, five pages are listed. Page 569 contains a brief discussion of different work ethics, page 723 is a reference to the gender differences in values, and page 831 refers to a question raised about whether sensitivity training is unethical. The reader has to get to a subsection in the last chapter of the book called "Leadership in the Twenty-First Century" before there is a two-page exposition on ethics. What we are treated to on the first page of the handbook is a meager grab bag of empirical studies and one fleeting reference to James MacGregor Burns's argument that transformational leaders foster moral virtue.[10]

Bernard Bass, the coauthor of the handbook and one of the most influential researchers in the leadership studies, offers an aesthetic definition of ethics as a "creative searching for human fulfillment and choosing it as good and beautiful." He goes on to criticize other areas of professional ethics because they focus too much on negative vices and not on the good things. As we will see, this is one of the major differences between the social science and philosophic approach to ethics in leadership studies. The social scientists tend to describe what makes a leader good while philosophers tend to examine the things that keep leaders from being good.[11] (This explains why positive psychology has had such an impact on leadership studies.)[12] We obviously need to study both the good and the bad. Bass believes that research about ethics "determines the connection between moral reasoning and moral behavior and how each depends on the issue involved."[13] After reading these two pages, one gets little information about ethics and leadership. What is most remarkable about this section of the handbook is that it offers little insight into what the research questions are in this area. It is not surprising that the standard reference work on leadership does not carry much information on ethics, in part because there was not much research on it at the time.[14]

At the end of my discussion of Bass's 3rd edition in my first version of this chapter, I had concluded that after "all of the research that went into this book, Bass seems to wing it when it comes to talking about ethics." Needless to say, Bass was not happy about my critique, and he told me so. He later said that he would change the ethics section in the 4th edition of the book and he did. In the 4th edition, published 18 years later in 2008, the ethics section of the handbook is significantly longer and ethics is placed under the section "Personal Attributes of Leaders."[15] The section on ethics is better but in some ways reflects the problem an interdisciplinary subject like leadership ethics. Bass's section consists of a curious combination of topics that are mostly from business ethics, such as responsible and irresponsible accounting statements and corporate social responsibility. This makes sense because the subtitle of the handbook is "Theory, Research & Managerial Applications." There are short sections on unethical leader behavior and corruption and a longer section moral reasoning that mostly concerns the social science literature. This is true when Bass refers to philosophic theories of ethics such as Immanuel Kant's. The reference is not to Kant's work but to a mention of Kant in an article on stereotyping in *The Dictionary of Psychology*.[16] Yet, the problem with is not that this section lacks philosophy or isn't about ethics but that except for the empirical studies, most of it is not really about ethics in leadership. It consists of a lot of little pieces that do not hang together. This problem illustrates why we need an interdisciplinary field of leadership ethics—to pull together the literature and insights of descriptive and normative literature on ethics.

LEADERSHIP AND THE ROSETTA STONE

One of the problems with leadership studies is that most of the work has been done from disciplines such as management and industrial psychology so a large part of the research rests on what Joe Rost calls the industrial paradigm, which views leadership is good management.[17] Rost criticizes the field for overemphasis on things that are peripheral to leadership such as traits, group facilitation, effectiveness, or the content of leadership, which includes the things that leaders must know to be effective.[18] This is clearly the case if you look at the contents of Bass's handbook. The largest section in the book is on the personal attributes of leaders and management of organizations.

Marta Calas and Linda Smircich also offer a provocative critique of the leadership studies that indirectly helps to explain why there has been little work on ethics in the field. They point out the positivist slant in much of the leadership research (particularly research on leadership in psychology and business). According to Calas and Smircich, the "saga" of leadership researchers is to find the Rosetta stone of leadership and break its codes. They argue that because the research community believes that society puts a premium on science, researchers' attempts to break the Rosetta Stone have to be "scientific." Hence the "scientists" keep breaking leadership into smaller and smaller pieces until the main code has been lost and can't be put together.[19] This fragmentation accounts for one of the reasons why there is so little work on ethics and leadership. Ethical analysis generally requires a broad perspective on a practice. For example, in business, ethical considerations of a problem often go hand in hand with taking a long-term view of a problem and the long-term interests of an organization. History and the rest of the humanities for that matter are fundamental to understanding human interactions such as leadership in groups and societies.

Calas and Smircich observe that the leadership literature seems irrelevant to practitioners, whereas researchers do not feel like they are getting anywhere—nobody seems happy. They believe that leadership researchers are frustrated because they are trying to do science, but they know they aren't doing good science. The researchers are also trying to do narrative, but the narrative is more concerned with sustaining the community of researchers, than helping explicate leadership. This may be even more the case today than it was when they wrote their article. Calas and Smircich, like many others in the field, emphasize the necessity of a multidisciplinary approach to leadership studies.

It is interesting to note that two respected figures in leadership studies, John W. Gardner and James MacGregor Burns, both take a historical and somewhat multidisciplinary approach to the subject. John W. Gardner's book, *On Leadership*, is a simple and readable outline of the basic issues in leadership studies. Gardner writes as a practitioner. He held many distinguished posts in the government and in business and taught at Stanford. He offers a good common sense discussion of ethics and leadership in his chapter "The Moral Dimension." The phrase, *the moral dimension of leadership*, is still used sometimes in the leadership literature. The conceptualization of morality as a *dimension* of leadership rather than a part or element is significant in that it implies that it is another way of seeing the whole of leadership rather than simply investigating a part of it.[20]

Gardner's chapter on ethics is a thoughtful piece that uses examples from several disciplines. One reason why it is often quoted is because he is a talented wordsmith, he uses engaging examples, and he offers wisdom that comes from experience. Gardner lines up the usual suspects of evil leadership, such as Hitler and the Ku Klux Klan, and peppers his discussion with a diverse set of examples from history and politics. For the most part, his discussion of ethics is hortatory. He says that we should hope that "our leaders will keep alive values that are not so easy to embed in laws—our caring for others, about honor and integrity, about tolerance and mutual respect, and about human fulfillment within a framework of values."[21] Gardner offers some good advice on ethics, but that's about all.

James MacGregor Burns's book, *Leadership*, is one of the most influential books in leadership studies. Burns is a political scientist, historian, and biographer. He builds his theory of transforming leadership around a set of moral commitments. His theory and observations are not drawn from experiments but from real leaders in history. I will discuss Burns's work in more detail later in this chapter. What makes Burns's work compelling is that the multidisciplinary approach allows him to understand leadership as a whole and not as a compilation of small fragments.

PARADIGM, SHIFTING PARADIGM, OR SHIFTY PARADIGM?

For an investigation into leadership ethics to be meaningful and useful, it has to be embedded in the study of leaders, followers, and leadership. Again, it is worthwhile to make an analogy to business ethics. If courses and research on business ethics ignore existing business research and practice, then the subject of ethics would become a mere appendage, a nice but not a crucial addition to a business school curriculum and knowledge about business. Research and teaching in areas like business ethics and leadership ethics should aim not only at making business people and leaders more ethical, and they should help us reconceptualizing the way that we think about the theory and practice of business and leadership. This is why both areas of applied ethics must embed themselves into their respective fields.

There are two ways to understand the state of leadership studies using Thomas Kuhn's analysis in *The Structure of Scientific Revolutions*. Given the criticisms of the field, one might argue that there exists a paradigm of leadership studies, based primarily on the work done in business and psychology. Prior to the establishment of a paradigm, writing a textbook would be prestigious, because you would be making a new contribution to the field.[22] Kuhn says that one way you can tell if a paradigm has been established is if scientists enhance their reputations by writing journal articles that are "addressed only to professional colleagues, the men whose knowledge of a shared paradigm can be assumed . . ."[23]

For some leadership scholars, there is a paradigm of leadership studies and it is defined by social science research in management. In some of the prominent journals, it remains difficult for a methodologically sound, well-written, and researched humanities article to make it through the review process unless it extensively cites various social science approaches to leadership.[24] There are also relatively few scholars with degrees in the humanities in leadership studies. Whereas a social scientist that writes about ethics is not required to cite or even properly cite relevant articles from philosophy, history, or other areas of the humanities. Social scientists can be quite sloppy when they use literature from the humanities in part because they often do not know or think that there is any method to humanities research. Philosophic sources are sometimes taken out of context, quoted from second or third hand sources, or simply misunderstood. In one frequently cited article that ties authentic leadership to Martin Heidegger's concept of authenticity, I discovered that the authors had seriously misrepresent what Heidegger said and I was amused by the fact that they referred to philosophers from the Middle Ages as "middle aged philosophers."[25] The problem is that there still are not many reviewers with humanities background and reviewers from each discipline are literally speaking another language—a problem that goes far beyond definitions and accounts for why the lion's share of recent research on ethics in leadership stems from a few questionnaires.[26]

According to Kuhn, when a paradigm is established and researchers engage in "normal science," there is little discussion about rules or definitions because they become researchers working in that paradigm internalized them. Kuhn says, "lack of a standard interpretation or of an agreed reduction to rules will not prevent a paradigm from guiding research."[27] He points out that over time, the meaning of important terms can shift along with theories, which seems to be what has happened in leadership studies. Kuhn believes that scientific progress would be impeded if the meaning of terms were overly rigid.

Rost believes that because researchers all have different definitions of leadership, that the field cannot progress unless there is a shared definition of leadership.[28] But as Kuhn points out, this sort of definition is not really necessary if researchers are working in a paradigm, because definitions are internalized and unarticulated. If researchers have radically different definitions of leadership, meaning that the term *leadership* denotes profoundly different things, then either there never was a well-formed paradigm (so leadership studies is in a preparadigm phase), or there exists a paradigm, and that paradigm is shifting. In both cases, there would be considerable debate over definitions. However, if there is a paradigm among some researchers and they are still arguing over definitions, then there is a third alternative. There is a paradigm of leadership studies, but it is a shifty one. By this I mean, scholars do not really trust this paradigm, but they nonetheless stick to it and keep doing research in the same old ways. This is why some of them still lament that there has been little progress in the field. In recent years, there is less discussion about definitions of leadership, but the debate over definitions is quite telling in terms of understanding the place of ethics in leadership. One might also argue that the "good paradigm" of leadership as management is alive and well because most journals and the gatekeepers of them come from this paradigm, despite the agreement among most scholars that leadership studies should be interdisciplinary.

LOCATING ETHICS: WHAT DO THE DEFINITIONS REALLY TELL US?

Leadership scholars have spent quite a bit of time and trouble worrying about the definition of leadership. Rost analyzes 221 definitions to make his point that there is not a common definition of leadership. What Rost does not make clear is what he means by a definition. Sometimes he sounds as if a definition supplies necessary and sufficient conditions for identifying leadership. He says, "neither scholars nor the practitioners have been able to define leadership with precision, accuracy, and conciseness so that people are able to label it correctly when they see it happening or when they engage in it."[29] He goes on to say that the various publications and the media all use leadership to mean different things that have little to do with what leadership really is.[30] In places Rost uses the word *definition* as if it were a theory or perhaps a paradigm. He says that a shared definition implies that there is a "school" of leadership. When the definition changes, there is a "paradigm shift."[31]

Rost's claim that what leadership studies need is a common definition of leadership, which is off the mark for two reasons. One would be hard-pressed to find a group of sociologists or historians who shared the exact same definition of sociology or history. It is also not clear that the various definitions that Rost examines are that different in terms of what they denote. I selected the following definitions from Rost's book on the basis of the ones that Rost says most representative of each particular era. We need to look at these definitions and ask: Are they so different that there is no family resemblance between them, that is, would researchers be talking about different things?[32] What do these definitions tell us about different periods of history? and What do these definitions tell us about the place of ethics in leadership studies?

1920s [Leadership is] the ability to impress the will of the leader on those led and induce obedience, respect, loyalty, and cooperation.[33]

1930s Leadership is a process in which the activities of many are organized to move in a specific direction by one.[34]

1940s Leadership is the result of an ability to persuade or direct men, apart from the prestige or power that comes from office or external circumstance.[35]

1950s [Leadership is what leaders do in groups.] The leader's authority is spontaneously accorded him by his fellow group members.[36]

1960s [Leadership is] acts by a person, which influence other persons in a shared direction.[37]

1970s Leadership is defined in terms of discretionary influence. Discretionary influence refers to those leader behaviors under control of the leader, which he may vary from individual to individual.[38]

1980s Regardless of the complexities involved in the study of leadership, its meaning is relatively simple. Leadership means to inspire others to undertake some form of purposeful action as determined by the leader.[39]

1990s Leadership is an influence relationship between leaders and followers who intend real changes that reflects their mutual purposes.[40]

If we look at the sample of definitions from different periods, we see that the problem is not that scholars have different meanings of leadership. The word *leadership* does not denote radically different things for different scholars. One can detect a family resemblance between the different definitions. All of them talk about leadership as some kind of process, act, or influence that in some way gets people to do something. A roomful of people, each holding one of these definitions, would understand each other.

Where the definitions differ is in their connotation, particularly in terms of their implications for the leader-follower relationship. In other words, *how* leaders get people to do things (impress, organize, persuade, influence, and inspire) and *how* what is to be done is decided (forced obedience or voluntary consent, determined by the leader, and as a reflection of mutual purposes) have normative implications. So perhaps what Rost is really talking about is not definitions, but theories about how people lead (or how people should lead) and the relationship of leaders and those who are led. His critique of particular definitions is really a critique of the way they do or do not describe the implicit underlying moral commitments of the leader-follower relationship. For example Burns also criticizes leadership studies for bifurcating literature on leadership and followership. He says that the leadership literature is elitist, projecting heroic leaders against the drab mass of powerless followers. The followership literature, according to Burns, tends to be populist in its approach, linking the masses with small overlapping circles of politicians, military officers and business people.[41]

If the definitions mentioned earlier imply that leadership is some sort of relationship between leaders and followers in which something happens or gets done, then the next question is: How should we describe this relationship? For people who embrace the values of a democratic society such as freedom, personal autonomy, and equality, the most morally unattractive definitions are those that appear to be coercive, manipulative and dictatorial. Rost clearly dislikes the theories from the 1920s, 1970s and 1980s, not because they are inaccurate definitions, but because he rejects the authoritarian values inherent in them. Yet, one's choice of a definition can be aesthetic and/or moral and/or political (if you control the definitions, you control the research agenda). Nonetheless, theories such as the ones from the 1920s, 1970s, and 1980s may be quite accurate descriptions of the way some corporate and world leaders behaved back then and today.

The most morally attractive definitions hail from the 1940s, 1950s, 1960s and Rost's own definition of the 1990s. They imply a noncoercive participatory and democratic relationship between leaders and followers. There are two morally attractive elements of these theories. First, rather than *induce*, these leaders *influence*, which implies that leaders recognize the autonomy of followers. Rost's definition uses the word *influence*, which carries an implication that there is some degree of voluntary compliance on the part of followers. In Rost's chapter on ethics, he says, "The leadership process is ethical if the people in the relationship (the leaders and followers) *freely* agree that the intended changes fairly reflect their mutual purposes."[42] For Rost consensus is an important part of what makes leadership *leadership*, and it does so because free choice is morally pleasing. This free choice is usually based on shared goals and values. Philosopher Eva Kort distinguishes between proper and purported leader. She says that someone is a proper leader if people freely choose to follow her because she is doing her job the right way, whereas a purported leader is someone you have to follow because of her position.[43]

Along with Kort, the morally attractive definitions also speak to a distinction frequently made between leadership and headship (or positional leadership). Holding a formal leadership position or position of power does not necessarily mean that a person exercises leadership. Furthermore, you do not have to hold a formal leadership role to exercise leadership. Leaders may wield force or authority using only their position and the resources and power that come with it.[44] This is an important distinction, but it does not get us out of what I call "the Hitler problem," or how do you answer the question, "Was Hitler a good leader?" Under the morally unattractive definitions he is a leader, perhaps even a great leader, albeit an immoral one. Ronald Heifetz argues that under the great man and trait theories of leadership you can put Hitler, Lincoln, and Gandhi in the same category because the underlying value of the theory is that leadership is influence over history.[45] However, under the morally attractive theories, Hitler was not a good leader or not a leader at all. He was a bully or tyrant or simply the head of Germany.

To muddy the waters even further, according to one of Warren Bennis's and Burt Nanus's characterizations of leadership, "The manager does things right and the leader does the right thing," one could argue that Hitler was neither unethical nor a leader, he was a manager.[46] Bennis and Nanus are among those management writers who talk as if leaders are wonderful and managers are morally flabby drones. However, what appears to be behind this in Bennis's and Nanus's work is the idea that leaders are supposed to be morally a head above everyone else. The leader/manager distinction is a troublesome one in the leadership literature. One problem is that *leadership* is an overused word and is often used in place of the word management. If we look at the formal positions of leaders and managers in organizations, the leader's job requires a broad perspective on the operation and on the moral significance of policies and actions of the organization (this is part of the "vision thing"). Managing requires a narrower perspective that focuses on accomplishing the work of the organization. What complicates this distinction is that sometimes managers think and act like leaders and leaders think and act like managers. So in a way, Bennis and Nanus seem to be right. However, it is not that managers are unethical, but rather that idea of managing is different from the idea of leading.

So what does this all mean? It looks like we are back to the problem of definition again. The first and obvious meaning is that definitions of leadership have normative implications (the old, "there is no such thing as a value-free social science"). Leadership scholars, like many people who write about leadership, are often messy about the language they use to describe and prescribe. While it is true that researchers have to be clear about when they are describing and when they are prescribing, the crisp fact/value distinction will not in itself improve our understanding of leadership.

Leadership scholars who worry about constructing the ultimate definition of leadership are asking the wrong question, but ultimately trying to answer the right one. As we have seen from the examination of definitions, the ultimate question in leadership studies is not "What *is* the definition of leadership?" The ultimate point of studying leadership is, "What is *good* leadership?" The use of word *good* here has two senses, morally good and technically good or effective. These two senses form a logical conjunction. In other words, for the statement "She is a good leader" to be true, it must be true that she is effective *and* true that she is ethical. The question of what constitutes a good leader lies at the heart of the public debate on leadership. We want our leaders to be good in both ways. It's easy to judge if they are effective and that is the focus of most leadership literature from the social sciences, but more difficult to judge if they are ethical because there is some confusion over what factors are relevant to making this kind of assessment.

ETHICS AND EFFECTIVENESS

The problem with the existing leadership research is that few studies investigate both senses of good and when they do, they usually do not fully explore the moral implications of their research questions or their results. The research on leadership effectiveness touches indirectly on the problem of explicitly articulating the normative implications of descriptive research. The Ohio studies and the Michigan studies both measured leadership effectiveness in terms of how leaders treated subordinates and how they got the job done. The Ohio studies measured leadership effectiveness in terms of consideration, the degree to which leaders act in friendly and supportive manner, and initiating structure, or the way that leaders structure their own role and the role of subordinates to obtain group goals.[47] The Michigan studies measured leaders on the basis of task orientation and relationship orientation.[48] These two studies influenced a number of other research programs and theories, including the situational leadership theory of Hersey and Blanchard, which looks at effectiveness in terms of how leaders adapt their leadership style to the requirements of a situation. Some situations require a task orientation, others a relationship orientation.[49]

Implicit in all of these theories and research programs is an ethical question. Are leaders more effective when they are nice to people, or are leaders more effective when they use certain techniques for structuring and ordering tasks?[50] One would hope that the answer is both, but that answer is not conclusive in the studies that have taken place over the least three decades. According to Gary Yukl, the only consistent findings that have come from this research are that considerate leaders usually have more satisfied followers.[51] The interesting question is, "What if this sort of research shows that you do not have to be kind and considerate of other people to run a country or a profitable organization?" Would scholars and practitioners draw an *ought* from the *is* of this research?[52] It's hard to tell when researchers are not explicit about their ethical commitments. The point is that no matter how much empirical information we get from the "scientific" study of leadership, it will always be inadequate if we neglect the moral implications because as we have seen, the very idea of a leader and leadership is not value neutral. The reason why leadership scholarship has not progressed very far is that most of the research focuses on explaining leadership not understanding it.[53]

I have argued that leadership ethics centers on a simple question: "What is the relationship between ethics and effectiveness?"[54] In modernity, we separate out what a person is good at doing from a person's moral character. For example John Stuart Mill argues that the intentions of a person tell you about the morality of the person and the results of an action tell you about the ethics of the action.[55] So good leaders can do bad things and bad leaders can do good things. The question of ethics and effectiveness is grounded in the ancient Greek notion of *arête* or virtue as an excellence that encompasses moral excellence and technical excellence.[56] The two come together if you use ethics to frame your idea of effectiveness. When you do this, the Hitler problem disappears because regardless of what he accomplished and his influence over history, he was a bad leader. When we analyze the quality of Hitler or anyone else as a leader, we really have to ask three moral questions: Did he do the right thing? Did he do it in the right way? And did he do it for the right reason? The ethical analysis comes in the assessment of what we mean by right in these three questions, which are of course related to a variety of moral principles as applied to particular situations and contexts.

The definition problem illustrates how when people think of leadership, they often think of *real* leadership as *good* leadership. Its meaning is both descriptive and normative because our ideas and perceptions of leadership are in part socially constructed. James R. Meindl, Sanford B. Ehrlich, and Janet M. Dukerich's classic article on the romance of leadership demonstrates how the meaning of *leader* has been romanticized to the point where people think that leaders can and do control the fates of their organizations and followers.[57] People attribute all kinds of personal and moral qualities to their leaders, some of which are unrealistic and can lead to disillusionment about leaders. Meindl et al. caution that empirical studies often filter out attributions that are a unique part of how people construct their idea of a leader. Many attributions are the normative qualities at the heart of what leadership means. As we have seen, researchers and ordinary people often talk about what leaders are when they really mean what leaders should be.

The discussion of definition locates where some of the ethical problems are in leadership studies. As we have seen, ethical commitments are central to how scholars define leadership and shape their research. Leadership scholars do not need to have one definition of leadership to understand each other, they just need to be clear about the values and normative assumptions that lie behind the way that they go about researching leadership. By doing so, we have a better chance of understanding the relationship between what leadership is and what we think leadership ought to be.

NORMATIVE THEORIES

So far I have located the place of leadership ethics in definitions and in some of the empirical research on leadership. Now we look at two of the older normative leadership theories of leadership and then two of the more recent ones. James MacGregor Burns's theory of transforming leadership is compelling because it rests on a set of moral assumptions about the relationship between leaders and followers. Burns uses the terms *transforming* and *transformational* in his book. However, he prefers to refer to his theory as *transforming* leadership. Burns's theory is clearly a prescriptive one about what values constitute morally *good* leadership. Drawing from Abraham Maslow's work on needs, Milton Rokeach's research on values development, and research on moral development from Lawrence Kohlberg, Jean Piaget, Erik Erickson, and Alfred Adler, Burns argues that leaders have to operate at higher need and value levels than those of followers. A leader's role is to exploit tension and conflict within people's value systems and play the role of raising people's consciousness.[58]

On Burns's account, transforming leaders have very strong values. They do not water down their values and moral ideals by consensus, but rather they elevate people by using conflict to engage followers and help them reassess their own values and needs. This is an area where Burns is quite different from Rost. Burns writes "despite his (Rost's) intense and impressive concern about the role of values, ethics, and morality in transforming leadership, he underestimates the crucial importance of these variables." Burns goes on to say, "Rost leans towards, or at least is tempted by, consensus procedures and goals that I believe erode such leadership."[59] In other words. just because people agree that something is ethical does not mean that it is.

The moral questions that drive Burns's theory of transforming leadership come from his work as a biographer and a historian. When biographers or historians study a leader, they struggle with the question of how to judge or keep from judging their subject. Throughout his book, Burns uses examples of a number of incidents where questionable means, such as lying and deception are used to achieve honorable ends or where the private life of a politician is morally questionable.[60] If you analyze the numerous historical examples in Burns's book, you find two pressing moral questions shape his leadership theory. The first is the morality of means and ends (and this also includes the moral use of power), and the second is the tension between the public and private morality of a leader. His theory of transforming leadership attempts to characterize good leadership by accounting for both of these questions.

Burns's distinction between transforming and transactional leadership and modal and end values offers a way to think about the question "What is a good leader?" in terms of the relationship to followers and the means and ends of actions. Transactional leadership rests on the values found in the means of an act. These are called modal values, which are things like, responsibility, fairness, honesty, and promise keeping. Transactional leadership helps leaders and followers reach their own goals by supplying lower-level wants and needs so that they can move up to higher needs. Transforming leadership is concerned with end values, such as liberty, justice, and equality. Transforming leaders raise their followers up through various stages of morality and need and turn their followers into leaders.[61] Ideally transforming leadership entails the withering away of the leader.

As a historian, Burns concerns himself with the ends of actions and the change that they initiate. In terms of his ethical theory, at times he appears to be a consequentialist, despite, his acknowledgment that, "insufficient attention to means can corrupt the ends."[62] However, because Burns does not really offer a systematic theory of ethics in the way that a philosopher might, he is difficult to categorize. Consider for example, Burns's two answers to the Hitler question. In the first part of the book, he says quite simply that once Hitler gained power and crushed all opposition, he was no longer a leader. He was a tyrant.[63] Later in the book, he offers three criteria for judging how Hitler would fare before "the bar of history." Burns says that Hitler would probably argue that he was a transforming leader who spoke for the true values of the German people and elevated them to a higher destiny. First, he would be tested by modal values of honor and integrity or the extent to which he advanced or thwarted the standards of good conduct in mankind. Second, he would be judged by the end values of equality and justice. Lastly, he would be judged on the impact that he had on the well-being of the people that he touched. The third test has an Aristotelian twist to it. The relationship of leaders and followers and the ends of that relationship must rest on *eudaimonia* or happiness that is understood as human flourishing or as Aristotle says "living well and faring well with being happy."[64] According to Burns, Hitler would fail all three tests. Burns doesn't consider Hitler a leader or a transforming leader, because of the means that he used, the ends that he achieved, and the impact of Hitler as a moral agent on his followers during the process of his leadership.

By looking at leadership as a process and not a set of individual acts, Burns's theory of good leadership is difficult to pigeonhole into one ethical theory and warrants closer analysis. The most appealing part of Burns's theory is the idea that a leader elevates her followers and makes them leaders. He is also clear that followers can also influence and improve the morality of leaders.[65] Near the end of his book, he reintroduces this idea with an anecdote about why President Johnson did not run for reelection in 1968. Burns tells us, "Perhaps he did not comprehend that the people he had led—as a result in part of the impact of his leadership—had created their own fresh leadership, which was now outrunning his." All of the people that Johnson helped the sick, the blacks, and the poor now had their own leadership. Burns says, "Leadership begat leadership and hardly recognized its off-spring."[66] Transforming leadership aims at empowering followers and making them independent of their leaders.

The second example of a normative theory of leadership is servant leadership. Robert K. Greenleaf's book, *Servant Leadership: A Journey into the Nature of Legitimate Power and Greatness*, presents a view of how leaders ought to be. However, the best way to understand servant leadership is to read *Journey to the East*, by Hermann Hesse.[67] Hesse's story is about a spiritual journey to the East. On the journey, a servant named Leo carries the bags and does the travelers' chores. There is something special about Leo. He keeps the group together with his presence and songs. When Leo mysteriously disappears, the group loses their way. Later in the book, the main character HH discovers that the servant Leo was actually the leader. The simple, but radical shift in emphasis goes from followers serving leaders to leaders serving followers. The idea of a servant leader is a very old view of leadership that can be found in ancient Eastern and Western thought and is often used to describe religious leaders.

Servant leadership has not gotten as much attention as transforming and transformational leadership in the literature. Yet students and business people find it a compelling characterization of leadership.[68] According to Robert Greenleaf, the servant leader leads because he or she wants to serve others. People follow servant leaders freely because they trust them. Like the transforming leader, the servant leader elevates people. Greenleaf says servant leadership must pass this test: "Do those served grow as persons? Do they *while being served* become healthier, wiser, freer, more autonomous, more likely themselves to become servants?" He goes on and adds a Rawlsian proviso, "*And, what is the effect on the least privileged in society?*"[69] As normative theories of leadership both servant leadership and transforming leadership are areas of leadership ethics that are open to ethical analysis and provide a foundation of ideas for developing normative theories of leadership.

Ethics by Questionnaire[70]

If you want to make a name for yourself in the social science paradigm of leadership studies, you need a good questionnaire. Most of the articles published on ethics in leadership studies are questionnaire studies. Burns's theory of transforming leadership inspired a number of descriptive studies that eventually led to an interest in ethics in leadership studies. While Burns's theory was groundbreaking, it was Bass's work on transformational leadership that shaped most of the empirical research we see today on ethics. Bass focuses on measuring transformational leadership. He and his colleague Bruce Avolio developed the Multifactor Leadership Questionnaire (MLQ), which is extensively used in leadership research.[71] Bass's theory of transformational leadership does not incorporate Burns's emphasis on conflict and the dialogue between leaders and followers about values, nor does it include normative considerations using end and modal values.[72] Instead Bass focuses on how leaders use their idealized influence (charisma), intellectual stimulation, individual consideration, and inspirational motivation to change followers so they perform well. These variables have moral implications, but unlike transforming leadership theory, they are not explicit.

In the first publication of this chapter, I criticized Bass's theory of transformational leadership because it depends on charismatic leaders who could be evil transformational leaders like Hitler. Bass then tried to put his theory on a moral footing by distinguishing transformational leaders who are ethical, with *pseudo*-transformational leaders who are unethical. In a later article, Bass and Steidlmeier distinguish between *pseudo*-transformational leadership and *authentic* transformational leadership.[73] They then describe the moral qualities that leaders should have and assert that only moral leaders are transformational. Bass's argument fits with my earlier observation about the strong normative connotation of leadership—only *real* or *authentic* leaders are ethical. As Terry Price argues, however, Bass's adjustment to his theory does not work because Bass assumes that altruism is adequate for ethical success, yet there are many cases where altruistic leaders are seriously misguided about the nature of morality.[74]

The theory of authentic leadership evolved out of Bass's work on authentic transformational leadership, positive psychology, and popular management literature on the subject. The Authentic Leadership Questionnaire (ALQ) measures self-awareness, balanced processing, internalized moral perspective, and relational transparency. There are many variations on this theory.[75] Some researchers define authentic leadership along the lines of Fred Luthans's and Bruce Avolio's definition—"a process that draws from both positive psychological capacities and a highly developed organizational context, which results in both greater self-awareness and self-regulated positive behaviors on the part of leaders and associates, fostering positive self-development."[76] This definition later takes on some explicit moral elements such as "a pattern of leader behavior that draws upon and promotes both positive psychological capacities and a positive ethical climate, to foster greater self-awareness, an internalized moral perspective, balanced processing of information, and relational transparency on the part of leaders working with followers, fostering positive self-development."[77] Authentic leadership focuses on how leaders' self-knowledge and transparency contributes to making them effective and ethical leaders. There appears to be an inherent circularity in the notion of morality in this theory. Morality seems to be both the result of a leader being authentic and a quality of authenticity.[78] Nevertheless, this is another example of a theory that connects moral leadership with leader effectiveness and characterizes *real* or authentic leaders as ethical leaders or, the only people we can call leaders are good leaders.

Ethical leadership theory has produced an extraordinary number of articles on ethics. As I mentioned earlier, the name is unfortunate because I confuses the topic of ethics in leadership with a particular construct. The authors of this theory, Michael E. Brown, Linda K. Treviño, and David Harrison, define ethical leadership "as the demonstration of normatively appropriate conduct through personal actions and interpersonal relationships, and the promotion of such conduct to followers through two way communication, reinforcement, and decision-making."[79] They ground their work in social learning theory and emphasize the idea of leaders as role models. The theory also draws on the literature on transformational and authentic transformational leadership. Brown et al. isolate moral variables such as honesty, trust, fairness, openness, and consideration and hypothesize that ethical leadership will be positively related to employees' satisfaction with their leaders and employee effectiveness. The name "ethical leadership theory" is somewhat misleading in that the instrument used in these studies only measures people's attributions of ethical leadership to their leaders. Again, the fact that the majority of people attribute ethical qualities to a leader is not sufficient to say that the leader is ethical. Here are the questions that are used in the ethical leadership questionnaire.

1. Listens to what employees have to say
2. Discusses business ethics or values with employees
3. Asks "What is the right thing to do?" when making decisions
4. Makes fair and balanced decisions
5. Can be trusted
6. Has the best interests of employees in mind
7. Defines success not just by results but also the way that they are obtained
8. Disciplines employees who violate ethical standards
9. Sets an example of how to do things the right way in terms of ethics
10. Conducts his or her personal life in an ethical manner

As you can see by the list of criteria in this study, it is a mixture of "good management" qualities and subjective ethical judgments. Listening to employees may or may not be an ethical behavior. How a leader conducts his or her personal life may depend on the values of the beholder. Having the interests of the employee in mind may be unethical, especially if it conflicts with duties to others and the organization. I could go on, but this will have to wait for another time.

Peter A. Harms did a statistical analysis in which he compared data from questionnaires on ethical leadership with data from questionnaires on authentic and transformational leadership. He found and found a strong correlation between the findings of the three constructs. As he and his colleague Mary Uhl-Bien concluded that all of these studies seem to implicitly be studies of leader effectiveness.[80] They note that all three constructs, like the Ohio studies seem to be measuring similar attitudes related to the likeability of leaders. Nonetheless, being likeable is related to but certainly not the same as being ethical.

The transformational, authentic, and ethical leadership constructs and their questionnaires have generated and extraordinary amount of literature. In a quick search of major databases that included books and journal articles, I discovered 44,392 articles on Bass's transformational leadership theory and 154,076 on authentic leadership theory. Literature concerning both of those theories paled in comparison to the whopping 226,573 articles on ethical leadership theory.[81] This is good news because it shows that researchers are interested in leadership ethics. It is bad news is that no matter how many people make use of the ethical leadership questionnaire or try to refine it, the data they collect only measure people's perceptions about whether a leader is ethical. It leaves quite a bit of territory still waiting to be explored concerning what is and is not ethical in leadership. Here is where disciplines such as philosophy, history, and other areas of the humanities can contribute.

CONCLUSION: LEADERSHIP ETHICS AND THE HUMANITIES

So where does this leave us? Research on leadership has always found itself leaning toward the study of traits, although most scholars understand the importance of contexts too. Social scientists describe the traits, qualities, and behaviors that constitute good leaders—this is the "Rosetta Stone." Descriptions of good leaders and theories like Brown et al.'s "ethical leadership" construct are a necessary part of leadership ethics but not all of it. We must also examine the ethical challenges that are distinctive to the roles of leaders and followers and their relationship with each other. Some obvious ones stem from the temptations of power, the problems of ego and self-interest, and the burdens of being responsible for the welling of groups, organizations, or nations that consist of people who have a variety of needs and interests. While as a phenomenon leadership is similar across contexts, its study is not well served when dominated by research that is mainly about business organizations. While we need to understand how leaders and followers behave, leadership ethics must encompass the personal and intellectual challenges of leading and following. To do this, it has to tap into areas such as history, literature, philosophy, and art for insights into human behavior and values.

Perhaps one of the most striking things about history is the fact that people seem to always hope for the same moral behavior from their leaders.[82] The romance of leadership is not new. The emerging field of leadership ethics offers a place where the humanities and social science sides of the field can come together and learn from each other. Leadership scholars need to move beyond the accumulation bits of information derived from surveys that are taken by employees or college students to knowledge that has the feel of being universal. Research on ethics from the humanities will help them get there.

The field of leadership ethics can serve to improve the field of leadership studies. As I have tried to show, it is almost impossible to talk about leadership without talking about ethics. The leader-follower relationship is a longstanding part of the human condition. We need to describe it, evaluate it, and explore the hopes fears and aspirations that people have and have had throughout history and across cultures. Lastly, leadership ethics can also serve as a critical theory that opens up new dialogues among researchers and practitioners. Multidisciplinary and interdisciplinary work in leadership ethics should generate different ways of thinking about research, leadership development, organizations, institutions, and societies. Moreover, it would provide different ways of asking research questions and new avenues of research. In conclusion, ethics is the heart of leadership studies and has veins that run though all leadership research. The study of leadership ethics has the potential to take us to new territories that are waiting to be explored.

NOTES

1. Joanne B. Ciulla, Mary Uhl-Bien, and Patricia H. Werhane, *Sage Benchmarks in Leadership: Leadership Ethics* (London: Sage Publications Ltd., 2013), xxi–xxii.

2. For a good collection on metaethics see: Andrew Fischer and Simon Kirchin (Eds.), *Arguing about Metaethics* (New York: Routledge, 2006).

3. Joseph Rost, *Leadership for the Twenty-First Century* (New York: Praeger, 1991), 172.

4. Ibid., 168.

5. James Rachels, *The Elements of Moral Philosophy* (New York: Random House, 1986); Mark Pastin, *The Hard Problems of Management: Gaining the Ethics Edge* (San Francisco: Jossey-Bass, 1986). I am not arguing about the quality of these books, but rather the quantity of research done by Rost.

6. Rost, 177.

7. Ibid. The works cited in his argument are Robert Bellah, Richard Madsen, William M. Sullivan, and Ann Swidler, *Habits of the Heart* (New York: Harper & Row, 1985); William M. Sullivan, *Reconstructing Public Philosophy* (Berkeley, CA: University of California Press, 1986); and Alasdair MacIntyre, *After Virtue* (Notre Dame, IN: University of Notre Dame Press, 1984).

8. Ibid., 177.

9. Bernard M. Bass, *Bass & Stogdill's Handbook of Leadership*, 3rd edition (New York: The Free Press, 1990). The quotes are taken from the back jacket of the book.

10. From James MacGregor Burns's book *Leadership* (New York: Harper Torchbooks, 1978).

11. There are books on bad leaders. One of the best ones is: Jean Lipman Blumen, *The Allure of Toxic Leaders: Why We Follow Destructive Bosses and Corrupt Politicians—and How We Can Survive Them* (New York: Oxford University Press, 2006).

12. For example see: K. S. Cameron, J. E. Dutton and R. E. Quinn (Eds.), *Positive Organizational Scholarship* (San Francisco: Berrett-Koehler, 2003).

13. Bass, 906.

14. For example, John Gardner is well known in the leadership area. His leadership paper, "The Moral Aspect of Leadership" was published in 1987. Burns's book was published in 1978 and contained a wealth of references that might have been useful.

15. Bernard M. Bass and Ruth Bass, *The Bass Handbook of Leadership: Theory, Research & Managerial Applications*, 4th edition (New York: Free Press, 2008), 199–238.

16. R. J. Corsini, "Stereotype." In *The Dictionary of Psychology* (Philadelphia, PA: Brunner/Mazel, 1999). Bass mentions other philosophers with dates after their names but most of those sources do not make it into the references, with the exception of John Rawls. My own work is also referred to but not discussed much in the piece.

17. Rost, 27.

18. Ibid., 3.

19. Marta Calas and Linda Smircich, "Reading Leadership as a Form of Cultural Analysis." In *Emerging Leadership Vistas*, edited by James G. Hunt, B. Rajaram Baliga, H. Peter Dachler, and Chester A. Schriesheim (Lexington, MA: Lexington Books, 1988), 222–226.

20. For example see: Thomas Sergiovanni, *Moral Leadership* (San Francisco: Jossey-Bass, 1992), xiii. Sergiovanni argues "rich leadership practice cannot be developed if one set of values or one basis of authority is simply substituted for another. What we need is an expanded theoretical and operational foundation for leadership practice that will give balance to a full range of values and bases of authority." He refers to this expanded foundation as the *moral dimension in leadership*.

21. John Gardner, *On Leadership* (New York: Free Press, 1990), 77.

22. Example of a leadership textbook is: Richard Hughes, Robert Ginnett, Gordon J. Curphy, *Leadership: Enhancing the Lessons of Experience* (New York: Irwin, 1993). One of the most popular textbooks is: Peter G. Northhouse, *Leadership: Theory and Practice*, 6th edition (Thousand Oaks, CA: Sage Publications, 2012).

23. Thomas Kuhn, *The Structure of Scientific Revolutions* (Chicago: University of Chicago Press, 1970), 20.

24. This is not sour grapes—I have never submitted an article to *The Leadership Quarterly.* I know of this problem because I have spent many years reviewing articles as a member of its editorial board.

25. They also spelled Descartes' first name wrong. See M. H. Kernis and B. M. Goldman, "A Multicomponent Conceptualization of Authenticity:

Theory and Research." In *Advances in Experimental Social Psychology*, volume 38, edited by M. P. Zanna (San Diego: Academic Press, 2006), 283–357.

26. Fortunately, there are new journals that do a better job of addressing this problem such as the journal *Leadership* (Sage Publishing). This journal publishes some of the most innovative work on leadership from a wide range of disciplines and perspectives. It has contributed to changing the research paradigm of leadership studies into one where new and innovative research in areas such as leadership ethics is possible. The other journal that will contribute to this paradigm is the *Leadership in the Humanities* (Edward Elgar Publishing). This journal has increased the volume and variety of literature from the humanities; may avoid some of the problems as the *Leadership Quarterly* because its editorial board has a good balance of academics from the social sciences and the humanities. Both provide outlets for writing about the ethics of leadership. However, the challenge of bringing insights from the humanities with insights from the social sciences remains formidable.

27. Kuhn, 20.

28. Rost, 6–7.

29. Rost, 6.

30. Ibid.

31. Ibid., 99.

32. The theory of meaning that I have in mind is from: Ludwig Wittgenstein, *Philosophical Investigations*, tr. G. E. M. Anscomb, 3rd edition (New York: Macmillan, 1968), 18–20, 241.

33. Rost, 47 from: B. V. Moore, "The May Conference on Leadership," *Personnel Journal* 6 (1927): 124.

34. Ibid., 47 from: E. S. Bogardus, *Leaders and Leadership* (New York: Appelton-Century, 1934), 5.

35. Ibid., 48 from: E. B. Reuter, *Handbook of Sociology* (New York: Dryden Press, 1941), 133.

36. Page 50. The bracket part is Rost's summary of the definition from: C. A. Gibb, "Leadership." In *Handbook of Social Psychology*, volume 2, edited by G. Lindzey (Cambridge, MA: Addison Wesley, 1954), 877–920.

37. Page 53 from: M. Seeman, *Social Status and Leadership* (Columbus: Ohio State University Bureau of Educational Research, 1960), 127.

38. Page 59 from: R. N. Osborn and J. G. Hunt, "An Adaptive Reactive Theory of Leadership." In *Leadership Frontiers*, edited by J. G. Hunt and L. L. Larson (Kent, OH: Kent State University Press, 1975), 28.

39. Page 72 from: S. C. Sarkesian, "A Personal Perspective." In *Military Leadership*, edited by J. H. Buck and L. J. Korb (Beverly Hills, CA: Sage, 1981), 243.

40. Rost, 102.

41. Burns, 1978, 3.

42. Rost, 161.

43. Eva D. Kort, "What, After All, Is Leadership? "Leadership" and Plural Action," *The Leadership Quarterly* 19 (2008): 409–25.

44. Leaders carry their own normative baggage in their definitions. For example: "A leader is a man who has the ability to get other people to do what they do not want to do, and like it." (Harry Truman)

"Clean examples have a curious method of multiplying themselves" (Gandhi)

"Whatever goal man has reached is due to his originality plus his brutality." (Adolf Hitler)

"If we do not win, we will blame neither heaven nor earth, only ourselves." (Mao)

These examples are from G. D. Paige's book, *The Scientific Study of Political Leadership*, 66. They are taken from Barbara Kellerman's, *Leadership: Multidisciplinary Perspectives* (Englewood Cliffs, NJ: Prentice-Hall, 1984), 71–72.

45. Ronald Heifetz. *Leadership without Easy Answers* (Cambridge, MA: Belknap/Harvard University Press, 1994), 17–18.

46. See Warren Bennis and Burt Nanus, *Leaders: The Strategies for Taking Charge* (New York: Harper Collins, 1985), 45.

47. See E. A. Fleishman, "The Description of Supervisory Behavior," *Personnel Psychology*, vol. 37 (1953): 1–6.

48. Results from the earlier and later Michigan studies are discussed in R. Likert's books, *New Patterns of Management* (New York: McGraw-Hill, 1961) and *The Human Organization: Its Management and Value* (New York: McGraw-Hill, 1967).

49. See P. Hersey and K. H. Blanchard, *The Management of Organizational Behavior*, 5th edition (Englewood Cliffs, NJ: Prentice Hall, 1993).

50. It would be worthwhile to look at some of the studies and ask how the subjects with high/high orientations solve ethical problems. Do they tend to find themselves trapped in between deontic and consequentialist approaches to the problem? Are people who score high on the task scale consequentialists when it comes to approaching ethical problems? etc.

51. See Gary Yukl, *Leadership in Organizations*, 2nd edition (Englewood Cliffs, NJ: Prentice Hall, 1989), 96.

52. Old metaethical problems such as G. E. Moore's naturalistic fallacy of drawing an *ought* from an *is* and more recent discussions of ethical realism take on a certain urgency in applied ethics. I find that the more work that I do in applied ethics, the more I lean toward the position that moral discourse is cognitive in that it expresses propositions that have truth value. However, I am still uncomfortable with drawing moral prescriptions from "scientific" studies of leadership. I have not really worked out a coherent position on these points of moral epistemology. For a good discussion of these issues see Geoffrey Sayre-McCord (Ed.), *Essays on Moral Realism* (Cornell: Cornell University Press, 1988). I find David Wiggins's and Geoffrey Sayre-McCord's articles on ethical realism to be particularly compelling.

53. This is the argument that the sciences provide explanation and the humanities understanding. See chapter 1 of G. H. von Wright, *Explanation and Understanding* (Ithaca, NY: Cornell University Press, 1971).

54. Joanne B. Ciulla, "Ethics and Effectiveness: The Nature of Good Leadership." In *The Nature of Leadership*, 2nd edition, edited by John Antonakis and David Day (Thousand Oaks, CA: Sage Publications, 2011), 508–40.

55. J. S. Mill, "What Utilitarianism Is." In *Utilitarianism and Other Essays*, edited by A. Ryan (New York: Penguin Books, 1987), 272–338.

56. Aristotle, *Nichomachean Ethics*. In *The Complete Works of Aristotle*, vol. 2, edited by Jonathan Barnes (Princeton, NJ: Princeton University Press, 1984), Book I sections 6–8 (1096a12-1098b8). Later in Book II, sections 13–16 (31104b).

57. J. R. Meindl, S. B. Ehrlich, and J. M. Dukerich, "The Romance of Leadership," *Administrative Science Quarterly* 30, no. 1 (1985): 78–102.

58. Burns, 1978, 42–43.

59. Rost, 1991, xii.

60. For example, see Burns's discussion of Roosevelt's treatment of Joe Kennedy, Burns, 1978, 32–33.

61. One of the problems with using the values approach to ethics is that it requires a very complicated taxonomy of values. The word *value* is also problematic because it encompasses so many different kinds of things. The values approach requires arguments for some sort of hierarchy of values that would serve to resolve conflicts of values. To make values something that people do rather than just have, Milton Rokeach offers a very awkward discussion of the ought character of values. "A person phenomenologically experiences 'ought-ness' to be objectively required by society in somewhat the same way that he perceives an incomplete circle as objectively requiring closure." See Milton Rokeach, *The Nature of Human Values* (New York: The Free Press, 1973), 9.

62. Burns, 1978, 426.

63. Ibid., 3.

64. Aristotle, *Nicomachean Ethics*, Book I (1095a19). In *The Complete Works of Aristotle*, volume 2, edited by Jonathan Barnes (Princeton, NJ: Princeton University Press, 1984), 1730.

65. Burns's description of the transforming process resembles Jurgen Habermas's discourse ethics, which frequently informs European discussions of leadership ethics. See Ju͏rgen Habermas, *The Theory of Communicative Action*, vol. 2. In *Lifeworld and System*, edited and translated by T. McCarthy (Boston: Beacon Press, 1987).

66. Burns, 1978, 424.

67. Greenleaf takes his theory from Hesse. See Robert K. Greenleaf, *Servant Leadership* (New York: Paulist Press, 1977). Hermann Hesse, *The Journey to the East* (New York: Farrar, Straus and Giroux, 1956).

68. The Robert K. Greenleaf Center in Indianapolis works with companies to implement this idea of leadership in organizations. https://greenleaf.org.

69. Greenleaf, 1977, 13–14.

70. Some of this discussion is adapted from, Ciulla, Uhl-Bien, and Werhane, 2013, Volume I, xxvii–xxx.

71. B. J. Avolio and B. M. Bass, *Full-range training of leadership manual* (Binghamton, NY: Bass/Avolio & Associates, 1991).

72. B. M. Bass, *Leadership and Performance beyond Expectations* (New York: Free Press, 1991).

73. B. M. Bass and P. Steidlmeier, "Ethics, Character, and Authentic Transformational Leadership Behavior," *Leadership Quarterly* 10, no. 2 (1999): 181–217.

74. T. L. Price, "The Ethics of Authentic Transformational Leadership," *The Leadership Quarterly* 14, no. 1 (2003): 67–81.

75. See William L. Gardner, Claudia C. Cogliser, Kelly M. Davis, and Matthew P. Dickens, "Authentic Leadership: A Review of the Literature and Research Agenda," *The Leadership Quarterly* 22 (2011): 1120–45.

76. F. Luthans and B. J. Avolio, "Authentic Leadership Development." In *Positive Organizational Scholarship*, edited by K. S. Cameron, J. E. Dutton, and R. E. Quinn (San Francisco: Berrett-Koehler, 2003), 241–61.

77. F. O. Walumbwa, B. J. Avolio, W. L Gardner, T. S. Wernsing, and S. J. Peterson, "Authentic Leadership: Development and Validation of a Theory Based Measure," *Journal of Management* 34 (2008): 94.

78. Joanne B. Ciulla, "Searching for Mandela: The Saint as a Sinner Who Keeps on Trying." In *Authentic Leadership: Clashes, Convergences and Coalescences*, edited by Donna Ladkin and Chellie Spiller (Northampton, CT: Edward Elgar, 2013), 152–175.

79. Michael E. Brown, Linda K. Treviño, and David A. Harrison, "Ethical Leadership: A Social Learning Perspective for Construct Development and Testing," *Organizational Behavior and Human Decision Processes* 97 (2005): 120.

80. Peter D. Harms, "What Are We Really Measuring? A closer look at the construct validity of leadership questionnaires." Presented at the University of Houston Leadership Symposium, Houston, TX (October, 2012).

81. This is just quick search of articles found in the University of Richmond Library's, One Search System on June 1, 2014. I searched for "transformational leadership theory," "authentic leadership theory," and "ethical leadership theory."

82. For example, see Joanne B. Ciulla, "Being There: Why Leaders Should Not 'Fiddle' While Rome Burns," *Presidential Studies Quarterly* 40, no. 1 (March 2010), 38–56.

2

Moral Leadership and Business Ethics

Al Gini and Ronald M. Green

Nothing great ever happens until leadership shows up.
—Mike Singletary[1]

President Calvin Coolidge was more than a little right when he said: "The business of America is business." Business of all kinds is the economic backbone of this society. "No group in America is more influential than business persons. Their influence, for good and evil, enters every life and every home."[2] Like it or not, business serves as the moral metronome for society. The meter and behavior established by business and business leaders help to set the tone, develop the vision, and shape the patterns of behavior for all of us.

When most of us think of business, we tend to think big. We think Fortune 500. We think megacorporations—American Express, Coca-Cola, General Electric, the Home Depot, McDonald's, Microsoft, and Verizon. Many of us think, naively, that business is what large corporations do. We are partially correct, but, if we only stopped there, we would be overlooking a vibrant and pulsating community of commercial entrepreneurs operating right down the block and all around us—Bonnie's Bakery, Danny's Deli, Tony's Tailor Shop, Sally's Hair Stylings, Barbara's Bookstore, Claire's Copy Center.

In the United States—and in the world—big business have clout because, whether they exist within a democratic government or not, big businesses make big money. Dollars have influence, dollars vote, and, in big business, big money gets to vote early and often. Nevertheless, in spite of the depth and power of an estimated 5,868,849 corporations with total revenues in excess of $28,762,923,553,000 (that's nearly $29 trillion), small businesses play a major role in our economy and in the way we live. Recent census data indicate that there are 29.6 million small and family businesses in the United States, and 99 percent of them employ fewer than 500 people each.[3]

Statistics aside, "business" as a concept, as a definition or description, is not an entity, a factory, a company, or a place. Nor is it a particular product, service, or thing. The essence of business is an action, an activity that occurs between two or more individuals. Business is something we do. Business is, most fundamentally, a transaction or a trade. We engage in trade by relinquishing some property rights (or services) and by acquiring other property rights (or services) through an exchange with another person. For example, you relinquish $2 to acquire a pack of six Pilot pens at Staples. Staples relinquishes a six-pen pack to acquire $2. Or you agree to provide legal services for a fee to Staples. You perform and they pay you. In all these cases, you have each relinquished and acquired, or exchanged, property rights or services. So, at its most fundamental level, business is the activity of executing exchange transactions. If Staples didn't engage in exchange transactions, it wouldn't be a business firm.

The issue of ethics in business arises at the very core, the nexus of what we mean by business—transactions, actions in regard to others. Both business and ethics begin with the admission that we are not alone in, or the center of, the universe. We are communally living creatures. We are in need of each other. We are dependent on each other to survive and thrive. Our collective existence requires us to continually make choices, be they good or bad, about "what we ought to do" in regard to others.

As students of business ethics, we are convinced that without the continuous commitment, enforcement, and modeling of leadership, standards of business ethics cannot and will not be achieved in any organization. The ethics of leadership—whether they be good or bad, positive or negative—affect the ethos of the workplace and thereby help to form the ethical choices and decisions of the workers in the workplace. Leaders help to set the tone, develop the vision, and shape the behavior of all those involved in organizational life. The critical point to understand here is that, like it or not, business and politics serve as the metronome for our society. And the meter and behavior established by leaders set the patterns and establish the models for our behavior as individuals and as a group. Although the terms *business ethics* and *moral leadership* are technically distinguishable, in fact, they are inseparable components in the life of every organization.

The fundamental principle that underlies our thesis regarding leadership and ethical conduct is age-old. In his *Nichomachean Ethics*, Aristotle suggested that morality cannot be learned simply by reading a treatise on virtue. The spirit of morality, said Aristotle, is awakened in the individual only through the witness and conduct of a moral person. The principle of the "witness of another," or what we now refer to as "patterning," "role modeling," or "mentoring," is predicated on a four-step process, three of which follow:

1. As communal creatures, we learn to conduct ourselves primarily through the actions of significant others.
2. When the behavior of others is repeated often enough and proves to be peer-group positive, we emulate these actions.
3. If and when our actions are in turn reinforced by others, they become acquired characteristics or behavioral habits.

According to B. F. Skinner, the process is now complete. In affecting the actions of individuals through modeling and reinforcement, the mentor in question (in Skinnerean terms, "the controller of the environmental stimuli") has succeeded in reproducing the type of behavior sought after or desired. For Skinner the primary goal of the process need not take into consideration either the value or worth of the action or the interests or intent of the reinforced or operant-conditioned actor. From Skinner's psychological perspective, the bottom line is simply the response evoked.[4] From a philosophical perspective, however, even role modeling that produces a positive or beneficial action does not fulfill the basic requirements of the ethical enterprise at either the descriptive or normative level. Modeling, emulation, habit, results—whether positive or negative—are neither the sufficient nor the final goal. The fourth and final step in the process much include reflection, evaluation, choice, and conscious intent on the part of the actor, because ethics is always "an inside-out proposition" involving free will.[5]

John Dewey argued that at the precritical, prerational, preautonomous level, morality starts as a set of culturally defined goals and rules that are external to the individual and are imposed or inculcated as habits. But real ethical thinking, said Dewey, begins at the evaluative period of our lives, when, as independent agents, we freely decide to accept, embrace, modify, or deny these rules. Dewey maintained that every serious ethical system rejects the notion that one's standard of conduct should simply and uncritically be an acceptance of the rules of the culture we happen to live in. Even when custom, habit, convention, public opinion, or law are correct in their mandates, to embrace them without critical reflection does not constitute a complete and formal ethical act and might be better labeled "ethical happenstance" or "ethics by virtue of circumstantial accident." According to Dewey, ethics is essentially "reflective conduct," and he believed that the distinction between custom and reflective morality is clearly marked. The former places the standard and rules of conduct solely on habit; the latter appeals to reason and choice. The distinction is as important as it is definite, for it shifts the center of gravity in morality. For Dewey, ethics is a two-part process; it is never enough simply to do the right thing.[6]

In claiming that workers/followers derive their models for ethical conduct by witnessing their leaders, we are in no way denying that workers/followers share responsibility for the overall conduct and culture of an organization. The burden of this chapter is not to exonerate the culpability of workers, but rather to explain the process involved: The witness of leaders both communicates the ethics of our institutions and establishes the desired standards and expectations leaders want and often demand from their fellow workers and followers. Although it would be naive to assert that employees simply and unreflectively absorb the manners and morals of the workplace, it would be equally naive to suggest that they are unaffected by the modeling and standards of their respective places of employment. Work is how we spend our lives, and the lessons we learn there, good or bad, play a part in the development of our moral perspective and the manner in which we formulate and adjudicate ethical choices. As business ethicists, we believe that without the active intervention of effective moral leadership, we are doomed to forever wage a rearguard action. Students of organizational development are never really surprised when poorly managed and badly lead businesses wind up doing unethical things.

ETHICS AND BUSINESS

Jean-Paul Sartre argued that, like it or not, we are *by definition* moral creatures because our collective existence "condemns" us continuously to make choices about "what we ought to do" in regard to others.[7] Ethics is primarily a communal, collective enterprise, not a solitary one. It is the study of our web of relationships with others. When Robinson Crusoe found himself marooned and alone on a tiny Pacific atoll, all things were possible. But when Friday appeared and they discovered pirates burying treasure on the beach, Crusoe was then involved in the universe of others, an ethical universe. As a communal exercise, ethics is the attempt to work out the rights and obligations we have and share with others. What is mine? What do I owe you?

According to John Rawls, given the presence of others and our need of these others both to survive and to thrive, ethics is elementally the pursuit of justice, fair play, and equity. For Rawls, building on the cliché that "ethics is how we decide to behave when we decide we belong together," the study of ethics has to do with developing standards for judging the conduct of one party whose behavior affects another. Minimally, "good behavior" intends no harm and respects the rights of all affected, and "bad behavior" is willfully or negligently trampling on the rights and interests of others.[8] Ethics, then, tries to find a way to protect one person's individual rights and needs against and alongside the rights and needs of others. Of course, the paradox and central tension of ethics lie in the fact that while we are by nature communal and in need of others, at the same time we are by disposition more or less egocentric and self-serving.[9]

If ethics is a part of life, so too are work, labor, and business. Work is not something detached from the rest of human life, but, rather, "man is born to labor, as a bird to fly." [10] What are work and business about? Earning a living? Yes. Producing a product or service? Sure. Making money or profit? Absolutely. In fact, most ethicists argue that business has a moral obligation to make a profit. But business is also about people—the people you work for and work with. Business is an interdependent, intertwined, symbiotic relationship. Life, labor, and business are all of a piece. They should not be seen as separate "games" played by different "rules." The enterprise of business is not distinct from the enterprise of life and living because they share the same bottom line—people. Therefore, as in the rest of life, business is required to ask the question, "What ought to be done in regard to others?"

While no one that we are aware of would argue seriously against the notion of ethics in our private lives, many would have it that ethics and business don't or can't mix. That is, many people believe that "business is business," and that the stakes and standards involved in business are simply different from, more important than and, perhaps, even antithetical to the principles and practices of ethics. Ethics is something we preach and practice at home in our private lives, but not at work. After all, it could cost us prestige, position, profits, and success.

Theologian Matthew Fox maintains that we lead schizophrenic lives because we either choose or are forced to abandon our personal beliefs and convictions "at the door" when we enter the workplace. The "destructive dualism" of the workplace, says Fox, separates our lives from our livelihood, our personal values from our work values, our personal needs from the needs of the community. Money becomes the sole reason for work, and success becomes the excuse we use to justify the immoral consequences of our behavior.[11] This "dualism" produces and perpetuates the kind of "occupational schizophrenia" once articulated by nationally known jurist Alan Dershowitz: "I would never do many of the things in my personal life that I have to do as a lawyer." [12]

According to ethicist Norman E. Bowie, the disconnection between business and ethics and the dualism of the workplace stem from the competing paradigms of human nature of economists and ethicists. Economics is the study of the betterment of self. Most economists, says Bowie, have an egoistic theory of human nature. Their analyses focus on how an individual rationally pursues desired tastes, wants, or preferences. Within the economic model, individuals behave rationally when they seek to strengthen their own perceived best interests. Individuals need only take the interests of others into account when and if such considerations work to their advantage. Economics, Bowie claims, is singular and radically subjective in its orientation. It takes all taste, wants, and desires as simply given, and does not evaluate whether the economic actor's preferences are good or bad. The focus remains on how the individual can achieve his/her wants and desires.

Ethics, on the other hand, is non-egoistic or pluralistic in nature. Its primary paradigm of evaluation is always self in relation to others. The ethical point of view, says Bowie, requires that an actor take into account the impact of his or her action on others. If and when the interests of the actor and those affected by the action conflict, the actor should at least consider suspending or modifying his or her action, and by so doing recognize the interests of the other. In other words, ethics requires that on occasion we "ought to act" contrary to our own self-interest and that on occasion a person "ought to" act actively on behalf of the interests of another. Economists ask, "What can I do to advance my best interests against others?" Ethicists ask, "In pursuing my best interests what must I do, what 'ought' I do in regard to others?" Whereas economics breeds competition, ethics encourages cooperation.[13]

For R. Edward Freeman, these competing paradigms are firmly entrenched in our collective psyches, and give rise to what he calls "the Problem of the Two Realms." One realm is the realm of business. It is the realm of hard, measurable facts: market studies, focus groups, longitudinal studies, production costs, managed inventory, stock value, research and development, profit and loss statements, quantitative analysis. The other realm is the realm of philosophy/ethics. This is the soft realm, says Freeman. This is the realm of the seemingly ineffable: myth, meaning, metaphor, purpose, quality, significance, rights, values. While the realm of business can be easily dissected, diagnosed, compared, and judged, the realm of philosophy is not open to precise interpretation, comparison, and evaluation. For Freeman, in a society that has absorbed and embraced the Marcusian adage "the goods of life are equal to the good life," these two realms are accorded separate but unequal status. Only in moments of desperation, disaster, or desire does the realm of business solicit the commentary and insights of the realm of ethics. Otherwise, the realm of business operates under the dictum of legal moralism: Everything is allowed which is not strictly forbidden.

For Freeman the assertion that "business is business" and that ethics is what we try to do in our private lives simply does not hold up to close scrutiny. Business is a human institution, a basic part of the communal fabric of life. Just as governments come to be out of the human need for order, security, and fulfillment, so too does business. The goal of all business, labor, and work is to make life more secure, more stable, more equitable. Business exists to serve more than just itself.

No business can view itself as an isolated entity, unaffected by the demands of individuals and society. As such, business is required to ask the question, "What ought to be done in regard to the others we work with and serve?" For Freeman, business ethics, rather than being an oxymoron, a contradiction in terms, is really a pleonasm, a redundancy in terms.[14] As Henry Ford, Sr., once said: "For a long time people believed that the only purpose of industry is to make a profit. They are wrong. Its purpose is to serve the general welfare." [15]

What business ethics advocates is that people apply in the workplace those commonsensical rules and standards learned at home, from the lectern, and from the pulpit. The moral issues facing a person are age-old, and these are essentially the same issues facing a business—only writ in large script.[16] According to Freeman, ethics is "how we treat each other, every day, person to person. If you want to know about a company's ethics, look at how it treats people—customers, suppliers, and employees. Business is about people. And business ethics is about how customers and employees are treated."[17]

What is being asked of the business community is neither extraordinary nor excessive: a decent product at a fair price; honesty in advertisements; fair treatment of employees, customers, suppliers, and competitors; a strong sense of responsibility to the communities it inhabits and serves; and a reasonable profit for the financial risk-taking of its stockholders and owners. In the words of General Robert Wood Johnson, founder of Johnson and Johnson:

> The day has passed when business was a private matter—if it even really was. In a business society, every act of business has social consequences and may arouse public interest. Every time business hires, builds, sells or buys, it is acting for the ... people as well as for itself, and it must be prepared to accept full responsibility.[18]

LEADERSHIP

According to Georges Enderle, business leadership would be relatively simple if corporations only had to produce a product or service, without being concerned about employees; management only had to deal with concepts, structures and strategies, without worrying about human relations; businesses just had to resolve their own problems, without being obligated to take the interests of individuals or society into consideration.[19] But such is not the case. Leadership is always about self and others. Like ethics, labor and business-leadership is a

symbiotic, communal relationship. It's about leaders, followers, constituencies, and all stakeholders involved. And, like ethics, labor and
business-leadership seems to be an intrinsic part of the human experience. Charles DeGaulle once observed that men can no more survive
without direction than they can without eating, drinking, or sleeping.
Putting aside the obvious fact that DeGaulle was a proponent of
"the great-person theory" of leadership, his point is a basic one.
Leadership is a necessary requirement of communal existence.
Minimally, it tries to offer perspective, focus, appropriate behavior,
guidance, and a plan by which to handle the seemingly random and
arbitrary events of life. Depending on the type of leadership-
followership involved, it can be achieved by consensus, fiat, or
cooperative orchestration. But whatever techniques are employed,
leadership is always, at bottom, about stewardship—"a person(s)
who manages or directs the affairs of others ... as the agent or
representative of others." Leadership, as stewardship, aims at positive
change in the life of an organization or community. This means that
leadership is always an ethical enterprise. Peter Drucker, one of the
most skilled observers of organizational life, concludes, on the basis
of more than 65 years of studying management, that the primary purpose of all business organizations and the grounds and rationale for all
forms of managerial authority is to make the human condition more
secure, more satisfactory, and more productive.[20] More colloquially,
Tony Dungy, former NFL coach, said: "It is not about you ... Your only
job [as a coach, as a leader] is to help your team be better."[21] Centuries
before Drucker or Dungy, St. Augustine, himself a formative leader of
early Christianity, clearly suggested in the *City of God* that the first and
final job of leaders is to attempt to serve the needs and well-being of
the people they lead.[22]

Although the phenomenon of leadership can and must be distinguishable and definable separately from our understanding of what
and who leaders are, we are convinced that leadership can only be
known and evaluated in the particular instantiation of a leader doing
a job. In other words, while the terms *leadership* and *leader* are not
strictly synonymous, the reality of leadership cannot be separated
from the person of the leader and the job of leadership. Given this cav-
eat, and leaning heavy on the research and insights of Joseph C. Rost,[23]
we can define leadership as follows: *Leadership is a power- and value-
laden relationship between leaders and followers/constituents who intend real
changes that reflect their mutual purposes and goals.* For our purposes, the

critical elements of this definition that need to be examined are, in order of importance: followership, values, mutual purposes and goals.

Followership

As Joseph Rost has pointed out, perhaps the single most important thesis developed in leadership studies in the last 20 years has been the evolution and now *almost* universal consensus regarding the role of followers in the leadership equation. Pulitzer prize-winning historian Garry Wills argues that we have long had a list of the leader's requisites—determination, focus, a clear goal, a sense of priorities, and so on. But until recently we overlooked or forgot the first and all encompassing need: "The leader most needs followers. When those are lacking, the best ideas, the strongest will, the most wonderful smile have no effect."[24] Followers set the terms of acceptance for leadership. Leadership is a "mutually determinative" activity on the part of the leader and the followers. Sometimes it's cooperative, sometimes it's a struggle and often it's a feud, but it's always collective. Although "the leader is one who mobilizes others toward a goal shared by leaders and followers," leaders are powerless to act without followers. In effect, Wills argues, successful leaders need to understand their followers far more than followers need to understand leaders.[25]

Leadership, like labor and ethics, is always plural; it always occurs in the context of others. E. P. Hollander has argued that while the leader is the central and often the most vital part of the leadership phenomenon, followers are important and necessary factors in the equation.[26] All leadership is interactive, and all leadership should be collaborative. In fact, except for the negative connotation sometimes associated with the term, perhaps the word *collaborator* is a more precise term than either *follower* or *constituent* to explain the leadership process.[27] But whichever term is used, as James MacGregor Burns wrote, one thing is clear, "leaders and followers are engaged in a common enterprise; they are dependent on each other, their fortunes rise and fall together."[28]

From an ethical perspective, the argument for the stewardship responsibilities of leadership is dependent on the recognition of the roles and rights of followers. Followership argues against the claim of Louis XIV, "l'etat c'est moi!" The principle of followership denies the Machiavellian assertions that "politics and ethics don't mix" and that the sole aim of any leader is "the acquisition of personal power."

Followership requires that leaders recognize their true role within the commonwealth. The choices and actions of leaders must take into consideration the rights and needs of followers. Leaders are not independent agents simply pursuing personal aggrandizement and career options. Like the "Guardians" of Plato's *Republic*, leaders must see their office as a social responsibility, a trust, a duty, and not as a symbol of their personal identity, prestige, and lofty status.[29] In more contemporary terms, James O'Toole and Lynn Sharp-Paine have separately argued that the central ethical issue in business is the rights of stakeholders and the obligation of business leaders to manage with due consideration for the rights of all stakeholders involved.[30]

In his cult classic *The Fifth Discipline*, management guru Peter Senge has stated that of all the jobs of leadership, being a steward is the most basic. Being a steward means recognizing that the ultimate purpose of one's work is others and not self; that leaders "do what they do" for something larger than themselves; that their "life's work" may be the "ability to lead," but that the final goal of this talent or craft is "other directed."[31] If the real "business of business" is not just to produce a product/service and a profit but to help "produce" people, then the same claim/demand can be made of leadership. Given the reality of the "presence of others," leadership, like ethics, must by definition confront the question, "What ought to be done with regard to others?"

Values

Ethics is about the assessment and evaluation of values, because all of life is value-laden. As Samuel Blumenfeld emphatically pointed out, "You have to be dead to be value-neutral." [32] Values are the ideas and beliefs that influence and direct our choices and actions. Whether they are right or wrong, good or bad, values, both consciously and unconsciously, mobilize and guide how we make decisions and the kinds of decisions we make. Reportedly, Eleanor Roosevelt once said, "If you want to know what people value, check their checkbooks!"

We believe that Tom Peters and Bob Waterman were correct when they asserted, "The real role of leadership is to manage the values of an organization."[33] All leadership is value-laden. And all leadership, whether good or bad, is moral leadership at the descriptive if not the normative level. To put it more accurately, all leadership is ideologically driven or motivated by a certain philosophical perspective, which on analysis and judgment may or may not prove to be morally acceptable in the colloquial sense. All leaders have an agenda, a series of beliefs, proposals, values, ideas, and issues that they wish to "put on the table." In fact, as Burns has suggested, leadership only asserts itself, and followers only become evident, when there is something at stake—ideas that need to be examined, issues to be determined, values to be adjudicated.[34] In the words of Eleanor's husband, Franklin D. Roosevelt:

> The Presidency is preeminently a place of moral leadership. All our great Presidents were leaders of thought at times when certain historic ideas in the life of the nation had to be clarified. . . .[35]

Although we would prefer to study the moral leadership of Lincoln, Churchill, Gandhi and Mother Teresa, like it or not we must also evaluate Hitler, Stalin, Saddam Hussein, and David Koresh within a moral context.

All ethical judgments are in some sense a "values-vs.-values" or "rights-vs.-rights" confrontation. Unfortunately, the question of "what we ought to do" in relation to the values and rights of others cannot be reduced to the analog of a simple litmus-paper test. In fact, I believe that all of ethics is based on what William James called the "will to believe." That is, we choose to believe, despite the ideas, arguments, and reasoning to the contrary, that individuals possess certain basic rights that cannot and should not be willfully disregarded or overridden by others. In "choosing to believe," said James, we establish this belief as a factual baseline of our thought process for all considerations in regard to others. Without this "reasoned choice," says James, the ethical enterprise loses its "vitality" in human interactions.[36]

If ethical behavior intends no harm and respects the rights of all affected, and unethical behavior willfully or negligently tramples on the rights and interests of others, then leaders cannot deny or disregard the rights of others. The leader's world view cannot be totally solipsistic. The leader's agenda should not be purely self-serving. Leaders should not see followers as potential adversaries to be bested, but rather as fellow travelers with similar aspirations and rights to be reckoned with.

How do we judge the ethics of a leader? Clearly, we cannot expect every decision and action of a leader to be perfect. As John Gardner has pointed out, particular consequences are never a reliable assessment of leadership.[37] The quality and worth of leadership can only be measured in terms of what a leader intends, values, believes in, or stands for—in other words, character. In *Character: America's Search for Leadership*, Gail Sheehy argues, as did Aristotle before her, that character is the most crucial and most elusive element of leadership. The root of the word *character* comes from the Greek word for *engraving*. As applied to human beings, it refers to the enduring marks or etched-in factors in our personality, which include our inborn talents as well as the learned and acquired traits imposed on us by life and experience. These engravings define us, set us apart, and motivate behavior.

In regard to leadership, says Sheehy, character is fundamental and prophetic. The "issues [of leadership] are today and will change in time. Character is what was yesterday and will be tomorrow."[38] Character establishes both our day-to-day demeanor and our destiny. Therefore, it is not only useful but essential to examine the character of those who desire to lead us. As a journalist and longtime observer of the political scene, Sheehy contends that the Watergate affair of the early 1970s serves as a perfect example of the links between character and leadership. As Richard Nixon demonstrated so well, says Sheehy, "The Presidency is not the place to work out one's personal pathology ..."[39] Leaders rule us, run things, and wield power. Therefore, says Sheehy, we must be careful about whom we choose to lead, because whom we chose is what we shall be. If, as Heraclitus wrote, "character is fate," the fate our leaders reap will also be our own.

Putting aside the particular players and the politics of the episode, Watergate has come to symbolize the failings and failures of people in high places. Watergate now serves as a watershed, a turning point, in our nation's concern for integrity, honesty, and fair play from all kinds of leaders. It is not a mere coincidence that the birth of business ethics as an independent, academic discipline can be dated from the Watergate affair and the trials that came out of it. No matter what our failings as individuals, Watergate sensitized us to the importance of ethical standards and conduct from those who direct the course of our political and public lives. What society is now demanding, and what business ethics is advocating, is that our business leaders and public servants should be held accountable to an even higher standard of behavior than we might demand and expect of ourselves.

Mutual Purposes and Goals

The character, goals, and aspirations of a leader are not developed in a vacuum. Leadership, even in the hands of a strong, confident, charismatic leader, remains, at bottom, relational. Leaders, good or bad, great or small, arise out of the needs and opportunities of a specific time and place. Leaders require causes, issues and, most important, a hungry and willing constituency. Leaders may devise plans, establish an agenda, bring new and often radical ideas to the table, but all of them are a response to the milieu and membership of which they are a part. If leadership is an active and ongoing relationship between leaders and followers, then a central requirement of the leadership process is for leaders to evoke and elicit consensus in their constituencies, and conversely for followers to inform and influence their leaders. This is done through the uses of power and education.

The term *power* comes from the Latin word *posse*: to do, to be able, to change, to influence or effect. To have power is to possess the capacity to control or direct change. All forms of leadership must make use of power. The central issue of power in leadership is not will it be used, but rather will it be used wisely and well. According to James MacGregor Burns, leadership is not just about directed results; it is also about offering followers a choice among real alternatives. Hence, leadership assumes competition, conflict, and debate, whereas brute power denies it.[40] "Leadership mobilizes," said Burns, "naked power coerces."[41] But power need not be dictatorial or punitive to be effective. Power can also be used in a noncoercive manner to orchestrate, direct, and guide members of an organization in the pursuit of a goal or series of objectives. Leaders must engage followers, not merely direct them. Leaders must serve as models and mentors, not martinets. Or to paraphrase novelist James Baldwin, power without morality is no longer power.

For Peter Senge, teaching is one of the primary jobs of leadership.[42] The "task of leader as teacher" is to empower people with information, offer insights, new knowledge, and alternative perspectives on reality. The "leader as teacher" is not just about "teaching" people how "to achieve their vision." Rather, it is about fostering learning, offering choices, and building consensus.[43] Effective leadership recognizes that to build and achieve community, followers must become reciprocally co-responsible in the pursuit of a common enterprise. Through their conduct and teaching, leaders must try to make their fellow constituents aware that they are all stakeholders in a conjoint activity that cannot succeed without their involvement and commitment. Successful leadership believes in and communicates some version of the now famous Hewlett Packard motto: "The achievements of an organization are the results of the combined efforts of each individual."

In the end, says Abraham Zaleznik, "leadership is based on a compact that binds those who lead with those who follow into the same moral, intellectual and emotional commitment."[44] However, as both Burns and Rost warn us, the nature of this "compact" is inherently unequal because the influence patterns existing between leaders and followers are not equal. Responsive and responsible leadership requires, as a minimum, that democratic mechanisms be put in place that recognize the right of followers to have adequate knowledge of alternative options, goals, and programs, as well as the capacity to choose among them. "In leadership writ large, mutually agreed upon purposes help people achieve consensus, assume responsibility, work for the common good, and build community."[45]

STRUCTURAL RESTRAINTS

There is, unfortunately, a dark side to the theory of the "witness of others." Howard S. Schwartz, in his radical but underappreciated managerial book, *Narcissistic Process and Corporate Decay*,[46] argues that corporations are not bastions of benign, other-directed ethical reasoning; nor can corporations because of the demands and requirements of business, be models and exemplars of moral behavior. The rule of business, says Schwartz, remains the "law of the jungle," "the survival of the fittest," and the goal of survival engenders a combative "us-against-them mentality," which condones the moral imperative of getting ahead by any means necessary. Schwartz calls this phenomenon "organizational totalitarianism": Organizations and the people who manage them create for themselves a self-contained, self-serving world view, which rationalizes anything done on their behalf and which does not require justification on any grounds outside of themselves.[47] The psychodynamics of this narcissistic perspective, says Schwartz, impose Draconian requirements on all participants in organizational life: Do your work; achieve organizational goals; obey and exhibit loyalty to your superiors; disregard personal values and beliefs; obey the law when necessary, obfuscate it whenever possible; and deny internal or external discrepant information at odds with the stated organizational world view. Within such a "totalitarian logic," neither leaders or followers or rank or file, operate as independent agents. To "maintain their place," to "get ahead," all must conform. The agenda of "organizational totalitarianism" is always the preservation of the status quo. Within such a logic, like begets like, and change is rarely possible. Except for extreme situations in which "systemic ineffectiveness" begins to breed "organization decay," transformation is never an option.

In *Moral Mazes*, Robert Jackall parallels much of Schwartz's analysis of organizational behavior, but from a sociological rather than a psychological perspective. According to critic and commentator Thomas W. Norton, both Jackall and Schwartz seek to understand why and how organizational ethics and behavior are so often reduced to either dumb loyalty or the simple adulation and mimicry of one's superiors. While Schwartz argues that individuals are captives of the impersonal structural logic of "organizational totalitarianism," Jackall contends that, "organizational actors become personally loyal to their superiors, always seeking their approval and are committed to them as persons rather than as representatives of the abstractions of organizational authority." But in either case, both authors maintain that organizational operatives are prisoners of the systems they serve.[48]

For Jackall, all business organizations are examples of "patrimonial bureaucracies," wherein "fealty relations of personal loyalty" are the rule and the glue of organizational life. Jackall argues that all corporations are like fiefdoms of the Middle Ages, wherein the lord of the manor (CEO, president) offers protection, prestige, and status to his vassals (managers) and serfs (workers) in return for homage (commitment) and service (work). In such a system, advancement and promotion are predicated on loyalty, trust, politics, and personality as much as, if not more than, on experience, education, ability, and actual accomplishments. The central concern of the worker/minion is to be known as a "can-do guy," a "team player," being at the right place at the right time and master of all the social rules. That's why in the corporate world, asserts Jackall, 1,000 "atta-boys" are wiped away with one "oh, shit!"

Jackall maintains that, as in the model of a feudal system, employees of a corporation are expected to become functionaries of the system and supporters of the status quo. Their loyalty is to the powers that be; their duty is to perpetuate performance and profit; and their values can be none other than those sanctioned by the organization. Jackall contends that the logic of every organization (place of business) and the collective personality of the workplace conspire to override the wants, desires, and aspirations of the individual worker. No matter what a person believes off the job, said Jackall, on the job all of us to a greater or lesser extent are required to suspend, bracket, or only selectively manifest our personal convictions.

What is right in the corporation is not what is right in a man's home or his church. What is right in the corporation is what the guy above you wants from you.[49]

For Jackall the primary imperative of every organization is to succeed. This logic of performance that he refers to as "institutional logic," leads to the creation of a private moral universe; a moral universe that, by definition, is totalitarian (self-sustained), solipsistic (self-defined), and narcissistic (self-centered). Within such a milieu, truth is socially defined and moral behavior is determined solely by organizational needs. The key virtues, for all alike, become the virtues of the organization: goal preoccupation, problem solving, survival/success and, most important, playing by the house rules. In time, says Jackall, those initiated and invested in the system come to believe that they live in a self-contained world that is above and independent of outside critique and evaluation.

For both Schwartz and Jackall, the logic of organizational life is rigid and unchanging. Corporations perpetuate themselves, both in their strengths and weakness, because corporate cultures clone their own. Even given the scenario of a benign organizational structure that produces positive behavior and beneficial results, the etiology of the problem and the opportunity for abuse that it offers represent the negative possibilities and inherent dangers of the "witness of others" as applied to leadership theory. Within the scope of Schwartz's and Jackall's allied analyses, "normative" moral leadership may not be possible. The model offered is both absolute and inflexible, and only "regular company guys" make it to the top. The maverick, the radical, the reformer are not long tolerated. The "institutional logic" of the system does not permit disruption, deviance, or default.

MORAL LEADERSHIP

Leadership is hard to define, and moral leadership is even harder. Perhaps, like pornography, we only recognize moral leadership when we see it. The problem is, we so rarely see it. Nevertheless, we are convinced that without the "witness" of moral leadership, standards of ethics in business and organizational life will neither emerge nor be sustained. Leadership, even when defined as a collaborative experience, is still about the influence of individual character and the impact of personal mentoring. Behavior does not always beget like behavior in a one-to-one ratio, but it does establish tone, set the stage, and offer options. Although to achieve ethical behavior, an entire organization, from top to bottom, must make a commitment to it, the model for that commitment has to originate from the top. Ethical leadership, whether in business or elsewhere, is not an outlier or an oxymoron. Rather, it expresses the true nature of the leadership challenge.

NOTES

1. Mike Singletary, quoted in "Mike Singletary Happy to Get Change with 49ers," *Chicago Tribune*, October 26, 2008. At http://articles.chicagotribune.com/2008-10-26/sports/0810250536_1_coach-ditka-49ers-safety-ronnie-lott-bears/2 (last accessed November 20, 2012).

2. Raymond C. Bauhmart, S.J., *An Honest Profit* (New York: Holt, Rinehart and Winston, 1968), xiii.

3. Rebel Cole, "Bank Credit, Trade Credit or No Credit: Evidence from the Surveys of Small Business Finances." http://www.sba.gov/advocacy/7540/4028.

4. B. F. Skinner, *Beyond Freedom and Dignity* (New York: Alfred A. Knopf, 1971), 107, 108, 150, 214, 215.

5. Stephen R. Covey, *The Seven Habits of Highly Effective People* (New York: A Fireside Book, 1990), 42, 43.

6. John Dewey, *Theory of The Moral Life* (New York: Holt Rinehart and Winston, 1960), 3–28.

7. Jean-Paul Sartre, *Existentialism and Human Emotions* (New York: The Wisdom Library, ND), 23, 24, 32, 33, 39, 40, 43, 44.

8. John Rawls, "Justice as Fairness: Political not Metaphysical," *Philosophy and Public Affairs* 14 (1985): 223–51.

9. The academic question about which system of ethics best answers the question "What we ought to do?" is a moot point and may in fact be an artificial one. However, the reality is, whichever way one decides to answer the question, "What we ought to do?" is an endemic requirement of the human condition.

10. Pope Pius XI, "Quadragesimo Anno (On Reconstructing the Social Order)" in David M. Byers, ed. *Justice in the Marketplace: A Collection of the Vatican and U.S. Catholic Bishops on Economic Policy, 1891–1984* (Washington, D.C.: United States Catholic Conference, 1985), 61.

11. Matthew Fox, *The Reinvention of Work* (San Francisco: Harper San Francisco, 1994), 298, 299.

12. "Tempo" section, *Chicago Tribune*, February 1, 1995, 2.

13. Norman E. Bowie, "Challenging the Egoistic Paradigm," *Business Ethics Quarterly*, vol. 1, no. 1 (1991): 1–21.

14. R. Edward Freeman, "The Problem of the Two Realms," speech, Loyola University Chicago, The Center for Ethics, Spring, 1992.

15. Henry Ford, Sr., quoted by Thomas Donaldson, *Corporations and Morality* (New Jersey: Prentice-Hall, Inc., 1982), 57.

16. Ibid., 14.

17. Freeman, "The Problem of the Two Realms."

18. General Robert Wood Johnson, quoted by Frederick G. Harmon and Gary Jacobs, "Company Personality: The Heart of the Matter," *Management Review* (Oct. 1985e): 10, 38, 74.

19. Georges Enderle, "Some Perspectives of Managerial Ethical Leadership," *Journal of Business Ethics*, 6 (1987): 657.

20. Peter F. Drucker with J. P. Maciarriello, *The Daily Drucker: 366 Days of Insight and Motivation for Getting the Right Things Done* (New York: Harper Business, 2004), 105, 195.

21. Tony Dungy with Nathan Whitaker, *The Mentor Leader* (Carol Stream, IL: Tyndale House Publishers, 2010).

22. Saint Augustine, *Basic Writings of Saint Augustine*, vol. 5.2: *The City of God*, edited by Whitney J. Ontes (New York: Random House, 1948), 490–91 (=book XIX, Chapter 14): "those who rule serve those whom they seem to command; for they rule not from the love of power, but from a sense of the duty they owe to others."

23. Joseph C. Rost, *Leadership for the Twenty-First Century* (Westport, CT: Praeger, 1993).

24. Garry Wills, *Certain Trumpets* (New York: Simon and Schuster, 1994), 13.

25. Ibid., 17.

26. E. P. Hollander, *Leadership Dynamics* (New York: The Free Press, 1978), 4, 5, 6, 12.

27. In an article published after his book, Joseph Rost made a change in his use of the word *followers*: "I now use the word *followers* when I write about leadership in the industrial paradigm. I use the word *collaborators* when I write about leadership in the postindustrial paradigm. This is a change from *Leadership In the Twenty-First Century*, in which I use the word *followers* all the time. The reason for the change is the unanimous feedback I received from numerous professionals throughout the nation. . . . After trying several alternative words, I settled on the word *collaborators* because it seemed to have the right denotative and connotative meanings. In other words, *collaborators* as a concept fits the language and values of the postindustrial paradigm and so its usage should not be a problem to those who want to articulate a new paradigm of leadership." See Rost, "Leadership Development in the New Millennium," *The Journal of Leadership Studies*, vol. 1, no. 1 (1993): 109, 110.

28. James MacGregor Burns, *Leadership* (New York: Harper Torchbooks, 1979), 426.

29. Al Gini, "Moral Leadership: An Overview," *Journal of Business Ethics*, vol. 16, no. 3 (1997): 323–30.

30. James O'Toole, *Leading Change* (San Francisco: Jossey-Bass, 1994); Lynn Sharp-Paine, "Managing for Organizational Integrity," *Harvard Business Review* (March–April 1994): 106–17.

31. Peter M. Senge, *The Fifth Discipline* (New York: Double/Currency Books, 1990), 345–52.

32. Christina Hoff Sommers, "Teaching the Virtues," *Chicago Tribune Magazine*, September 12, 1993, 16.

33. Thomas J. Peters and Robert H. Waterman, Jr., *In Search of Excellence* (New York: Harper and Row, 1982), 245.

34. Burns, chapters 2, 5.

35. Ibid., xi.

36. William James, *The Will to Believe* (New York: Dover Publications, Inc., 1956), 1–31, 184–215.

37. John W. Gardner, *On Leadership* (New York: The Free Press, 1990), 8.

38. Gail Sheehy, *Character: America's Search for Leadership* (New York: Bantam Books, 1990), 311.

39. Ibid., 66.

40. Burns, 36.

41. Ibid., 439.

42. For Senge the three primary tasks of leadership include: leader as designer; leader as steward; leader as teacher.

43. Senge, 353.

44. Abraham Zaleznik, "The Leadership Gap," *Academy of Management Executives*, vol. 4, no. 1 (1990): 12.

45. Joseph C. Rost, *Leadership for the Twenty-First Century*, p. 124.

46. Howard S. Schwartz, *Narcissistic Process and Corporate Decay* (New York: New York University Press, 1990).

47. Howard S. Schwartz, "Narcissistic Project and Corporate Decay: The Case of General Motors," *Business Ethics Quarterly*, vol. 1, no. 3 (1991): 250.

48. Thomas W. Norton, "The Narcissism and Moral Mazes of Corporate Life: A Commentary on the Writings of H. Schwartz and R. Jackall," *Business Ethics Quarterly*, vol. 2, no. 1 (1992): 76.

49. Robert Jackall, *Moral Mazes* (New York: Oxford University Press, 1988), 6.

Part II

The Moral Relationship between Leaders and Followers

3

Further Ethical Challenges in the Leader-Follower Relationship

Edwin P. Hollander

INTRODUCTION

Ethics and power are basic to leader-follower relations. They are interdependent, and ethical behavior is often seen associated with differential access to power. Practically speaking, ethics represents "fair dealing," essential to developing loyalty and trust in a relationship, which includes open communication. Exercising power to get one's way can thwart ethical behavior. Newer leadership practices encourage power-sharing through good teamwork, as a departure from traditional top-down power-wielding. Performing well at an organization's peak depends on the CEO's capacity as team leader doing so.[1] With such organizational effectiveness, there should be a favorable climate for ethical practices with truly open, shared communications in the team and with its support systems.

Making information available is a key to such practices. However, because information is used as a commodity of power, withholding it, by failing to inform, or wanting *not* to be informed, for deniability of responsibility, are ethical failings. They impair successful operations because some leaders are determined to maintain their power and its advantages. This includes far out risks involving secrecy and deception, even with their boards, and close followers. A case that occurred at Merrill Lynch, a troubled financial firm, involved its CEO, Stanley O'Neal, failing to inform its board of his activities, especially the extent of its substantial financial losses. He had also kept from them his secret dealings with Wachovia Bank about a possible merger/acquisition. Their import, within his noninclusive leadership style, led to his removal. Its lesson was deeply confounded though by $150 million given to him by that ending.[2]

Accepting greater compensation and status, despite failing to perform well, signals an inability to recognize "distributive justice."[3] Such leaders are found to be uncaring about how their actions are actually seen and reacted to by followers, and dismissive of consultation. Top-down leading, called "leader-centric," prevents having the benefits of shared functions, including decision-making and other participative practices, as Peter Drucker among others has warned.[4] It also may invite ethical lapses by a leader's display of such dysfunctional conduct as arrogance, insularity, and impetuousness.

SOURCES OF ETHICAL CHALLENGES

Ethical conduct and considerations of moral values are significant for leader-follower relations, but also are a source of challenge in them. Joseph Rost, emphasized that leadership is an influence relationship that should reflect *mutual purposes*,[5] and stressed that ethics had a place in leadership regarding both process and ends.

In contrast to leader-centrism, leadership is now better seen to be a process rather than a person or state. This process is essentially a shared experience, a voyage through time, with benefits to be gained and hazards to be surmounted by the parties involved. A leader is not a sole voyager, but a key figure whose actions or inactions can determine others' well-being and the broader good. Nonetheless, communal social health as well as reaching a desired destination are usually influenced by a leader's judgment and the information and values on which it is based, with what inputs from whom.

The leadership process is therefore especially fraught with ethical challenges. Christopher Hodgkinson considered leadership to be "intrinsically valuational," as "philosophy-in-action." He wrote, "Logic may set limits for and parameters within the field of value action but value phenomena determine what occurs within the field. They are indeed the essential constituents of the field of executive action ... If this were not true then leadership behavior could be routinized and, ultimately, computerized."[6] John Gardner also saw values as part of "the moral framework that permits us to judge some purposes as good and others as bad" in leadership.[7]

This view extends to avoiding coercion in making a change, and at least to informing those affected of its basis. Indeed, in most instances, Drucker said, change is not necessarily planned, but the result of a variety of factors: an unexpected success, failure, or sudden event; an incongruity between what is expected and what occurs; a process need that produces an invention; a market and industry condition; shifts in perceptions and meanings; and new knowledge.[8] Change is best achieved by a consultative process, rather than being forced based on one person's judgment, and potentially faulty decision. A more productive way is by being inclusive, involving wider participation.

INCLUSIVE LEADERSHIP (IL)

"Doing things with people, rather than to people" is the essence of inclusive leadership (IL), and it goes beyond mainly directing them.[9] It is an effective way a leader can relate to followers for mutual benefit, by "giving them a place at the table." Listening is important as a sign emphasizing respect, recognition, responsiveness, and responsibility, both ways. The goal is to achieve distributed leadership and improved outcomes.[10]

Participation is essential to IL, given that leadership need not be the total responsibility of only one person, or those with formal authority, but may be generated by informal processes called "upward influence" from followers. Having such influence can optimize organizational functioning, especially as followers perceive leaders to be competent and accountable in directing them ethically. These are elements needed to sustain followers' trust and loyalty. This approach also fits path-goal theory regarding motives leading followers toward rewarding goals.[11]

Traditionally, leader and follower roles were seen as sharply distinctive, as were leadership and followership, but they are better seen as interdependent.[12] This newer emphasis departs from a "leader-centric" model and opens an avenue for participation by followers in such processes as shared decision making. Increasing participation has been justified on grounds of the higher-order value of involvement, democratic action, increased effectiveness, and an ethical imperative. It can help to improve the quality and success of decisions and their implementation, exemplified by "workers' councils" in Europe. Recent polling of American workers indicated that only 30 percent say they are engaged at work.[13] Joanne Ciulla,[14] in this book, finds that "bogus empowerment" that does not give real power of discretion, doesn't change the leader-follower relationship.

Cultural differences, but also universals, have been found in the way that followers perceive leaders and respond to them, regarding follower expectations. The Globe Research Program[15] is an international study of leadership across world societies. Its goal was to learn what is considered effective leadership, regarding criteria of psychological welfare and international competitiveness. Worldwide, in 62 societies, it involved 17,000 respondents completing questionnaires administered in over 900 organizations.

As regards ethics, "integrity" was one of the 21 leader attributes that were found to be universally positive, and eight impediments (e.g., irritability) that were negative. "Another 35 were found to vary in different cultures; sensitivity, for example, was seen as a positive leader attribute in the US and a negative one in Russia. Some of the main propositions from the Program's integrated theory resonate with the inclusive leadership approach."[16] Among major findings from this program are these:

> Whether or not the leader is accepted depends on how well the leader's attributes and behaviors fit with the culturally endorsed implicit leadership theories (ILTs). The better the fit, the more accepted the leader will be.

> How effective a leader is depends on how well the leader's attributes and behaviors fit with the strategic organizational contingencies. The better the fit, the more effective the leader will be.

> Leaders who are accepted by their followers are more effective than leaders who are not. An effective leader will, over time, be increasingly accepted because a leader's demonstration of competence improves follower's attitudes toward the leader, resulting in increased acceptance.[17]

Inclusion seeks to improve the leader-follower relationship to yield effective team performance in groups and organizations. Bill Gates, a founder who headed Microsoft, was described by a former coworker as "trying to get the right answer ... not his answer ... always great about saying 'What do you think?' "[18] Gates earned respect by opening up discussion and then probing intently, seeking a conclusion with them. "He was not losing, but gaining, respect by listening for good suggestions. ..."[19] Here is a formal leader attaining credit. On the other hand, Dick Fuld, former CEO of Lehman Brothers, a famous investment bank with a much-publicized end, was known to squelch staff members who spoke out at meetings, especially stating opinions or questions.[20]

A typical case of excluding vital stakeholders, who were left outside, was the two-year study concluding in 2013 by the Transportation Security Administration (TSA) resulting in changing policy to allow small knives (up to 2.36 inches) again to be brought on aircraft. John S. Pistole, TSA administrator said the proposed change would free the agency to concentrate on larger threats. However, *the flying public and flight crews were not asked for input on the policy.* The nearly 90,000 *flight attendants* union coalition expressed "outrage," [protesting] "with some pilots' unions and a few major airlines. ... 'We are the last line of defense in aviation security', the coalition statement said. Pistole conceded, 'I could have done a better job of bringing them in earlier'."[21] An obvious question is what had stopped him? Eventually, two days before this policy change was to take effect, the TSA announced a delay to accommodate feedback from an advisory committee of aviation industry, consumer, and law enforcement officials.

The leader role is still seen as preeminent in directing activity and often decisive in decision-making, so it was Mr. Pistole who had the ethical responsibility to consider interests of affected parties, before making a new policy. Instead, he let his role be more an exercise of power, rather than coordinating interests that serve people who need an organizational system.[22]

In the security sector, a practical ethics issue resides in "The actual dangers from not attending to information from those 'in the know' on the working front ... [It] is revealed in Karen Cerulo's informative book, *Never Saw It Coming.*[23] A general point she made is that American optimism tends to override warnings to be concerned about disasters that might befall us. She reported that the FBI leaders in Washington headquarters repeatedly disregarded warnings of the signs of a possible terrorist assault in the United States by air, including the significant alert in the noteworthy 'Phoenix Memo' from FBI field agents before the 9/11/01 airplane attacks. Institutional leader-centrism and attitudes of superiority kept such information as these warnings from being attended to. The FBI's dominant pattern was to have directives flow down from headquarters, rather than fostering a two-way and even multiple interchange of such information."[24]

A major contrast comes from the sixth century BC, in China, when Lao Tzu wrote about the "wise leader" in his *Tao Te Ching*.[25] His philosophy made a significant contribution to the theme of sharing leadership with followers: "The wise leader settles for good work and then lets others have the floor. The leader does not take all the credit for what happens and has no need for fame."[26] This does not mean that formal leaders are to be disengaged, or their views dismissed. The intention, rather, though having the position power to be persuasive, is still to encourage and listen to other comments. Even the brightest can benefit from information and criticism, but often resist them.

Many so-called truths are actually biases out of one's particular position and culture. To a saying that, "Truth is more a liquid than a solid," one might add, "sometimes it's a gas." Ethical conduct depends on regard for verifiable truths and not their evasion. The respected late Senator, Daniel Patrick Moynihan from New York, said, "You are entitled to your own opinions, but not your own facts."

Encouraging follower involvement in decision-making and power-sharing is evident in the team emphasis in such practices as group-based management. This can be a significant benefit to an organization's functioning.[27] However, proper conditions are needed for the effectiveness of participation. As Victor Vroom and Arthur Jago assert, variability in the effectiveness of participation is dependent on specific situational variables.[28] Their contingency approach takes account of those variables that may enhance or diminish participation to yield successful outcomes. These include availability of time to consider alternatives, and shared information relevant to the particular decision task. Therefore, candor in being open about "the facts" becomes an ethical necessity. Hiding them is unethical, and a peril to good decisions and relationships.

Though leaders and their qualities are central to much leadership study, it is in engaging followers that these qualities become especially relevant for good leaders. An essential ingredient is their willingness to involve followers authentically in such matters as decision-making. Two-way influence, and the perception and counter-perception of leader and followers, is basic to the process. Hadley Cantril said the leader must be able to perceive the reality worlds of followers and have sensitivity to guide intuitions, if a common consensus and mutual trust rather than "mere power, force, or cunning" are to develop and prevail.[29] Identification with the leader is exemplified in Freud's concept of the leader as a shared "ego-ideal" with whom members of a group mutually identify.[30] They have a common bond on which life itself may depend, as in the military. Similarly, identification is enhanced in workplaces where managers have closer contact with their workforce, even in the cafeteria, and wearing similar attire.

LEADER PERFORMANCE AND "MISLEADERS"

Peter Drucker famously stated, "leadership is performance," and that it is "doing, not dash," the latter regarding charisma, which comes here later.[31] He also coined the term *misleaders* for those who are poor at leading. The central question is "What earns a favorable judgment on a leader's performance?" Obviously one important answer has to do with success in achieving group goals. But such goals may be set by the leader who thereby defines—and may redefine—the criteria for judgment within the system. In the political sphere, notably the macro-leadership of the presidency, this is "setting the agenda," and frequently involves a process of "getting on the right side of an issue." This usually requires value expression, particularly about the leader's statements about what is desirable and to be sought. The element of trust is likely to provide credit that allows a leader latitude for action.

Other things equal, positive or negative outcomes are more likely to be attributed to the leader, so that when things go wrong he or she is more readily faulted and even removed. In Jeffrey Pfeffer's causal attribution terms, leaders are symbols who can be fired to convey a sense of rooting out the basis for the problem.[32] For Sartre "To be a leader is to be responsible," but the reality too often is that responsibility and accountability are lacking. There is also the troublesome problem of misleaders who are dysfunctional, and remain on nonetheless. Evidence of higher values from such leaders is usually not forthcoming. Equity, responsibility, and accountability in the exercise of power are precious commodities. Nick Emler and Robert Hogan said, "There is no inbuilt tendency to use power responsibly. You cannot randomly allocate leadership responsibility and expect the interests of justice or society to be well served. Those in charge have a responsibility to make moral decisions greater than those they command ... (and) those differences become more consequential the further up the hierarchy one goes."[33]

The CEO and Chairman of the Board of JPMorgan Chase, Jamie Dimon, was challenged by a stockholders' rebellion in the Spring 2013 annual meeting. A majority vote, though not binding, would have him give up the latter post so another person can also oversee how the nation's largest bank is managed.[34] In 2012, this proposal garnered 40 percent of the shares in favor, but this time about 32 percent. The justification for this change, among others, was a decline in trust from the damage of a mulibillion dollar trading loss, and a crisis that became a debacle after. There is persisting concern that major banks have not altered their risky investment strategies, even after being bailed out with taxpayer funds from very costly ventures that brought on the 2008 financial recession. But Chase did not need or take any money from the government. Still, though Dimon was credited with having managed through it well, this general backdrop left little tolerance for deception and a lack of accountability central to Chase's huge 2012 risk-taking bet.

Chase's risk was in hedging bank funds with a loss initially stated as $2 billion ($2,000 million). The immense scope of this risk and loss made it the lead story riveting. Dimon, however, dismissed it as a stupid mistake, a "tempest in a teapot," though later apologized, when brought to a congressional hearing. Two months after, Dimon updated the loss, on July 13, to $5.8 billion. At an "investors' day" meeting in February 2013, the press said he "jokingly dismissed" a question from an analyst, by saying, "I'm richer than you."[35] A bipartisan U.S. Senate report in March 2013 then announced the loss as $6.2 billion, and implicated Dimon as more involved than originally denied.[36]

The damage had earlier been blamed on a rogue bank trader in London, called the "London Whale," who was said to have not been properly monitored. His chief, in charge of the investment office that dealt with trading, Ina Drew, testified that "she played no role in revising the risk model that, in part, led to the huge loss. Nonetheless, she admitted knowing the portfolio was regularly in 'breach' of the firm's risk limits in early 2012. She also said that 'senior management' at JPMorgan [agreed] on delaying a move that would have stopped the portfolio from growing significantly in early 2012."[37]

The *Times*'s business editor, Floyd Norris wrote of the report's revelations that it posed the question of whether "playing in the modern world of derivatives [should be conducted with] government-backed deposit insurance? ... Much of the attention has focused on what Jamie Dimon ... knew and when he knew it, and the extent to which the bank intentionally deceived regulators and investors as the investment strategy was blowing up." But, Norris said, "I, on the other hand, was struck by the sheer incompetence and stupidity documented in the report."[38] In that same issue, March 22, 2013, the *Times* editorialized that the revealing report and hearing showed that "recklessness, tied to speculation in derivatives," "[still is] in the banking system" and "puts the public at risk."

Ina Drew retired with her $16 million compensation package in 2012, and Dimon's salary was reduced from $23 to $11.5 million for 2013. Although Dimon accepted ultimate responsibility, his direct involvement in authorizing this risky trading process only came to light reluctantly by his emails required for this latest Senate report. Troubling issues remain about who and what were hurt, and related ethical considerations, including attempts to deceive depositors, investors, and regulators. On August 10, 2013, the *New York Times*'s front-page lead article said two of JPMorgan Chase's former London employees were reported to be facing criminal fraud charges for their role in covering up the size of this huge loss. Even after this distressing revelation of speculative excess, some in banking still pointed out it was small relative to regular banking profits.[39]

Equity, accountability, and responsibility are all of concern here. In the wake of this episode, still not closed, came demands again that the big banks be divided up so that they no longer are "Too big to fail"[40] and need to be bailed out with public, taxpayer funds again. Sandy Weill, who had been a major creator of the giant bank known as Citigroup, and earlier was Dimon's boss there, changed his long-time opposition to such division and publicly asserted he was now in favor of breaking them up.[41] U.S. Attorney General Eric Holder had then gone even further, in explaining a lack of cases against banks. Provoking controversy, he said it was because of their size that, "if we do bring a criminal charge—it will have a negative impact on the national economy, perhaps even the world economy."[42]

How such leader's statements and actions are perceived by followers has broader ethical and performance consequences. One effect of the attributional view is to make even more explicit the significance of how leaders are evaluated, not least regarding expectations about leader competence and motivation. A pointed example of this is shown in the classic research on "derailment" by Morgan McCall, Michael Lombardo, and Ann Morrison with 400 promising managers, seen to be on a fast track.[43] Those who failed to reach their expected potential were more often found to lack skills in relating to others, but not a deficit in their technical skills. Other research by Jim Kouzes and Barry Posner, with a sample of 3,400 organizational respondents, dealt with qualities they admired in their leaders, and also found the relational realm significant.[44]

The followers' view is instructive in understanding leader behavior and its effects. Our own research program, begun by Hollander and Kelly[45] used the "critical incidents technique,"[46] a mode of event analysis. We drew our total sample of 293 respondents, about half male and half female, primarily from organizationally based master's degree students enrolled in evening university courses on organizational behavior or leadership. Two-thirds held professional and/or administrative positions, and the great majority (four-fifths) were employed full time.

We asked these respondents to write a description of an incident that had occurred between them and a superior in which either good leadership (the set given one-half of the respondents) or bad leadership (given the other half) was displayed. To protect anonymity, no names or other identifying information was requested. Other follow-up questions then asked what they found rewarding or not from what that superior did or said as leader, what their own response was, and what effect this event had on the relationship with this superior. Respondents also rated the leader on six-point Likert rating scales of seven leader characteristics (e.g., involvement and directiveness), as representative of major qualities of leader reported in the literature. In addition, respondents evaluated the leader in the incident on 10 six-point semantic differential scales (e.g., capable-incapable and helpful-unhelpful).

Content analyses of the first open-ended question indicated that, in good leadership, leaders were seen to be supportive, have good communication skills in providing clarity and/or being good listeners, be action/results oriented, delegate to and/or empower subordinates, and be fair. In bad leadership, leaders were reported to be unsupportive, showing a lack of communication skills; to be uninvolving, unfair, angry or harsh, autocratic; and at times to be poor managers of resources.

The major findings of this research showed that relational qualities were emphasized in reports and evaluations distinguishing good from bad leadership. Most notably, these included providing personal and professional support, communicating clearly as well as listening, taking needed action, and delegating. Examples on the negative, dysfunctional side included instances of character flaws, unfairness, self-seeking at others' expense, lying, misjudgment, vacillation, and illegal conduct, all of which detract from the leader's standing with followers. Perhaps most important, we studied the consequences of the good or bad leadership incident with regard to the effect on the relationship and subsequent actions. This approach parallels the work of Judith Komaki on followers knowing consequences of their behavior.[47] We found that the experience of good leadership was associated most with such intangible rewards as communicating (e.g., "provided a clear message that helped me interact more effectively") and support (e.g., "backed up his staff"). Conversely, bad leadership elicited accounts of poor communication and such unrewarding behaviors as unfairness (e.g., "rules do not go for everyone") and harshness (e.g., "constantly sought to demean me"). Respondents in the good condition reported that the incident developed/strengthened their relationship with the leader and increased their respect for him or her. In the bad condition, respondents often mentioned a loss of respect, passivity/withholding, discouragement, alienation, and weakening of that relationship, ending in departure from the unit or organization.

Failure to maintain "unit cohesion" in the U.S. Army in combat conditions in the Vietnam War was due to inadequate and inattentive leadership, according to military historians Richard Gabriel and Paul Savage.[48] Gabriel and Savage said, ". . . the officer corps grew in inverse proportion to its quality . . . (and) could be described as both bloated in number and poorer in quality. . . . One result was My Lai [where many noncombatant civilians were killed by American soldiers]. Even the staunchest defenders of the Army agree that in normal times a man of [their leader] Lieutenant Calley's low intelligence and predispositions would never have been allowed to hold a commission. . . . The lowering of standards was a wound that the officer corps inflicted on itself" (p. 10). They also detail the way that the senior officer corps successfully managed to put themselves farther to the rear of action than before.

Coming to the present time, the highest-ranking U.S. military officer, General Martin E. Dempsey, publicly stated that he was "disturbed about the misconduct issues" of top commanders. Chairman of the Joint Chiefs of Staff since mid-2012, he was speaking as much as any other issue about ethical conduct. He said its basis in character has become significant to address, after a series of scandals involving high-ranking officers in the American military. "For the first time, [he] will require generals and admirals to be evaluated by their peers and the people they command on qualities including personal character, as part of a broad overhaul of training and development programs for generals and admirals. ... He said that evaluations of top officers needed to go beyond the traditional assessment of professional performance by superior officers alone ... [and] decided the changes were necessary 'to assess both competence and character in a richer way.' "[49]

Though misleaders are dysfunctional, many still continue to stay in place, and their ranks are large. From a 10-year survey, David DeVries estimated that the base rate for executive incompetence was at least 50 percent.[50] More recently, Marilyn Gowing, who had been director of personnel research in the U.S. Office of Personnel Management (OPM) reported that a similar figure had resulted from a survey conducted in the Federal Civil Service.[51] Hogan, Raskin, and Fazzini (1990) found that organizational climate studies from the mid-1950s onward show 60 to 75 percent of organizational respondents reporting their immediate supervisor as the worst or most stressful aspect of their job. Michael Argyle and Monika Henderson found similar results, with their international survey of workers.[52]

Poor performance also can seriously impede the organization's successful operations, but as already noted, rewards are given to those in charge, nonetheless. Their responsibility for performance is somehow deflected from them, as a classic case showed. Many decades ago, Roger Smith, chairman of General Motors (GM) from 1981 to 1990, presided over an unprecedented drop of almost 20 percent of his company's share in the U.S. market. For many at GM and elsewhere, Smith was considered to be rigid and unresponsive to the challenges of consumer needs and foreign competition. Asked by *Fortune* magazine to explain what went wrong, he replied, "I don't know. It's a mysterious thing." Commenting on this statement, Robert Samuelson said, "As a society, we have spent the past decade paying for mistakes like Smith's."[53] Yet the organization continued its reward pattern: On his retirement, the GM board increased his already generous pension to over a million dollars a year, a truly fabulous sum more than 30 years ago, and highly questionable, given it further reduced shareholders' value, as was complained.

The usual acquiescence to board favoritism by large payments to top executives was challenged in 2012 in a much-publicized rare case of stockholders rebelling against the $15 million salary to be paid to a CEO, Vikram Pandit at Citicorp. That vote was seemingly the first time shareholders had come together to oppose compensation at a giant financial firm. It occurred during a period of drastic slumps. Though a nonbinding resolution, the board eventually dismissed him in October 2012 with a reported $6.7 million payment. His financial stake was secure, though, because when he became CEO in 2007, he sold his hedge fund to Citicorp for $165 million, and in the intervening years acquired a vast amount of stock options in the corporation, some of which did well.

This contentious system for compensation contrasts with one that would show the discipline and unity of purpose represented in "teamwork" aimed at openly stated performance goals and related procedures.[54] Truly achieving these goals demands a concern for leader-follower relations that maintain responsibility, accountability, authenticity, and integrity. Indeed, a so-called crisis of leadership usually reveals a severe lack of these elements.[55] It is purposeful to value them as universally applicable to the political and organizational spheres. Though this position comes out of a democratic tradition, its general utility is basic to organizational psychology's views of effective leadership practices.[56]

FOLLOWER ACCEPTANCE OF A LEADER'S LEGITIMACY AND GAINING IDIOSYNCRASY CREDIT (IC)

Acceptance by followers can be seen as essential to the legitimacy of and trust in leaders. This vital follower role in perceiving the attributes, actions, and motives of a leader has come to be viewed as basic to a leader's effects on followers.[57] Fundamentally, leadership begins with a leader having legitimacy, based on whether and how he or she is seen to have become a leader, as in election or appointment. It is activated when others acknowledge his or her status as a leader, by accepting his or her direction.[58]

Central to leader-follower relations is the mutual need of followers to perceive and respond to the leader, and for the leader to them. This relationship is based on the reality that there is no leadership without followership, and raises recurring questions about how and why people follow.[59] Some answers in brief are that it depends on follower perceptions of the leader's legitimacy, how the leader behaves toward them, how the leader succeeds or fails in reaching mutual goals and in fulfilling their needs.

To bring these elements together, it is useful to conceive followers giving credit to a leader, when seen as "one of us" and performing well. Called "idiosyncrasy credit" (IC), it exists in others' perceptions and can account for leader emergence and added latitude of leader action, beyond legitimacy of authority. Followers accord such credits to a leader as a way of exercising "upward influence" so that ICs can augment and enrich transforming and other leadership practices. The relevance of the IC concept is seen in everyday speech, where "giving or taking credit" and "being discredited" are understood as expressing approval or disapproval.

Leaders may behave in ways that would be considered "non-conformist" if displayed by others. The followers make judgments about a leader who accord them ICs for performing well as an accepted member of the group who gets good results. These credits may then be used to initiate action, likely to be perceived favorably, over and above what the leader has as "legitimacy" from election or anointment to the leader role. Building on this credit concept, Terry Price considers leaders to have an allowance for "exceptionalism."[60] Given this wider berth, they can get away with acting differently, and innovating as a feature of their role, that others could not.

POWER DISTANCE: COMPENSATION, NONINCLUSION, AND LOSS OF SUPPORT

In his classic conception of powerholding, David Kipnis identified four corrupting influences of power affecting the powerholder and those in a relationship with that individual. Briefly, what he called these "metamorphic effects" are (1) power becomes desired as an end in itself, to be sought at virtually any cost; (2) holding power tempts the individual to use organizational resources for self-benefit, even illegally; (3) creates the basis for false feedback and an exalted sense of self-worth; (4) and a corresponding devaluation of others' worth, with a desire to avoid close contact with them.[61] Mauk Mulder has extended the last point especially in his concept of "power distance."[62] Such distance heightens the gap between leader and followers that exists because of disparities in available information or other resources. This gap is made smaller with processes of identification and sharing.

Because well-being is at stake, other important features of this relationship are equity, equality, and need, with the potential for perception of injustice.[63] These issues are especially salient in a condition where one person depends on another with a great power difference between them. On this point, Emerson said that the explicit recognition of dependence by a lower power person on one of higher power can promote resentment by the former.[64] This effect can undermine mutual efforts, though it has not received as much attention as more tangible rewards, such as markedly different economic benefits.[65] Clearly, the element of trust may be undercut by a leader's self-serving activity, especially the lack of accountability when he or she is manifestly failing.

Given their traditional superior role, leaders may be prone to self-serving biases beyond those that exist in other social relationships. In his analysis of some key psychological processes involved, Anthony Greenwald gave an interpretation of how the leader's ego or self incorporates several distinctive cognitive biases.[66] These include the self as focus of knowledge, "beneffectance" as the perception of responsibility for desired, but not undesired, outcomes, and resistance to change.

These tendencies are further enhanced by power over others and a sense of being different, with accompanying social distance, and potential manipulation of them as objects. A necessary corrective is for the leader to be attuned to the needs of followers, their perceptions and expectancies. However, the narcissism associated with leaders who draw on the affection of followers often deprives them of this corrective.[67] As a derivative of their identification, followers may be affected by perceptual distortions of the self-serving bias to boost their self-image.

Though they are a major strategic audience, followers still may be subjected to power distance keeping them from participating, while the leader retains full control of activities and ever greater financial benefits. The founder of Total Quality Management (TQM), W. Edwards Deming, believed that the enormous financial incentives executives receive have destroyed teamwork at many American companies.[68] In a trend dating back three decades, "CEO pay spiked 725 percent between 1978 and 2011, while worker pay rose just 5.7 percent, according to a study by the Economic Policy Institute ... Income inequality between CEOs and workers has consequently exploded, with CEOs last year [2011] earning 209.4 times more than workers, compared to just 26.5 times more in 1978—meaning CEOs are taking home a larger percentage of company gains. That trend comes despite workers nearly doubling their productivity ... when compensation barely rose. Worker productivity spiked 93 percent between 1978 and 2011 on a per-hour basis, and 5 percent on a per-person basis, according to the Federal Reserve Bank of St. Louis."[69]

Marvin Bower, who began and was the long-time head of McKinsey, a major consulting firm, said regarding CEO compensation, "Excessive pay will make people in the company feel that the chief executive . . . is not putting the business ahead of personal interests. These attitudes are demotivating to people in any company . . ."[70] The thrust of his concerns are the negative consequences of challenges to believing in the "team," the "social contract," and of not "playing fair," which can impede successful leadership.

Some leaders have become so removed from followers' perceptions and needs that they are unaware of how their actions affect the "team" they wish to muster. They may have little or no ICs, or even negative credit, as with the opposite of charisma, dubbed "derisma," from derisive or deride. Nevertheless, examples are seen of highly compensated American CEOs performing poorly, having what years ago was identified as "CEO Disease" by John Byrne, William Symonds, and Julia Flynn Siler and others.[71] *Business Week*, *Forbes*, and *Fortune* are among major business publications having featured such stories.

Criticisms have centered also on how these sums enormously exceed the pay of the average worker, as compared to foreign competitors whose ratio is far lower, despite manifestly poor outcomes for some American firms. These disparities may produce even more alienation of followers from their leaders. Though leaders are recognized as needed, they also may be resented for having a position of authority that accords them special benefits, as seen now for instance in the contempt many hold for members of Congress, though not centered on financial grounds. However, congressional salaries have grown from $30,000 in 1967 to $130,000 in 1991, and then were most recently raised to $174,000. The average annual salary in the United States has *not* increased anything like that, but as a fraction of what Congress earns, along with its coveted pensions and health care plans.

Leaders whose performance is substandard, but who remain well-rewarded, are less able to encourage good followership by gaining and retaining loyalty and trust. Indeed, it is quite to the contrary, in part, because of the inability to show concern for equity to followers. An example is at American Airlines' where pilots and flight attendants' unions had protested that their agreeing to "give-backs" in salary and benefits to save the airline resulted in selective benefits paid only to already well-compensated executives. A spokesman for the pilots said that when things were bad, workers and executives were together, but when things got better, executives salaries improved while those flying the planes continued to get reduced wages.

One reason proposed for why there are not as many complaints in the United States about the unfairness of pay disparities as there are elsewhere is that individual success is valued more here. The point is made that there is identification with those who succeed in making a great deal of money, with hopes that you will be able to get there, too. Another reason mentioned, on the pragmatic side, is that with per-sisting unemployment and corporate downsizing, a sense of threat to their job opportunities makes employees grateful for having a job at all. This may be so despite dissatisfaction with work conditions, including pay stagnating or reduced.

Signs of off-the-scale executive compensation exist not only in the corporate political sector but are observed widely, as former Harvard president Derek Bokhas reported.[72] Excess has been seen in some charitable and nonprofit organizations, and among some university presidents. In the first category was the well-publicized case of the president of United Way of America whose annual salary and benefits, apart from other perquisites, was about half a million dollars, over two decades ago, for a charitable organization.[73] Not long after that revelation, he reluctantly agreed to resign, at his board's urging. Other disclosures were made about his self-dealing activities, includ-ing the appointment he created for his son as president of a spin-off firm to market United Way products. Then came the word that the most recent president of the largest affiliate of United Way, the Tri-State (New York, New Jersey, Connecticut) division, had resigned in 1989 with a $3.3 million pension payment from that affiliate's chari-table funds. Its constituent groups voiced considerable displeasure when that fact surfaced, but after the payment was made.

In a pace-setting case, the president of the public University of Pittsburgh retired in 1991 with a multimillion dollar package plus a guaranteed annual salary of $309,000 for life. When reported in a local newspaper, this practice was found offensive by faculty and students paying ever-higher tuition.[74] In the decades since, public and private institutions have also paid generous sums to their executives, though they are supposedly nonprofit educational entities. The most publi-cized recent cases were at private New York University (NYU), where departing officials, below the presidency, leaving voluntarily, were given huge severance pay, over a million dollars. A critic on the NYU faculty was quoted in the *New York Times* saying, "Most faculty find these numbers to be obscene ... To students with a crushing debt burden, they are unfathomable."[75]

The *Times* article concluded with U.S. Senator Charles Grassley's (R-Iowa) comment that, "The problem of colleges that always seem to find money for the executive suite even as they raise tuition is not unique to New York University. However, [it] is among the most expensive, has a well-funded endowment, and has high student debt loads." He added that these expenditures demand to be explained as to "why necessary to its educational mission?" Meanwhile, the campus community was understandably aroused by revelations that President John Sexton has received or will receive considerable sums from the institution's funds, including a $1.4 million salary, $2.5 million bonus on retirement ... [extended from 2015 to 2016], plus a guaranteed additional $800,000 a year for life.[76] A question posed by Jeff Goodwin, a sociology faculty member, was that, considering NYU students have the highest debt load of any university in the country, "Rather than expanding, or paying huge salaries to top administrators, why doesn't NYU help its alumni pay off their debts?"[77]

A no-confidence resolution in Dr. Sexton was passed 298–224 by the NYU Arts and Sciences faculty in March 2013, the first in NYU history. Professor Goodwin summed up the situation in an op-ed article in the *New York Times*, saying, "How did Dr. Sexton lose the confidence of so many faculty members? By ignoring us. ... [A]bove all [he] consistently refused to address concerns about plans to expand NYU offices and dorms for ['NYU 2031'] the year in which all the building will be complete. The very name told us we'd be living on a construction site for a couple of decades [and] this did not go over very well with many faculty members. We were also concerned about where the money would come from ... as no business plan for the project had been made public. Thirty-nine departments and schools passed resolutions last year against the 2031 plan ... typically passed unanimously or nearly [so]. And yet Dr. Sexton's response was a deafening silence. [Before the recent vote] he ... professed his sincere belief in the principle of 'shared governance' ... [and] admitted he had not done all that he might to include faculty in the decision-making process at NYU. But how long can a university president continue in office when he has lost the support of so many faculty members."[78]

The other side's official view came in a reply from the chairman of the NYU Board of Trustees, Martin Lipton, longtime NYU law school alumnus, in a letter in the *Times* several days later. He stated that the 2031 expansion plan had received "wide editorial approval" [and] "overwhelming city approval ... after insuring that it was well within the university's ability to afford." He also said that, "Dr. Sexton has responded to concerns about faculty involvement for each initiative in decision-making by appointing faculty committees and has given them significant compensation packages for senior administrators ... Compensation at NYU is in line with that at the top research universities with which NYU competes, both for administrators and for faculty."[79] Notably, a shared role for "faculty governance" is invoked, however practiced, by each side. Indeed, it is supposed to singularly distinguish higher education from for-profit corporations.[80] Four faculties have since voted no-confidence against President Sexton, but the law school, where he had been dean, rejected it with only two in favor.[81] Other professional schools, medicine, dentistry, and nursing, did not conduct no-confidence votes, but their administrators stated faculty members supported Sexton.

BOARDS OF DIRECTORS AND EXECUTIVE COMPENSATION

A usually crucial audience for organizational leaders is their board of directors, to whom they are supposed to report. It can be very friendly to top leaders because leaders often select them. Though voted on in public corporations by shareholders, they rarely disapprove those selected. In general, corporate board members are almost always reelected. Of 17,081 who were up for reelection in the United States in 2012, only 61 or 0.36 percent, three-eighths of 1 percent, failed to be reelected; so well over 99 percent stayed on.[82] Boards can reward or oust executives, even do both on very generous terms. That was the case with two corporate CEOs, Citigroup's Charles Prince and Merrill Lynch's Stanley O'Neal, already mentioned. Both of them received nine-figure departure payouts despite disappointing performance, and the loss of top executives, during their tenure, who might have been their successors.

The compensation of top executives is made up of a salary, which though generous may be just a small part of the total actually received.

Bonuses are another component, and may pay much more than stipulated salary. By far the most enriching element in the package are stock options letting their owners receive or buy large blocks of stock shares at low price to sell later at hoped-for higher price, pocketing the difference, which can run up to hundreds of millions of dollars.

Still further, there also is severance pay, the so-called *golden parachute*, usually promising an additional mass of money if and when things don't work out later and they must leave. Leo Apotheker made something of a record by getting fired as CEO of Hewlett-Packard (HP) after 11 months, with a $13 million severance, and having lasted just 7 months as CEO with his previous job at SAP for an unreported parting sum.[83] The HP board chairman, Raymond Lane, who had urged hiring him, reluctantly resigned two weeks after a weak reelection, but insisted on staying on the board. Two other members who also had poor support departed under pressure finally.[84]

Andrew Mason, 32-year-old CEO of Groupon, was dismissed for decisions said to be behind a bad earnings report. At the end of February 2013, he wrote to Groupon employees, with a light touch, "... after four and a half intense and wonderful years as CEO of Groupon, I've decided that I'd like to spend more time with my family. Just kidding—I was fired today ... If you're wondering why ... you haven't been paying attention."[85] Not to worry, he had already made his nine-figure bundle. An article in *Forbes*, headed "Don't cry for Groupon's Andrew Mason," said he was personally worth over $200 million in company stock he had already cashed in or still owned.[86]

Viewing organizational leadership critically, Rost said that the emphasis seems to be that management is the essence of effective leadership.[87] While that is open to debate, it may explain in part the enormous differential in pay for CEOs and other top executives. In the original version of this chapter, published in the mid-1990s, the ratio of CEO pay to the average American worker in 1991 was 85 to 1, with Britain then 35 to 1, and Japan 17 to 1. These ratios have widened immensely since then, based on organizations using the same favorable compensation calculation methods that have accelerated expansion of these pay packages. They strive to exceed comparable organizations in bidding for executives. Especially damaging to teamwork is the case of those continuing to receive immense rewards despite unsatisfactory performance. This damage occurs too, as already mentioned, when top executives are discharged with large golden parachutes, though failing, and even in the context of corporate layoffs and downsizing they have instituted before departing.

Problems of excessive compensation are also of great concern in the European Community, which has attempted to impose restrictions. As a case in point, in 2012, "British banks have been suffering amid dismal earnings, scandals, and regulatory investigations, but three of the country's largest firms handed out seven-figure pay packages to hundreds of employees. . . . In the latest disclosures, the Royal Bank of Scotland, which is 82% owned by the British government after receiving a bailout during the financial crisis, announced . . . that 93 of its employees earned more than a million pounds, $1.5 million, last year."[88]

A still dominant corporate view in America favors no restrictions on compensation, and it has succeeded in maintaining big payouts by arguing their necessity to meet competition to keep staff. As a result, organizations continue to pay executives what are seen as "competitive" salaries and bonuses that are ever increasing at a rate far beyond other employees' pay.

CHARISMA AND ITS EFFECTS, ETHICALLY AND OTHERWISE

Contemporary with Freud's concept of the leader as an *"ego-ideal"* was the idea of the *"charismatic leader,"* to whom followers are drawn with loyalty and devotion, according to Max Weber, a German sociologist who studied bureaucracy.[89] However, he stated that charisma is not just a quality of the leader but an attribute invested by followers, especially in a time of crisis. He said charisma may be withdrawn by them if the leader is "long unsuccessful." Therefore, though the term comes from the Greek word for *divine gift*, it can be viewed as followers giving a great amount of credit to a leader. Weber had conceived charisma to be one part of acceptance by followers of a leader's various bases for claiming legitimacy. Barnard dealt with this issue in his "acceptance theory of authority," about more "rational" conditions, stated here earlier, that permitted a follower to judge a leader's order as authoritative.[90]

Ethically speaking, the leader also may use his or her charismatic appeal for personal or social gain, so charisma is not seen as an unmixed good.[91] Hodgkinson said, "Beware charisma,"[92] and Jane Howell and Bruce Avolio have observed the need to distinguish more between ethical and unethical charismatic leaders.[93] In the organizational sphere, they cite the dubious ethical conduct associated with Robert Campeau, John DeLorean, and Michael Milken, all of whom were acknowledged to have charisma for many of their followers. Unethical leaders are more likely to use charisma to enhance power over followers, for self-serving ends, in a calculated, manipulative way. Ethical leaders are likelier to use charisma in constructive ways, to serve others and social goals.

When James MacGregor Burns advanced his concept of the *transforming leader*, who changes the attitudes and behavior of followers, he regarded it as having a moral basis, yielding beneficial ends.[94] Yet, charisma was considered in connection with such leaders, as the quality often imputed to them,[95] even though Burns said it "... is so overburdened as to collapse under close analysis."[96] Charisma usually is invoked still as a term of almost general approval. In the corporate world, as well as in politics, charismatic leaders are often sought as saviors. But they may present difficulties, such as tendencies toward narcissism,[97] in addition to unethical conduct. Drucker also warned to be wary of their belief in their own infallibility.[98]

CONCLUSIONS

Although this presentation is organizationally based, its themes and emphases have larger implications at the societal level, resonating with concerns about the effects of power and distance. One point clearly is that leader characteristics affect followers by shaping their perceptions and responses. Indeed, this link between perceptions and behavior tests the ethics of a leader's actions as well as other attributes perceived by followers, and their response to those attributes.[99] At the other end of the scale, poor leaders create conditions for a lack of success, as Hackman has pointed out.[100] He specified several that can operate to cause this outcome. Prominent among these are assigning a task to a group that could be done by an individual; failing to let the group function as one in terms of its judgments; managing by being dictatorial or laissez-faire; depriving the group of needed resources and structure.

Clearly, there are ethical challenges in the use of authority and power, highlighted here in regard to open communication. Among these are the potential for destructive effects on the social contract between the leader and followers. Being a leader allows more influence and power over others' outcomes, and events more broadly. The leader also has many benefits and privileges, including higher financial rewards and the freedom to keep at a distance, if desired.

But these benefits come at the price of responsibility and accountability. Where the leader is seen to be power-oriented, exploitative, and self-serving, especially in the face of failures, the goal of mutual identification is hardly attainable. Instead, followers may feel alienated and that prospect continues to be a vital challenge.

NOTES

1. Nelson D. Schwartz, "C.E.O. Evolution Phase 3: After Empire Builders and Repair Experts, the Team Captain," *New York Times*, November 10, 2007.

2. Landon Thomas Jr. and Jenny Anderson, "A Risk-Taker's Reign at Merrill Ends with a Swift, Messy Fall," *New York Times*, October 29, 2007.

3. George Caspar Homans, *Social Behavior: Its Elementary Forms* (New York: Harcourt, Brace & World, 1961).

4. Peter F. Drucker, "Toward the New Organization," *Leader to Leader* 3 (1997): 6–8.

5. Joseph C. Rost, *Leadership for the Twenty-First Century* (New York: Praeger, 1991).

6. Christopher Hodgkinson, *The Philosophy of Leadership* (Oxford, England: Basil Blackwell, 1983), 202.

7. John W. Gardner, *On Leadership* (New York: Free Press/Macmillan,1990), 66–67.

8. Peter F. Drucker, *Innovation and Entrepreneurship: Practice and Principles* (New York: Harper & Row, 1985), 34–35.

9. Edwin P. Hollander, *Inclusive Leadership: The Essential Leader-Follower Relationship* (New York: Routledge/Psychology Press, Taylor & Francis, 2009).

10. David V. Day, Peter Gronn, and Eduardo Salas, "Leadership Capacity in Teams," *The Leadership Quarterly* 15, no. 6 (2004): 857–80.

11. See Martin G. Evans, "The Effects of Supervisory Behavior on the Path-goal Relationships," *Organizational Behavior and Human Performance* 5 (1970): 277–98. See also Robert J. House and Terrence R. Mitchell, "Path-Goal Theory of Leadership," *Journal of Contemporary Business* 3, no. 4 (1974): 11, 13.

12. Edwin P. Hollander, "American Presidential Leadership: Leader Credit, Follower Inclusion, and Obama's Turn," in *Exploring Distance in Leader-Follower Relationships: When Far is Near and Near is Far*, edited by Michelle C. Bligh and Ronald E. Riggio (New York: Routledge, 2013), 274–313. See also Edwin P. Hollander, "Inclusive Leadership and Idiosyncrasy Credit in Leader-Follower Relations," in *The Oxford Handbook of Leadership*, edited by M. G. Rumsey (New York: Oxford University Press, 2013), 122–141.

13. Gallup Poll, "Poll Watch," *The Week*, July 5–12, 2013.

14. Joanne B. Ciulla, "Leadership and the Problem of the Bogus Empowerment," in *Ethics, the Heart of Leadership*, edited by Joanne B. Ciulla (Westport, CT: Praeger, 1998).

15. Robert J. House, Paul John Hanges, Mansour Javidan, Peter W. Dorfman, and Vipin Gupta, *Culture, Leadership, and Organizations: The GLOBE Study of 62 Societies* (Thousand Oaks, CA: Sage, 2004).

16. Edwin P. Hollander, *Inclusive Leadership: The Essential Leader-Follower Relationship* (New York: Routledge/Psychology Press/Taylor & Francis, 2009), 6, 7, 8.

17. House, Hanges, Jadivan, Dorfman, and Gupta, *Culture, Leadership, and Organizations.*

18. Gregory Maffei, "Sure, Take Me on. You Might Get a Promotion," *New York Times,* January 8, 2011, Business p. 2.

19. Hollander, "Inclusive Leadership and Idiosyncrasy Credit. . ." in *The Oxford Handbook of Leadership,* edited by M. G. Rumsey (2013), 124.

20. Andrew R. Sorkin, *Too Big to Fail* (New York: Viking, 2009).

21. Joe Sharkey, "Small Knives, Small Risk? Not Everyone Thinks So," *New York Times,* March 19, 2013.

22. See, for example, Robert K. Greenleaf, *Servant Leadership: A Journey into the Nature of Legitimate Power and Greatness* (New York: Paulist Press, 1977) and Max De Pree, *Leadership Is an Art* (New York: Doubleday Dell, 1989).

23. Karen Cerulo, *Never Saw It Coming: Cultural Challenges to Envisioning the Worst* (Chicago: University of Chicago Press, 2006).

24. Hollander, *Inclusive Leadership,* 2009, 11.

25. K. O. Schmidt, *Tao Te Ching* (Lakemont, GA: CSA Press, 1975).

26. John Heider, "The Leader Who Knows How to Make Things Happen," *Journal of Humanistic Psychology* 27, no. 3 (1982): 33–39.

27. Edwin P. Hollander and Lynn Offermann, "Power and Leadership in Organizations: Relationships in Transition," *American Psychologist* 45 (1990): 179–89

28. Victor H. Vroom and Arthur G. Jago, "The Role of the Situation in Leadership," *American Psychologist* 62 (2007): 17–24.

29. Hadley Cantril, "Effective Democratic Leadership: A Psychological Interpretation," *Journal of Individual Psychology* 14 (1958): 128, 138.

30. Sigmund Freud, *Group Psychology and the Analysis of the Ego* (New York: Bantam: 1960. Originally published in German in 1921.

31. Peter F. Drucker, "Leadership: More Doing Than Dash," *Wall Street Journal,* January 6, 1998.

32. Jeffrey Pfeffer, "The Ambiguity of Leadership," in *Leadership; Where Else Can We Go?,* edited by. Morgan W. McCall, Jr., and Michael M. Lombardo (Durham, NC: Duke University Press, 1977).

33. Nick Emler and Robert Hogan, "Moral Psychology and Public Policy," in *Handbook of Moral Behavior and Development,* volume 3, edited by W. M. Kertines and J. L. Gewirtz (Hillsdale, NJ: Lawrence Erlbaum, 1991), 69–93.

34. Susanne Craig and Jessica Silver-Greenberg, "A Call for New Blood on the JPMorgan Board," *New York Times,* May 6, 2013.

35. Ben Protess and Jessica Silver-Greenberg, "Trading Hearings Put Focus Back on JPMorgan's Chief," *New York Times,* March 18, 2013.

36. Jessica Silver-Greenberg and Ben Protess, "Senate Inquiry Faults JPMorgan on Trading Loss," *New York Times,* March 15, 2013.

37. Stephen Gandel, "Former London Whale Boss: I Was Misled," *CNN Money,* March 15, 2013.

38. Floyd Norris, "Masked by Gibberish, the Risks Run Amok," *New York Times,* March 22, 2013.

39. Ben Protess and Jessica Silver-Greenberg, "U.S. Said to Arrest Pair in Big Bank Loss," *New York Times,* August 10, 2013.

40. Sorkin, "Too Big to Fail," 2009.

41. Sanford I. Weill was quoted in Michael J. de la Merced, "Deal Maker Now Doubts Megabanks," *New York Times,* July 26, 2012.

42. Andrew Ross Sorkin, "Realities Behind Prosecuting Big Banks," *New York Times*, March 12, 2013.

43. Morgan W. McCall, Michael M. Lombardo, and Ann M. Morrison, *The Lessons of Experience: How Successful Executives Develop on the Job* (Lexington, MA: Lexington Books, 1988).

44. Jim Kouzes and Barry Posner, *The Leadership Challenge: How to Get Extraordinary Things Done in Organizations* (San Francisco: Jossey-Bass, 1987).

45. Edwin P. Hollander and Dennis R. Kelly, "Rewards from Leaders as Perceived by Followers" (paper, Eastern Psychological Association, Philadelphia, March 30, 1990); Edwin P. Hollander and Dennis R. Kelly, "Appraising Relational Qualities of Leadership and Followership" (paper, 25th International Congress of Psychology, Brussels, July 24, 1992).

46. John C. Flanagan, "The Critical Incident Technique," *Psychological Bulletin* 51 (1954): 327–58.

47. Judith L. Komaki, *Leadership from an Operant Perspective* (London: Routledge, 1998).

48. Richard Gabriel and Paul Savage, *Crisis in Command* (New York: Hill and Wang, 1978).

49. Thom Shanker, "Conduct at Issue as Subordinates Review Officers," *New York Times*, April 14, 2013.

50. David L. DeVries, "Executive Selection: Advances but No Progress," *Issues and Observations* 12 (1992): 1–5

51. Marilyn Gowing, Personal Communication, March, 2006

52. Michael Argyle and Monika Henderson, *The Anatomy of Relationships* (London: Heinemann, 1985).

53. Robert Samuelson, "The Death of Management," *Newsweek*, May 10, 1993, 55.

54. See, for example, J. Richard Hackman, *Groups That Work (and Those That Don't)* (San Francisco: Jossey-Bass, 1989) and Jon R. Katzenbach and Douglas K. Smith, *The Wisdom of Teams: Creating the High-Performance Organization* (Cambridge, MA: Harvard Business School Press, 1993).

55. Edwin P. Hollander, "What Is the Crisis of Leadership?" *Humanitas* 14 (1978): 285–96.

56. John W. Gardner, *On Leadership* (New York: Free Press/Macmillan, 1990); Edwin P. Hollander, *Leadership Dynamics: A Practical Guide to Effective Relationships* (New York: Free Press/Macmillan, 1978); Charles Manz and Henry Sims, *Super-Leadership: Leading Others to Lead Themselves* (New York: Prentice Hall Press, 1989).

57. Robert E. Kelley, "In Praise of Followers," *Harvard Business Review* 88 (1988): 142–48; Robert E. Kelley, *The Power of Followership* (New York: Doubleday, 1992).

58. Chester I. Barnard, *The Functions of the Executive* (Cambridge, MA: Harvard University Press, 1938); Mary Parker Follett, "The Essentials of Leadership," in *Freedom and Coordination*, edited by L. Urwick (London: Management Publication Trust), 47–60.

59. Michael Maccoby, "What Kind of Leader Do People Want to Follow?," in *The Art of Followership*, edited by Ronald E. Riggio, Ira Chaleff, and Jean Lipman-Blumen (San Francisco: Jossey-Bass, 2008), 209–17.

60. Terry L. Price, *Leadership Ethics: An Introduction* (New York: Cambridge University, 2008).

61. David Kipnis, *The Powerholders* (Chicago: University of Chicago Press, 1976).

62. Mauk Mulder, "On the Quantity and Quality of Power and the Q.W.L." (paper, International Conference on the Quality of Work Life, Toronto, 1981).

63. Morton Deutsch, "Equity, Equality, and Need: What Determines Which Value Will Be Used as the Basis of Distributive Justice?," *Journal of Social Issues* 31 (1975): 137–49.

64. Emerson, "Power-Dependence Relations."

65. Derek Bok, *The Cost of Talent* (New York: Free Press, 1993).

66. Anthony Greenwald, "Totalitarian Egos in the Personalities of Democratic Leaders" (paper, International Society of Political Psychology Annual Meeting, Washington, D.C., June 20, 1985).

67. Jerrold M. Post, "Narcissism and the Charismatic Leader-Follower Relationship," *Political Psychology* 7 (1986): 675–88.

68. W. Edwards Deming, Quoted in *The Economist*, February 1, 1992, 19.

69. Bonnie Kavoussi, "CEO Pay Grew 127 Times Faster Than Worker Pay Over Last 30 Years, Study Finds," *Huffington Post*, July 4, 2012, Business p. 1.

70. Marvin Bower, *The Will to Lead* (Boston: Harvard Business School Press, 1997), 127.

71. John A. Byrne, William C. Symonds, and Julia Flynn Siler, "CEO Disease," *Business Week*, April 1, 1991, 52–60. See also Graef S. Crystal, *In Search of Excess: The Overcompensation of American Executives* (New York: W. W. Norton, 1991).

72. Bok, *The Cost of Talent*, 1993.

73. Dennis Hevesi, "United Ways Challenge Method Used to Divide Their Donations," *New York Times*, March 20, 1992.

74. Frank Reeves, "Pitt Misled Us, Lawmaker Asserts," *Pittsburgh Post-Gazette*, April 25, 1991.

75. Ariel Kaminer, "More Than One N.Y.U. Star Got Lavish Parting Gift," *New York Times*, March 4, 2013.

76. Ibid.

77. Jeff Goodwin, "The War in Washington Square," *New York Times*, March 21, 2013.

78. Ibid.

79. Martin Lipton, "Letter to the New York Times from Chairman of NYU Board of Trustees," *New York Times*, March 26, 2013.

80. Edwin P. Hollander, "Leadership in Higher Education," in *The Oxford Handbook of Leadership*, edited by M. G. Rumsey (New York: Oxford University Press, 2013), 311–26.

81. Ariel Kaminer, "Fourth No Confidence Vote for the President of N.Y.U.," *New York Times*, May 11, 2013.

82. James B. Stewart, "Bad Directors and Why They Aren't Thrown Out," *New York Times*, March 30, 2013.

83. James B. Stewart, "When Shareholder Democracy is Sham Democracy," *New York Times*, April 13, 2013.

84. Quentin Hardy, "H.P. Chairman Steps Down as 2 Resign from Board," *New York Times*, April 5, 2013.

85. David Streitfeld, "Groupon Dismisses Chief after a Dismal Quarter," *New York Times*, March 1, 2013.

86. Joan Lappin, "Don't Cry for Groupon's Andrew Mason," *Forbes*, February 5, 2013.

87. Rost, *Leadership for the Twenty-First Century*, 1991.

88. Julia Werdigier and Mark Scott, "A Bad Year in Britain for Banks, Not Bankers," *New York Times*, March 9, 2013.

89. Max Weber, "The Sociology of Charismatic Authority," in *From Max Weber: Essays in Sociology*, translated and edited by Hans H. Gerth and C. Wright Mills (New York: Oxford University Press, 1946), 245–52. Original in 1921 in German.

90. Barnard, *The Functions of the Executive* (Cambridge, MA: Harvard University Press, 1938).

91. Robert J. House and Boas Shamir, "Toward the Integration of Transformational, Charismatic and Visionary Theories," in *Leadership Theory and Research: Perspectives and Directions*, edited by Martin M. Chemers and Roya Ayman (San Diego, CA: Academic Press, 1993), 81–107.

92. Hodgkinson, *The Philosophy of Leadership*, 187.

93. Jane M. Howell and Bruce J. Avolio, "The Ethics of Charismatic Leadership: Submission or Liberation?" *Academy of Management Executive* 6 (1992): 43–54.

94. James MacGregor Burns, *Leadership* (New York: Harper & Row, 1978).

95. James MacGregor Burns, *Leadership*; Bernard M. Bass, *Leadership and Performance Beyond Expectations* (New York: Free Press, 1985).

96. Burns, *Leadership*, 1978, 243.

97. See Post, "Narcissism and the Charismatic Leader-Follower Relationship," 1986.

98. Drucker, "Leadership: More Doing Than Dash," 1988.

99. See Robert G. Lord and Karen J. Maher, "Leadership Perceptions and Leadership Performance: Two Distinct but Interdependent Processes," in *Advances in Applied Social Psychology: Business Settings*, edited by John S. Carroll (Hillsdale, NJ: Erlbaum, 1990), 4: 129–54.

100. Hackman, *Groups That Work*, 1989.

4

The Bogus Empowerment of Followers

Joanne B. Ciulla

Empowerment conjures up pictures of inspired and confident people or groups of people who are ready and able to take control of their lives and better their world. The empowered are the neighbors in a community who band together and take action to drive out drug dealers; the long-time welfare mother who gets a job and goes on to start a business; the child who learns to read and to ride a bike. Power is a relationship between people with mutual intentions or purposes.[1] Empowerment is about giving people the confidence, competence, freedom, and resources to act on their own judgments. Hence, when a person or group of people is empowered, they undergo a change in their relationship to other people who hold power and with whom they share mutual goals. In a community, empowering citizens changes their relationship to each other and to other holders of power such as business and government. In a business, empowering employees changes their relationship to each other, management, and the work process.

You can hardly pick up a popular business book without seeing the words *leadership, empowerment, trust,* or *commitment* either on the cover or in the text. Gone are the bosses of the industrial era. Since industrialization, organizations have entered a new age where employees are partners and part of the team. Not only are managers supposed to be leaders—all employees are supposed to be leaders in their own way. This is good. It's democratic. It shows respect for persons and it sounds very ethical. So why isn't everyone happy? Why do business leaders worry about trust and loyalty? Why are employees cynical? One reason is that people are not secure in their jobs because of the recession, technology, and competition from the global labor market. The other reason, and focus of this chapter, is that in many organizations promises of empowerment are bogus. The word *bogus* is a term used to express anger, disappointment, and disgust over hypocrisy, lies, and misrepresentations. This is how people feel when they are told that they are being empowered, but they know that they are not. When leaders promise empowerment, they raise the moral stakes in their relationship to followers. Failure to deliver can lead to even greater cynicism about leadership, alienation, and abdication of moral responsibility by employees and/or citizens.

When you empower others, you do at least one of the following: You help them recognize the power that they already have, you recover power that they once had and lost, or you give them power that they never had before. In his study of grassroots empowerment, Richard Couto says there are two main kinds of empowerment. The first kind he calls psycho-political empowerment. It increases people's self-esteem and results in a change in the distribution of resources and/or the actions of others. In other words, empowerment entails the confidence, desire and, most important, the ability of people to bring about real change. This is probably what most people think of when they think of empowerment. Couto calls the second form of empowerment psycho-symbolic empowerment. It raises people's self-esteem or ability to cope with what is basically an unchanged set of circumstances.[2] More often than not, leaders promise or appear to promise the first kind of empowerment but actually deliver the second.

In this chapter, I argue that authentic empowerment entails a distinct set of moral understandings and commitments between leaders and followers, all based on honesty. I begin by looking at the cultural values behind the idea of empowerment, particularly as it applies in the workplace. My primary focus is on business organizations, but much of what I have to say about the moral aspects of empowerment applies to leaders and followers in community, nonprofit, and political contexts as well. I briefly outline how the idea of empowerment has evolved in management theory and practice. Critical analysis of this history and the ways in which empowerment is manipulative and unauthentic, will then help establish some of the moral aspects of empowerment and their implications for leadership.

THE SOCIAL VALUES BEHIND EMPOWERMENT

The idea of empowerment has its charm. U.S. citizens treasure democracy and its accompanying values of liberty and equality. If democracy were the only goal of empowerment, U.S. citizens would have the most democratic workplaces in the world, but they don't. As Tom Wren points out, ever since U.S. independence, there has been a conflict between the values of equality and authority.[3] This tension is clearly evident in all organizational life. However, there are other values in our culture that shape the leadership and values of the workplace. Philosopher Charles Taylor identifies three values of the modern age that he says cause personal anxiety and social malaise. They are individualism, instrumental reason (which causes disenchantment with the world), and freedom (which people seem to be losing because of individualism and instrumentalism).[4] Ideally empowerment is what makes humans triumph over the anxiety they have over these values and provides the antidotes to the social malaise.

In the workplace are constant tensions among individualism, freedom, and instrumental value and/or economic efficiency (I count these as two aspects of the same value). In a society where people value individualism and freedom, the challenge of leadership in organizations is the challenge of leading cats, not sheep.[5] This means leaders have to use more powerful means of control than they would in a culture where people live in accepted hierarchies. For example, Americans were smitten with Japanese management in the late 1970s because it was effective and seemed so democratic. What they failed to realize was that the Japanese could afford to be democratic because the social controls imposed by hierarchy and community were internalized in workers, hence requiring less overt control by managers. U.S. business leaders face the challenge of maintaining control without overtly chipping away at individualism and democratic ideals. This is why the language of empowerment is so attractive.

Economic efficiency and instrumentalism are the most powerful and divisive values in the workplace. They trump all other values, and our current faith in the market makes it difficult to sustain plausibly any other ethical values in an organization. The market is a nasty, ruthless boss. Instrumentalism or the value of getting the job done is more important than the means and people used to get it done. Business leadership is effective if it gets results. Leaders and their organizations are successful if they make the most amount of money or do the most amount of work in the least amount of time. Not only are the ends more important than the means, there is little if any room for things that have intrinsic but noninstrumental value in business. The greatest of all impediments to empowerment in business, and increasingly in all areas of life, is economic efficiency. It acts on rules that refuse to take into account special circumstances.

In addition to the values of instrumentalism, individualism, and freedom, I add a fourth social value that I call "niceness." It might sound strange to say that U.S. culture values niceness at a time when there seems to be little civility. Niceness is not civility. Historian Norbert Elias traces the origin of civility to the sixteenth-century Dutch philosopher Erasmus. His book, *De Civilitate Morum Puerilium* or *On Civility in Children*, chronicles the proper behavior of people in society, with a special emphasis on outward physical behavior. In short, it is an etiquette book about properly blowing one's nose, eating at the table, and relieving oneself. Published in 130 editions and translated into English, French, Czech, and German, Erasmus's book established the concept of civility as behavior that was considerate of other people in a society.[6] Immanuel Kant later points out that civility is not morality (because it doesn't require a good will), but the similitude of morality—an outward decency.[7] Civility is the behavior that citizens should have toward their fellow citizens. It includes an obligation of citizens to be polite and respectful of the private rights of others.

Whereas the concept of civility develops as a form of outward consideration for others (e.g., not picking your nose in public), niceness is used as a means of gaining the favor and trust of others by showing a willingness to serve. Niceness fits the description of courtly behavior from which we get the term *courtesy*. The following selection from the *Zeldler Universal Lexicon of 1736* captures the basic elements of commercial niceness:

> The courts of great lords are a theater where everyone wants to make his fortune. This can only be done by winning favor with the prince and the most important people of his court. One therefore takes all conceivable pains to make oneself agreeable to them. Nothing does this better than making the other believe that we are ready to serve him to the utmost capacity under all conditions. Nevertheless we are not always in a

position to do this, and may not want to, often for good reasons. Courtesy serves as a substitute for all this. By it we give the other so much reassurance, through our outward show, that he has a favorable anticipation of our readiness to serve him. This wins us the other's trust, from which an affection for us develops imperceptibly, as a result of which he becomes eager to do good to us.[8]

There are other distinctive facets of niceness that are embedded in the observations of social critics since the mid-twentieth century. The first element of niceness is the belief that social harmony means lack of conflict. In *An American Dilemma*, Gunnar Myrdal explains one facet of niceness. He argues that U.S. social scientists derived their idea of social harmony from liberalism based on the Enlightenment ideal of *communum bonum* or common good. Radical liberals wanted to reformulate corrupt institutions into places where natural laws could function. The radical liberal, who could be a communist, socialist, or anarchist, wanted to dismantle power structures of privilege, property, and authority. In the utopia of the radical liberal, the concept of empowerment would not be useful. People would not need to be given power or made to feel powerful, because the restraints that institutions had on their lives would in theory be removed. However, the dominant view in the social sciences (and certainly among those who were management theorists) was conservative liberalism. The conservative liberal takes society as it is and, under the influence of economics, adopts the idea of social harmony as stable equilibrium.[9] The social scientists studied empirically observable situations and terms such as balance, harmony, equilibrium, function, and social process. They pretended that these terms gave a "do-nothing" valuation of a situation, but these words carry a veiled set of value judgments. Myrdal notes:

> When we speak of a social situation being in harmony, or having equilibrium, or its forces organized, accommodated, or adjusted to each other, there is almost inevitable implication that some sort of ideal has been attained, whether in terms of "individual happiness" or "the common welfare."[10]

Traditionally, management theorists have tacitly accepted the valuations behind these terms. Empowerment, like harmony, is assumed to be a good that brings about individual happiness. Social harmony in an organization meant accommodating and adjusting people. Conflict or disharmony was a sign of failed leadership. Niceness comes out of this one-dimensional picture of stable equilibrium and harmony. If no one complains and yells at work, then there is social harmony. Furthermore, the "do-nothing" value-free stance of social scientists is in part responsible for some of the manipulative theories and practices in management.

David Riesman captured another root of niceness in his 1950 description of the emerging U.S. character. In *The Lonely Crowd*, Riesman described inner-directed people who can cope with society because they are directed by internal, general goals implanted in them by their elders. Riesman observed that these people are becoming far and few between. Inner-directed people have less need for empowerment because they have what they need built-in. The more prevalent character type identified by Riesman is the other-directed person. These people are shallower, friendlier, and more uncertain of themselves.[11] Other-directed people take more of their clues on values and goals from the outside: They want to be liked and have a strong need to belong.

In his book, Riesman describes a society dominated by other-directed people, in which manipulative skill overshadows craft skill and expense accounts overshadow bank accounts. Business is supposed to be fun and managers are supposed to be glad-handers who joke with staff and charm their bosses and clients. Most importantly, Riesman notes the trend that continues today of rewarding highly skilled people with management positions and power over other people. Hence the skilled engineer who gets promoted has to become a skilled glad-hander. The growth of the service industry shaped this character type into the model leader-manager and employee. To be successful in a service, one has to be friendly, likable, and nice. Since Riesman's day, bank accounts matter more and expense accounts are smaller. What remains the same is the powerful value of the glad-hander. Our society may be less civil, and perhaps because of it niceness has been commercialized into the courtly norm of friendly bosses, bankers, and waiters all intent on gaining favor with customers and superiors to facilitate a smooth transaction.

As practiced in business, niceness consists of not getting into disputes and behaving in a commercially friendly fashion. Because people don't seem to behave this way naturally, we need the help of the therapist to attain niceness. In *The Triumph of the Therapeutic*, Philip Rieff says that truth has become a highly personal matter he calls "psychic truth."[12] He thinks that *therapeutic effectiveness* has replaced the value of truth in our culture. Truths that make people feel better and help them adjust and fit in are far more desirable than truths that rock the boat. If our culture places more importance on psychic truths than on real truths, and if some "truths" or therapeutic fictions are effective because they make people happier, then leaders only have an obligation to make people *feel* empowered. They do not have to give them actual power.

It is obvious why niceness, based on therapeutic lies and conflict-free environments and a kind of bland friendliness that we experience when we go the store or a bank, is one of the values that lurk behind the history of empowerment in business for an obvious reason. Leaders often prefer the "nice" kind of empowerment to the kind that leads to chaos and loss of control. It is a form of politeness in which leaders pretend that followers have a choice. It is "would you take the time to do this?" rather than "do this," but the meaning is the same. As I have said, there is empowerment and bogus empowerment. I describe bogus empowerment as the use of therapeutic fictions to make people feel better about themselves, eliminate conflict, and satisfy their desire to belong (niceness), so that they will freely choose to work toward the goals of the organization (control of individualism), and be productive (instrumentalism). Leaders who offer bogus empowerment are insincere and disrespectful of others. They believe that they can trick followers into believing they have been given power when in fact they have none.

EMPOWERMENT AND THE ORGANIZATION MAN

The sociologist C. Wright Mills offers one of the earliest and clearest articulations of bogus empowerment:

> The moral problem of social control in America today is less the explicit domination of men than their manipulation into self-coordinated and altogether cheerful subordinates.[13]

Mills believed that management's real goal was to "conquer the problem of alienation within the bounds of work alienation."[14] By this he meant that the problems of the workplace had to be defined and solved in terms of the values and goals of the workplace itself. By controlling the meanings and the terms under which alienation was conquered and satisfaction found, employers could maintain control without alienating workers. William H. Whyte echoed Mills's concern about psychological manipulation in *The Organization Man*, only Whyte zeroed in on people's need to belong. The workplace of the late 1950s is both radically different from and strikingly similar to today's workplace. Whyte criticized the social ethic that makes morally legitimate the pressure of society against the individual. The social ethic rationalizes the organization's demand for loyalty and gives employees who offer themselves wholeheartedly a sense of dedication and satisfaction. The social ethic includes a belief that the group is a source of creativity. A sense of belonging is the ultimate need of the individual, and social science can create ways to achieve this sense of belonging.[15]

Whyte feared that psychologists and social engineers would strip people of their creativity and identity. He attacked the use of personality tests to weed out people who don't fit in. He also challenged the notion that organizations should be free from conflict. The critique of the workplace in Whyte's book is similar to the critiques that liberals have of communitarianism. Community-oriented life looks good, but it is ultimately oppressive and authoritarian. In the fifties social critics worried about the conformity of people to institutions and the values of suburban life. Today we worry about lack of consensus about values, political polarization, and the breakdown of urban and suburban communities. Organizations often want to build teams and emphasize the value of group work. No one seems worried about loss of creativity and submission of individual identity to group identity. Managers care more about the problem of the individual who is not a team player and most management theorists believe that groups and teams are the foundation of all that is good and productive.

Whyte says, "The most misguided attempt at false collectivization is the attempt to see the group as a creative vehicle."[16] Contrary to popular management thinking today, Whyte does not believe that people think or create groups. Groups, he says, just give order to the administration of work. Whyte describes an experiment done at the National Training Lab on leaderless groups. Theoretically, when the group "jelled," the leader would fade into the background, to be consulted for his expertise only. These groups resulted in chaos, but as Whyte puts it, the trainers hoped that the resulting "feeling draining" of the group would be a valuable catharsis and a prelude to agreement.[17] According to Whyte, the individual has to enter into the process somewhere. If everyone wants to do what the group wants to do, and nothing gets done, then the individual has to play a role in the process. However, Whyte wonders if we should openly bring individuals into the process or "bootleg," it in an expression of group sentiment. Basically, he sees the leaderless group as intellectual hypocrisy. The power and authority of groups simply mask the real power and authority of leaders.

It is useful to compare Whyte's observations to those of later studies such as James Surowiecki's book *The Wisdom of Crowds*. Surowiecki argues that crowds can make better decisions than individuals under the right conditions.[18] The conditions require that the individuals in the crowd are independent of each other, have diverse opinions, are not located in a centralized place, and have some method of aggregating opinions. As described, the crowd avoids the problems that White sees with groups in organizations. The same is true of the kind of crowdsourcing that is the backbone of creative endeavors such as Wikipedia. Technology has found a way around Whyte's problem with groups by empowering everyone individually, which has allowed groups of unrelated strangers engage in creative endeavors. This sort of empowerment does not always translate to the workplace where there is usually still a desire to control employees and behavior of individuals and groups.

In his book, Whyte also urges people to cheat on all psychological tests given during job interviews and at the workplace. He pits the individual against the organization and what he sees as the social scientist's coercive idea of belongingness. Another famous illustration of the struggle against the organization is in Sloan Wilson's novel, *The Man in the Gray Flannel Suit*, published a year before Whyte's book. In the novel, a personnel manager asks the main character, Tom Rath, to write an autobiography in which the last line reads, "The most significant thing about me is . . ." Revolted by the exercise, Rath debates whether to say what the company wants to hear (the therapeutic lie) or write about his most significant memory, concerning a woman he met during the war. Caught between truth and fiction, Rath holds on to his dignity by stating the facts—his place of birth, his schooling, and the number of children in his family. He writes that the most significant thing about him is the fact that he is applying for the job. He also says that he does not want to write an autobiography as part of his application.[19]

Rath draws a fine line between himself and the organization. Whyte misses the moral in the first scene of Wilson's book: telling the truth strikes a much stronger blow for individual dignity than beating the organization at its own game. Wilson's novel might still resonate with students today because all of them at some time will have to decide how truthful they have to be in a job interview or with an employer and how much of themselves they are willing to give to an organization. It is sometimes difficult to tell the truth when you want someone to like you. The fine line is not about the amount of hours or work one does. It is the boundary that people draw between their inner self and the parts of them needed to do their job. It is the line that allows a person to be both an individual and part of a group. In today's workplace, it isn't always easy to draw this line, especially when social media allows people to display aspects of their personal lives and thoughts to the world. Some people discover that what they want their friends and family to know about them is not what they want their employer or future employer to know.

THE RACE FOR THE WORKER'S SOUL

In the 1960s, the centralized bureaucratic organization of the fifties gave way to the sensitive approach to management. The National Training Labs developed sensitivity training and T-Groups to transform bossy managers into participative ones. After much crawling around on the floor together and getting in touch with their inner feelings, few managers were transformed. During the seventies and eighties, management fads designed to capture the souls of workers bombarded the workplace. Fueled by global competitive pressures, managers were ready to try anything to increase productivity and competitiveness. In 1981, William Ouchi's *Theory Z* and Richard Pascal's and Anthony Athos's *The Art of Japanese Management* were best sellers. The "new" idea from Japan was job enrichment and quality circles—after all, it worked for the Japanese. In 1982, the mystical Eastern touch of these two books gave way to Thomas J. Peters's and Robert H. Waterman's blatantly evangelical book *In Search of Excellence*. Peters and Waterman realized outright that the role of a manager is to make meaning for employees and create excitement. They argued that excellent organizations do not produce the conformist described by Whyte. They assure us that "In the very same institutions in which culture is so dominant, the highest levels of true autonomy occur. The culture regulates rigorously the few variables that do count, and it provides meaning."[20] Nonetheless, in these organizations people are encouraged to "stick out, to innovate."

If a strong culture provided meaning, it could reach to the very souls of employees, hence allowing for great freedom and creativity within the boundaries of the culture and the meanings provided by the culture. This kind of organization is designed to foster Mills's cheerful subordinates.

In the eighties and nineties, the word *leadership* began taking the place of the word *management* in business books. The semantic change is also a conceptual change from the idea of a manager as a boss who commanded and controlled the process of production to the leader who inspires people to work toward mutual goals. Joe Rost says that in the old industrial paradigm, leadership was nothing more than good management.[21] Empowerment is at least implied in most recent articulations of leadership in business books today. What is confusing about this literature is that it continues to be written for people who usually hold the position of manager. In ordinary discourse, people talk about managers who lead and managers who manage. The carefully crafted distinctions between leaders and managers that are made in the scholarly leadership literature are not always present in popular usage. What we do see in ordinary U.S. discourse is that leadership has positive connotations and is sometimes used as an honorific, whereas management is either neutral or slightly negative.

The management fads from the 1980s until today have appealed to business leaders (and those who aspire to be business leaders) because they make them feel powerful, inspiring, adventuresome, and lovable all at the same time. The lovable leader is an attractive image, especially given the lack of respect and trust for some authority figures in business and politics today. Lovable leaders are nice because they are democratic and they do not openly exert power over others. Practicing lovable leadership requires some therapeutic fictions. CEOs of large corporations have spent fortunes on consultants and training programs. The goal of most of the programs has been to make work seem more enjoyable and participatory and to push power relationships between employees and management into the background. All of this is done in hope of creating a more competitive business. Sometimes these programs backfire. Consider the case of Pacific Bell.

In 1987, the California Public Utilities Commission asked Pacific Bell to stop its leadership-development program. The program intended to move away from the old AT&T culture, empower low-level managers and give them more responsibilities, cut middle managers, and become more customer-focused. At Pacific Bell 23,000 of 67,000 employees took the two-day training.[22] Charles Krone created the leadership development program that came to be called "Kroning." This New Age program aimed at getting all employees to use the same language and think at all times about the six essentials of organizational health: expansion, freedom, identity, concentration, order, and interaction. The program was based vaguely on the Armenian mystic Gurdjieff's Law of Three, which teaches that there are no constraints that can't be reconciled.[23]

After a two-month investigation of this $40 million training program, the commission reported that employees complained of brainwashing. An employee survey turned up repeated descriptions of the program as Big Brother, thought control, and mind restructuring. Employees also claimed that the Krone program used obtuse language and unnecessary concepts that made some people feel stupid. The irony was that the investigation discovered that a large majority of employees expressed a love of and commitment to Pacific Bell and mistrust of its management.[24] A Meridian survey of 2,000 Pacific Bell employees concluded that top managers at Bell "blame the employees for the lack of productivity and are trying to make them think better. However, the Pacific Bell workforce already knows how to think."[25]

In 1987, *California Business* surveyed 500 corporate owners and presidents and found that half their companies used some form of consciousness-raising.[26] These programs focused on the same themes espoused today: empowerment, leadership, and positive thinking. They are distinctive because they used such unorthodox training techniques as meditation, biofeedback, and hypnosis. For example, a company called Energy Unlimited escorted executives across hot coals as a means of empowering people. Today ropes courses that claim to teach leadership and team building are popular forms of training for business, government, and educational institutions. Although many of these programs now look silly to the outsider, they have serious followers among corporate managers. Their impact on other employees is unclear. We rarely hear about cases in which employees complain about a company motivational program. That's why the Krone's scandal is so interesting.

In 2012 U.S. businesses spent an estimated $170 billion on leadership training programs.[27] Employees tend to be a captive audience: Their success in the organization is contingent on buying into these programs. Motivational human potential courses often create a short-lived sense of euphoria among employees and/or a Hawthorne effect.

They raise the expectation that employees will be enriched and empowered, however, after the dust settles, everything seems the same until the next initiative. Today leadership training continues to have the same problems that it had in the past. As one critic of leadership training programs notes, "My problem with training is it *presumes* the need for indoctrination on systems, processes and techniques. Moreover, training *assumes* that said systems, processes and techniques are the right way to do things."[28] No training program will have the same sustainable impact unless employers treat employees as autonomous human beings capable of making decisions about how they do their work. Empowerment and/or leadership development are about helping people think critically not conform to the template of a training program or organization.

EMPOWERMENT AND PARTICIPATION

Discussions about worker participation, including issues such as empowerment and the team approach, derived from two sources: industrial relations research and management research (largely based on organizational behavior). On the industrial relations side, discussion in the 1970s focused on workplace democracy. Admirable models of workplace democracy included democratic worker councils employed at the time in Yugoslavian industries. These councils allowed workers to play an active part in all facets of the business. Employees even elected their own managers. Other researchers in the sixties and seventies studied worker cooperatives in hopes of finding clues to constructing new forms of truly democratic organizations.[29] The workplace-democracy advocates wanted employees to have control of the organization as a whole and to discover new possibilities for organizing work.[30] Behind their thinking was the idea that participation was central to democracy, where citizens had a say in all significant institutions, including family, school, and work.[31] Worker participation fit Couto's model of psycho-political empowerment. However, back in the Cold War era, real democracy in the workplace was considered un-American.

Researchers on the management side focused on quality of worklife, job enrichment, and motivation. They were interested in giving employees more discretion over the actual task that they performed, not over the organization itself. A major emphasis was on making the employee feel good about work. This approach, which is usually emphasized in business schools, aimed toward therapeutic effectiveness and tended to fall into Couto's category of psycho-symbolic empowerment. One of the biggest problems with empowerment schemes is that the language used often raises unrealistic expectations about how much power and control employees actually gain over their work. They also fail to see any change in their relationship to other powerholders. When employees discover the limits of their participation, they are disappointed. Even employees who have a high level of expertise find initiatives that are feasible and beneficial to the organization overridden, by people who know less but have either positional or political power. It is also the case that employees may suggest changes on the production line, but not changes in their work hours. Many managers were ambivalent about giving away their own supervisory power.

The 1935 Labor Relations Act recognized the need to protect workers from bogus empowerment of participatory programs. Under it, quality circles and other similar participatory schemes are illegal unless employees have the right to choose their representatives and have a genuine voice in decisions. The act prohibited "sham unions" or in-house unions formed by employers attempting to keep out real unions. Because it is obvious to most people today that employers have to forge a cooperative partnership with employees to be competitive, the 1935 act may look like an atavism that ought to be eliminated. However, the law recognized that companies prefer cooperation and participation of their employees on their own terms. Most important, companies fear the loss of control that would come with unionization. In most businesses, empowering employees does not change the balance of power within the organization. Unions are still the only institution in history that ever addressed the asymmetry of power between employers and employees. Unions can be a strong form of empowerment because they give employees an independent voice over things like salaries, work hours, and work rules that terrifies most employers. Businesses have always feared the power of unions, and in the United States, they have been very successful at demonizing unions. Businesses have fairly and unfairly held unions responsible for their own failures and inability to be competitive in a global economy. In recent years, politicians have jumped on the bandwagon and blamed public service unions for the deterioration of K-12 education and budget deficits in state and local governments.

Management language in the 2000s is a continuation of terms that started in the 1960s. We have moved from the concept of *worker involvement* or participation to *empowerment* to the now over-used term *leadership*. Employees are now called upon to be leaders, but leadership like empowerment does not mean much without the power to actually do things such as make real choices and initiate changes on the job. The emphasis on power in all of these concepts gets at what most business leaders failed to deliver despite their claims over the past 30 years. What has become abundantly clear in research done on productivity is that workers do a better job when they have a say in the way they do their work, the redesign of their jobs, and the introduction of technology into the workplace. Research has also shown that employees work better when they see the meaning of their work or understand impact of their work on others.[32] Yet, over the past century, some managers and management theorists seem constantly amazed by this, which tells us something about the respect they have for their employees.

At this point, some readers may be irritated by the cynical and unkind portrayal of management practices that most people consider a vast improvement over scientific management and traditional bureaucratic forms of work. Clearly there are sincere and committed business leaders all over the United States who really respect their employees and try to make their work more rewarding. I do not claim that all of the management theories and programs of the past hundred years or so have been designed to fool the U.S. worker, nor am I saying that all of the social scientists behind these theories and the consultants who develop these programs are evil manipulators. Yet I do ask the reader to consider the irony that despite the effort and resources put into empowerment programs, workplaces today are not much more democratic or participatory than they were 50 years ago. Not all empowerment and leadership initiatives are intended to manipulate people. Some leaders really do want to empower their followers. However, to do so they must be sincere and authentic.

SINCERITY AND AUTHENTICITY

In his book, *Sincerity and Authenticity*, Lionel Trilling notes that the public value of sincerity, like the concept of civility, emerged during the sixteenth century, a period of increasing social mobility in England and France. The art of acting with guile and expressing certain false emotions publicly became a tool for taking advantage of new social opportunities. Trilling says that sincerity was devalued when mobility and acting became accepted behaviors in a mobile society. People considered the sincere person stupid and unsophisticated. Audiences were no longer interested in seeing plays about "hypocrite-villains and conscious dissemblers."[33] It was more interesting to read or watch plays about self-deception. Authenticity replaced the notion of sincerity as a subject of dramatic interest. Hence, it is not surprising that the concept of authenticity would become prominent in the leadership literature.[34] This literature assumes that leaders who are "true to themselves" would be ethical and effective. Most studies show that they tend to be effective, but authenticity is neither a necessary or sufficient condition for being an ethical leader.[35]

According to Trilling, we have deprecated the value of sincerity by treating it as such a common commodity in society and the market place. If this is true, then the really valuable emotional commodities are authenticity and "true" emotions. Thus, either people who serve customers will require even better acting skills, or training will have to dig even deeper into the employee to evoke the appropriate real emotions. If training programs could get at people's real feelings, find the hot buttons, employees would either no longer have to act, or they could engage in "deep acting." This may be the real reason for the use of intrusive motivational programs like the Krone program. It also lurks in the background of the ideology of strong cultures. Make the workplace your family and carry to it all the sense of caring and responsibility that you feel naturally for family members. Although this sounds sinister, it is true that most organizations want their employees to have a certain "genuine" feeling about their work, the people they work with, and the organization. At Pacific Bell, employees really cared and were concerned about the company. Perhaps one thing that we learn from the Krone's case is that attempts at engineering appropriate attitudes and emotions can actually undercut genuine feelings for a company. If a workplace is run honestly, people do care and are friendly; however, their emotions have to be free to be real. Nonetheless, the broader issues at stake remain the line between motivation and manipulation of emotions, and the claims that an organization can make on the inner self and emotions of an employee.

The principle of authenticity applies to organizations as well as individuals and leaders. Often motivational programs and leadership programs are just polite lies within a company. Employee involvement programs and redesigned jobs benefit employees by making their work more interesting. They intend to make employees feel

empowered and feel that the organization cares about their development. Nonetheless, there is a difference between feeling empowered
and really being empowered. One wonders if employees willingly
buy into the fiction of empowerment because of their own need to
believe that they have power and control. If so, symbolic empowerment works because employees are unauthentic.

HONESTY AND SECURITY

The obvious difference between authentic and bogus empowerment
rests on the honesty of the relationship between leaders and followers.
Honesty entails a set of specific practical and moral obligations and is
a necessary condition for empowerment. In the beginning, I outlined
three social values behind empowerment: individualism; freedom;
and instrumentalism and economic efficiency. The fourth value, which
encompasses the first three, I have called niceness. I characterized the
value of niceness as a kind of self-interested social harmony, commercial friendliness, and therapeutic truth. All the values color the way
people view the context of their work. To empower people, leaders
must take into account the social and economic conditions under
which they operate.

In some ways, employees today have more power. On the one hand,
the use of and access to information technologies in the workplace
give employees far more power than they had in the past. On the other
hand, computerized control systems can impose even stricter discipline on workers and replace layers of management. Power shifts
occur inside organizations not necessarily because one group intentionally gives up power, but because the demands of technology and
economic efficiency require a new distribution of power. Why does
this matter? It matters because empowerment requires good faith.
It is a kind of giving. You do not tell people that you are giving them
power that they have already gotten through structural and techno-
logical changes.

Perhaps the greatest obstacle to empowerment today is job insecurity. The social contract that once said, if you do your job well, you
can keep it no longer exists. In an era of high unemployment, employers have the upper hand, wages stagnate, and employees often ask for
and expect little from employers when the chances of getting another
job look bleak. The threat of not getting a good job strikes fear into
the hearts of all workers because it reminds them of the fundamental

way in which they are totally powerless over their lives, especially when business leaders claim that they are powerless to do anything but cut their workforces. It would seem difficult to empower people in organizations that do not at least attempt to find ways to keep their workers employed through good times and bad. The economic orthodoxy that says labor is *the* expendable variable and that cutting labor costs is the most rational way to save money, balance the budget, or be competitive is so entrenched in business that it sounds crazy to suggest otherwise. Nonetheless, workers who lack security also lack power. They need both to produce the creative and innovative products needed to be competitive in the world market. Although many companies try smoke and mirror leadership or empowerment programs, moral action is stronger and longer lasting than therapeutic intervention.

EMPOWERMENT AS A RECIPROCAL MORAL AGREEMENT

When leaders really empower people, they give them the responsibility that comes with that power. But this does not mean that with less power, leaders have less responsibility. This point is often misunderstood. Perhaps one of the most ethically distinctive features of being a leader is that leaders are responsible for the actions of their followers. For example, transformational leaders don't have less responsibility for their followers when they transform them; the followers have chosen to take on more. Couto offers a good example of a bogus empowerment relationship. Couto says he listened in amazement as a hospital administrator "told federal health-policy makers about her hospital's patient advocacy program that empowered low-income patients to find means to pay their hospital bills."[36] Is the administrator really giving people power, or is she simply unloading the hospital's moral responsibility on them? In the workplace, employees can only take full responsibility if they have the power and access to resources to influence outcomes. Empowerment programs that give employees responsibility without control are cruel and stressful. Real empowerment gives employees control over outcomes so that they can be responsible for their work.

When empowering employees, leaders must keep their promises. The best way to do this is to make promises that they can keep. When leaders empower employees, they need to be clear about the extent of that power and avoid the temptation of engaging in hyperbole about the democratic nature of the organization. An organization can always give employees more responsibility, but employees feel betrayed when they discover that they have been given less than the leadership's rhetoric implied. A leader who keeps his or her promises establishes the dependability necessary for trust.

Leadership rests on two ideals that often conflict with each other—trust and power.[37] Trust has taken over from authority as the modern foundation of leadership. The moral concepts behind empowerment—responsibility, trust, respect, and loyalty—are reciprocal moral concepts; that is, they only exist if they are part of the relationship between followers and leaders. Like all the other moral principles that I have been examining in relationship to leadership and empowerment, they are related to truth and honesty. Honesty is one way to resolve the tension between power and trust. It is morally wrong to lie because lying shows lack of respect for the dignity of a person. This is why bogus empowerment is so devastating. Employees are made to feel foolish about falling for inflated claims and undelivered promises. Leaders lose credibility and respect because they have blatantly failed to respect their employees. Business leaders often overlook the reciprocal nature of these moral concepts, particularly the notion of loyalty or commitment. If leaders don't demonstrate in substantive ways that they are loyal and committed to their employees through good times and bad, they simply cannot expect employees to be loyal to them, and therapeutic interventions will be short-lived at best.

Lastly, if leaders are to establish a moral relationship with employees that allows for authentic empowerment, they need to think about constructively reapplying the traditional values behind empowerment. They must consider how to protect individualism even in team settings. Individualism has many flaws when it is selfish and uncaring, but there are some ethically important aspects to individualism, such as recognition and tolerance of difference and diversity.[38] Teamwork without tolerance of difference in opinion, gender, racial, or cultural background is unacceptable. Morally imaginative business leaders should challenge the dogma of instrumentalism and economic efficiency that sometimes mindlessly dominates all business decisions. It is difficult to say whether employees are more or less free on the job today than they were in the past. Although many are liberated from harsh physical toil and a dictatorial boss, others are caged in by competition, job insecurity, and peer pressure. Empowerment means more than discretion on the job. It also requires freedom from emotional manipulation, freedom to choose, and most importantly real viable choices.

To empower people authentically, business leaders have to be ready to overthrow some of the aspects of niceness. The truth is not always pleasant. It can disrupt the harmony of an organization and introduce conflict. When you really empower people, you don't just empower them to agree with you. Employees don't always feel good when they hear the truth and leaders don't like to deliver bad news. As a result of the therapeutic fictions that are part of niceness, managers aren't forthright in their assessment of employees' work and teachers aren't forthright about the quality of their students' work. Assessment inflation makes people feel good in the short run, but it does not build the self-esteem necessary for empowerment in the long run.

I close with the notion of authenticity. Leaders cannot empower people unless they have the moral courage to be honest and sincere in their intention to change the power relationship that they have with their followers. If leaders want to be authentic about empowering people, they must first be honest with themselves. Too many leaders are not authentic. They talk about empowerment and participation and even believe that they are participatory, but in practice they lead in autocratic ways. Employees are "empowered" to organize their work but when they do, management steps in and tells them how to do it their way.

James MacGregor Burns uses Franklin Roosevelt's decision to support the Wagner Act as an example of authentic empowerment. According to Burns, Roosevelt knew that giving people the right to organize into unions, gave a substantial amount of power to the people. He didn't necessarily like this fact; nevertheless, he supported the act.[39] Authentic empowerment requires leaders to know what they are giving away and how they are changing the relationship between themselves and their followers. This is the only way that they can commit to keeping their part of the empowerment relationship. It is difficult for leaders to give away their own power and even more difficult for them to take away power from others.

Leadership is a distinct kind of moral relationship between people. Power is a defining aspect of this relationship. Whenever there is a change in the distribution of power between leaders and followers, there is a change in the specific rights, responsibilities, and duties in the relationship. Both sides have to be honest when they make these changes and have to fully understand what they mean. Bogus empowerment attempts to give employees or followers power without changing the moral relationship between leaders and followers. Empowerment changes the rights, responsibilities, and duties of leaders as well as followers. It is not something one does to be nice to gain favor with people. For decades business leaders have tried to harness the insights of psychology to make people feel empowered. These attempts have often failed and led to cynicism among employees because business leaders have ignored the moral commitments of empowerment. Without honesty, sincerity, and authenticity, empowerment is bogus and it makes a mockery of one of America's most cherished values, the freedom to choose.

NOTES

1. James MacGregor Burns, *Leadership* (New York: Harper & Row, 1978), 13.

2. Richard Couto, "Grassroots Policies of Empowerment" (paper presented at the annual meeting of the American Political Science Association, September 1992), 13.

3. J. Thomas Wren, "Historical Background of Values in Leadership," *Kellogg Working Papers* (University of Maryland, 1996).

4. Charles Taylor, *The Ethics of Authenticity* (Cambridge, MA: Harvard University Press, 1991), 2–9.

5. James O'Toole, *Leading Change* (San Francisco: Jossey-Bass, 1994).

6. Norbert Elias, *The History of Manners* (New York: Pantheon Books, 1978), 53–55.

7. Immanuel Kant, "Idea for a Universal History with a Cosmopolitan Intent," *Perpetual Peace and Other Essays*, translated by Ted Humphrey (Indianapolis, IN: Hackett Publishing, 1983), 31–32.

8. Elias, 9.

9. Gunnar Myrdal, *An American Dilemma*, vol. 2 (New York: Harper & Row, 1962), 1046–47.

10. Ibid., 1055.

11. David Riesman, *The Lonely Crowd* (New Haven, CT: Yale University Press, 1950), 14–21.

12. Philip Rieff, *The Triumph of the Therapeutic* (New York: Harper & Row, 1966), 137. A similar point is made in Robert Bellah et al., *Habits of the Heart* (Berkeley, CA: University of California Press, 1985), ch. 2.

13. C. Wright Mills, "Crawling to the Top," *New York Times Book Review*, December 9, 1956.

14. C. Wright Mills, *White Collar* (New York: Oxford University Press, 1951), 232–37.

15. William H. Whyte, Jr., *The Organization Man* (New York: Simon & Schuster, 1956), 6–7.

16. Ibid., 51.

17. Ibid., 54.

18. James Surowiecki, *The Wisdom of Crowds* (New York: Anchor Books, 2005).

19. Sloan Wilson, *The Man in the Gray Flannel Suit* (New York: Arbor House, 1955), 14.

20. Thomas J. Peters and Robert H. Waterman, Jr., *In Search of Excellence* (New York: Warner Books, 1982), 105.

21. Joseph C. Rost, *Leadership for the Twenty-First Century* (New York: Praeger, 1991).

22. *Telephony*, June 22, 1987, 15.

23. Annetta Miller and Pamela Abramson, "Corporate Mind Control," *Newsweek*, May 4, 1987.

24. Ibid., 6.

25. Sanford Bingham, *Management*, July 1987, 14.

26. *Venture*, March 1987, 54.

27. Mike Myatt, "The #1 Reason Leadership Development Fails," *Forbes Magazine*, December 12, 2012, http://www.forbes.com/sites/mikemyatt/2012/12/19/the-1-reason-leadership-development-fails/.

28. Ibid.

29. Two good studies of cooperatives are Joyce Rothschild and Allen Whitt, *The Cooperative Workplace* (New York: Cambridge University Press, 1986); and Edward S. Greenberg, *Workplace Democracy* (Ithaca, NY: Cornell University Press, 1986).

30. For example, see Martin Carnoy and Derek Shearer, *Economic Democracy: The Challenge of the 1980s* (Armonk, NY: Sharpe, Inc., 1980); and Gerry Hunnius, G. David Garson, and John Case (Eds.), *Workers' Control* (New York: Vintage Books, 1973).

31. See Carol Pateman, *Participation and Democratic Theory* (London: Cambridge University Press, 1970).

32. Adam Grant, "Leading with Meaning," *Academy of Management Journal* 55, no. 2 (April 2012): 458–76.

33. Lionel Trilling, *Sincerity and Authenticity* (Cambridge, MA: Harvard University Press, 1972), 13.

34. B. J. Avolio and T. S. Wernsing, "Practicing Authentic Leadership." In *Positive Psychology: Exploring the Best in People*, edited by S. J. Lopez (Westport, CT: Greenwood Publishing Group, 2008), 147–65.

35. Joanne B. Ciulla, "Searching for Mandela: The Saint as a Sinner Who Keeps on Trying." In *Authentic Leadership: Clashes, Convergences and Coalescences*, edited by Donna Ladkin and Chellie Spiller (Northampton, CT: Edward Elgar, 2013), 152–75.

36. Couto, 2.

37. See Francis Sejersted, "Managers as Consultants and Manipulators: Reflections on the Suspension of Ethics," *Business Ethics Quarterly* 6, no. 1 (January 1996): 77.

38. Taylor, 37.

39. My thanks to James MacGregor Burns for this example and for his other helpful comments on the first formulation of this chapter.

5

Emotions and Trust: Beyond "Charisma"

Robert C. Solomon

I should begin by saying that I am a novice on the subject of leadership, but after years of research and consulting in business ethics, I have become convinced that morally sensitive leaders are the essential feature of any good organization. I have never been a leader—although one hopes that teachers and especially philosophy teachers might share a few of the attributes of leaders in terms of inspiration and impact—and I confess that, although I pride myself on my trustworthiness and loyalty, I have never been much of a follower, either. Too many leaders, as Voltaire complained of heroes, "are so noisy." Perhaps that is why I have never before delved into the subject as I should, for so much of what I have noticed about leadership is the noise.

Much of the noise has to do with the well-known but little-understood phenomenon of Weberian charisma, the excited appeal supposedly generated and accordingly cultivated by leaders. *Charisma*, in other words, has much to do with emotion, but not just the emotion generated by leaders. It is also, first and foremost, the passion *of* the leader. It is strange then, that the nature of emotions, the very heart of charisma, has been neglected by leadership scholars for so long. What has also been neglected is the intimate relationship between the emotions and ethics. This relationship speaks to several of the more controversial debates about leadership: the role and desirability of charisma; the nature of leadership itself; the dangers of evil leaders (Ciulla's "Hitler problem"[1]); the nature of ethical leadership; and the nature of the relationship between leaders and the led. (I prefer the word *led* mainly by virtue of its length. I do not deny that following may be as active and autonomous a choice as leading, and in a sense, perhaps more so.)[2] In this essay, therefore, I want to approach the topic of leadership by way of an often exciting but rarely analyzed set of connections: the connection between emotions and leadership; the connection between emotions and ethics; and, consequently, the connections among emotions, leadership, and ethics. To summarize, I would like to suggest that ethical leadership is essentially based on an emotional relationship, with the emphasis on charisma replaced by the much more mundane (but no less evasive) notion of trust. Whereas charisma is celebrated as a mysterious attribute of a leader, trust, obviously, is a relationship between a leader and his or her followers. The practical applications will, I hope, be apparent. The focus on leadership will bear fruit only if, unlike some lovelorn cowboys, we don't go looking for leaders in all the wrong places.[3]

THE ROLE OF EMOTIONS

Emotions are rarely the focus of discussions on leadership. When they are discussed, it is usually in terms of their arousal.[4] Emotions tend to be dismissed or ignored in almost every realm of hardheaded business, political, philosophical, and scientific discussion. Emotions, after all, are subjective. They are, according to the popular prejudice, "squishy," "ineffable," and "hard to get hold of." They are—because they are inner and private—immeasurable. Answers to survey questions, by contrast, are readily quantifiable, easily subject to statistical analysis, and need to deal with emotions only in an indirect way. ("Do you have confidence in the leaders of your organization?" "Do you approve of the direction in which the country is going?") By contrast, I would like to explore the role of emotions in a direct manner, in part through what one might call "phenomenology," an appeal to our shared experience. This does not mean that I am only describing my emotions, nor does it mean that I think it is worth placing too much faith on the much-touted "method" of "empathy" or *Verstehen* that has played such an enormous role in the history of anthropology and sociology. But what has emerged from my research on emotions over the years are the conclusions that many, if not most emotions are cognitively and evaluatively rich and insightful, not the brute forces or mere "arousal" discussed by many theorists. In short, emotions are essential to ethics. Emotional sensitivity, rather than only rationality and obeying the rules, is what ethics is all about. Furthermore, emotions are largely socially constituted—not in their biological origins, perhaps, but in their aims, expressions, and nuances.[5] In terms of the present discussion, this means that emotions should be understood in terms of emotional relationships.

There are ordinary and extraordinary leaders, who often but not always correspond or fail to respond to ordinary and extraordinary situations. It is not surprising that much of the literature on leadership focuses on extraordinary leaders in extraordinary times: for example, Lincoln, Churchill, and Truman, to limit ourselves to three relatively recent Anglo-American examples. At such times (in the course of a civil war, a world war, the use of the first thermonuclear bomb), the emotions of the whole world are extraordinary too. Extraordinary emotions motivate and provoke extraordinary behavior, which in turn produce and provoke even more extraordinary emotions. In extraordinary situations, predictions are extraordinarily difficult to make, if only because the extraordinary is by its very nature also relatively rare. We continue to study questions such as, how people will behave in war, under fire, in circumstances in which their everyday bearings and sources of security and routine have been destroyed or rendered irrelevant, but the behavior of supposedly ordinary people is no less fascinating than the behavior of the most distinguished and extraordinary leaders.

But what do I know of the emotions of a Martin Luther King, facing down the dogs and bullhorns of a well-armed and hostile Alabama police force? For that matter, what do I know of the emotions of those who stood with him, trusted him, confident in the face of their own fear that what they were doing was both important and effective? What can I imagine of the emotions of a Roosevelt or Churchill, a Stalin or a Mao, or, for that matter, a Bin Laden or their benighted followers? Accordingly, I want to approach the subject of emotion in leadership in rather ordinary situations. But by understanding such ordinary feelings and emotions, we need not pretend that we are easily capable of imagining or projecting ourselves into dramatic, tragic, or heroic situations that in fact lie quite beyond most of our experiences. That, I think, is part of the difficulty of understanding the greatest as well as the most evil leaders. What we tend to understand is just those aspects of their personalities that are most common, most like ourselves, most "human-all-too-human," as Nietzsche called it. The extraordinariness escapes our study. On the other hand, by examining ordinary situations, we can bypass such captivating but perhaps impossible questions such as, "Why can we not now find or produce an extraordinary leader of the ilk of a Lincoln, Churchill or a Mandela?" One probable answer, of course, is that we do not want and will not allow for one.

But our society is filled with leaders—heads of departments, agencies, associations, and corporations. It would be a mistake to dismiss them all as something less than real leaders, as mere "managers," because they do not have that sparkle and celebrity usually identified as "charisma." And so my focus will be on corporate executives and institutional administrators, university presidents and deans, cabinet ministers, and trade union leaders rather than on heroes. What sorts of emotions enter into their success and failure? The too familiar reply is couched in terms of "cool," unflappable, and an imperviousness or immunity to emotions. In other words, the less prone leaders are to "emotional" behavior the more effective. (Taoism teaches that lessened emotional involvement results in a more intuitive response, but then, the Taoists did not believe in leaders.) First, I would like to undermine and utterly reject that viewpoint. Second, I would like to insist that a rich and energetic emotional life is very different from the rather unflattering notion of behaving "emotionally" that is "out of control." Leadership intimately involves the former, not the latter.[6]

EMOTIONS AND DEFINITIONS OF LEADERSHIP

A dominant theme in the current literature is the search for an all-encompassing definition (paradigm, model) of leadership.[7] I am not interested in joining the search here, nor am I impressed with the use of singular "definitions" to analyze complex and ambiguous social phenomena.[8] But I would like to make a point or two about the underlying emotional themes that are to be found in virtually all of such attempts to define "leadership." I have highlighted certain terms that keep recurring. I have also retained the distinctively male references in brackets to remind us of how embarrassingly sexist the field has been. This is not incidental to my point, of course. The assumption that leaders are men (with distinctively "masculine" virtues) as opposed to women (whose "feminine" features almost inevitably include some form of sentimentality or supposedly excessive emotionality) explains in part, why the emotions have been ignored in favor of such dispassionate notions as "influence" and bureaucratic "management skills." This also goes some distance in explaining why the distinction between "leader" and "manager" has been so problematic. So long as leadership is defined instrumentally or simply in terms of change versus status, without explicit reference to and analysis of the emotions involved both in leading and in being led, the distinction is a negligible one, and leadership might be just as well reduced to the role of a mere "organizer."[9] I will come back to this point in a moment.

Consider the following definitions of leadership[10]:

1. "the ability to *impress* the will of the leader on those led and *induce* obedience, *respect, loyalty,* and cooperation" (B. V. Moore, 1927);
2. "an ability to *persuade* or direct [men]" (Reuter, 1941);
3. "authority *spontaneously* accorded [him] by [his] [fellow] group members" (C. A. Gibb, 1954);
4. "acts by a person which *influence* other persons in a shared direction" (M. Seeman, 1960);
5. "discretionary *influence*" (R. N. Osborn, J. G. Hunt, 1975);
6. "a [man] who has the ability to get other people to do what they don't want to do, and *like* it" (Harry Truman).

I have highlighted the terms *impress, induce, respect, loyalty, persuade, spontaneously, influence,* and *like* because they all strongly suggest (though obviously do not entail) emotional evocation. To be sure, there are skills and techniques of leadership (whether learned or "natural"), but leadership is not just instrumentality; "getting things done." It is also *moving* people, in both senses of that term. It involves stimulating their emotions, and it involves motivating them. Burns is perhaps most explicit about this, and his terms *exploiting tensions, raising consciousness, strong values,* all suggest strong emotion. What are *strong values,* for example? They are values deeply held, values that are deemed important, but also, therefore, values with enormous emotional significance. *Transactional* leadership is, for him, a highly emotionally charged and infectious process. So, too, even when Joseph Rost employs the much more modest terminology of *an influence relationship* we immediately want to know "what kind of influence," and some reference to emotions and affections is unavoidable.[11]

According to much of the recent literature, a leader is one who inspires and motivates, not just resolves or "manages." (The disdain heaped on the concept of "management" as a result of the search for "leadership" is a phenomenon that requires a detailed investigation of its own.) I think we might well distinguish between moral leadership and *moral leadership*, where the latter is truly inspirational and deeply emotional and the former is routine moral sensitivity. The latter may be what fascinates us, but the former, I would argue, is much more important for maintaining ethical organizations, institutions, and communities. To limit the honorific phrase *ethical leadership* to moral heroes is, again, to deny or demean what is perhaps most substantial to ethics and leadership, and no less based on emotion. More to the point of this essay, however, one might notice that, in terms of the earlier definitions, most of the emotions of leadership tend to fall on the side of the led, the "followers," rather than the leader. This suggests an unfortunate paradigm, one unhappily much in evidence in the behavior of any number of demagogues. They certainly provoke emotions, often violent and extremely effective and well-directed emotions, but they often evidence very little of those same passions themselves. Thus we should avoid the temptation to suggest that leadership does not so much involve emotions (i.e., the emotions of the leader) as it does the emotional impact or effect of the leader on the led. This would reduce leadership to manipulation, perhaps even to creating appearances that affect followers, perhaps to mere "acting," and raise the question of *authenticity*. The emotions of leadership must, in part, be the emotions of the leader. He or she is not a puppeteer, a strategic manipulator of other people's feelings. He or she is, first of all, the subject of passions.

Leadership is the very opposite of "control," and to say that leadership is a matter of emotions is not to say that it is a matter of emotional control or, for that matter, manipulation either. *Control* is a quasi-mechanical term, and, in human relationships, implies at the very least some sort of coercion, which virtually every leadership theorist has rightly distinguished from leadership. For example, leadership through naked terror—imperatives backed up by threats—is hardly leadership. Thus we do not think of those military commanders who threaten to shoot their own troops if they retreat as "leaders." So, too, "manipulating" emotions, as if they were circuits simply to be stimulated, is not leadership either. If Hitler had wholly relied on the Gestapo and threats of violence against his own people, or if he had only pressed the red buttons of prejudice against gypsies and Jews, his "leadership" would not be so problematic. He would not be considered a leader at all. But instead, he evidently did inspire real devotion and action, although the values he represented and the horrible results of his leadership haunt our use of this term.[12] Because emotions are often (mis)conceived as involuntary, appealing to people's emotions is too easily (mis)conceived as trying to control or manipulate them; thus our highly negative reactions to mawkish leadership pleas and overt appeals to our baser passions. But emotions occupy an intermediate and problematic position between straightforward voluntary rational decision-making and the merely mechanical. For example, zombies and robots may be commanded to behave without reference to their "will," but we do not think of someone as a "loyal follower" if he or she is merely a zombie or a robot. Thus we talk in politics as well as romance about "winning hearts." When Harry Truman defines leadership as getting people to do something they did not want to do initially and "liking" it, he is not conferring retrospective approval or necessarily any kind of enjoyment. Rather, he captures in the simplest language the idea that emotional behavior is voluntary behavior, and what leaders do with their followers to "move" their emotions in the direction already passionately chosen by the leader. This choice, however, need not be thought out or fully understood (although one might argue, not always convincingly, that the more thought and understanding, the better the leader). This brings to the surface a rather difficult point about *knowledge* in leadership. It is often said that leadership is a skill or set of skills (which it certainly is) and that skills by their very nature require knowledge. This is so, but such "know-how" is not always articulated or propositional knowledge. Just as people need not know the direction in which they are being led, it does not follow that the leaders themselves know the direction in which they are leading. Hegel captured that lack of clarity in his stunning phrase "the cunning of reason." Tolstoy illustrated the thesis in detail in his unflattering treatment of the principals in the 1812 Napoleonic invasion of Russia and the battle of Borodino in particular. But "not knowing the direction" does not mean "in complete ignorance." The leader may well be "feeling his way along" or "following his intuitions," and his followers may know only that they trust him and are faithfully following. To be a bit polemical, we might say that too much is made of the role of knowledge in leadership and not enough of such emotional features as trust and loyalty. More plainly, knowledge (e.g., managerial knowledge) is effective in leadership only insofar as that knowledge is in the service of the appropriate emotions.

That demand, that "knowledge be in the service of the appropriate emotions," is the beginning of an all-important answer to the most devastating challenge to the role of emotions in leadership. It is often noted that Hitler inspired at least as great devotion as Roosevelt and considerably more than Lincoln, and so the question raised is how one set of emotions can be judged superior to another. In ethics this is often referred to as the problem of "relativism," that is, whether a set of values held sacred by a community is thereby *right and proper for them*, and beyond criticism from anyone else. This assumes that there are no common "nonrelative" values or, in the case of emotions, that there are no standards for emotion apart from those already contained within the emotion. But there are such common values, and there are such standards: social harmony and well-being, to begin with. Thus we might suggest a criterion to distinguish between effective but evil leadership and ethical leadership: the promotion of harmony and the public good. But these are not self-contained within a society, nor can they apply to one part of a society without including consideration of all other parts as well. "Us versus them" leadership always contains at least the potential for evil (although when an oppressed group is struggling against an oppressor group, this danger may remain invisible for some time). The "appropriate emotions," therefore, will be those that are conducive to these larger concerns as well as sensitive to the nuances of the current situation. In short, an ethical leader is one who shares with his or her followers the emotions of fairness, mutual well-being, and harmony. In corporations, all of this might well be stated in terms of real concerns for "stakeholders" rather than the tempting but ultimately divisive focus on "the bottom line." In politics, it would be stated in terms of the urgency of winning elections. The "appropriate emotions" in ethical leadership motivate not the grudging decision to sacrifice profits or lose an election but rather the overriding passion to do the right thing.

FALSE LEADS: THE MYTH OF CHARISMA

"Charisma" is shorthand for the emotional power of certain rare leaders, but unfortunately, it is without ethical value and I will argue, without much explanatory value either. It is one of the most frequently recurrent terms in discussions of leadership. Derived in its current usage from the German sociologist Max Weber, it is perhaps the only such term that so explicitly refers to the emotional quality of leadership, albeit at considerable cost to clarity, imbued as the term is with mystery and magic. It is also used at great cost to an adequate understanding of emotions, because the very notion of charisma connotes an irrational as opposed to a rational influence. Although Weber is noted for his analysis of institutions and bureaucracy in terms of "rationality," he himself was an ethical noncognitivist and viewed rationality and rationalization as a costly "disenchantment" with the world. At the end of his famous book, *The Protestant Ethic and the Spirit of Capitalism*,[13] he argued that rationalism is destructive of value, an "iron cage" in which both freedom and meaning are sacrificed to efficiency. One should not be surprised, therefore, that for him charisma offered a significantly religious promise.[14]

The *American Heritage Dictionary* defines the Weberian term *charisma* as follows: "1.a. A rare personal quality attributed to leaders who arouse fervent popular devotion and enthusiasm. b. Personal magnetism or charm. 2. Theology. An extraordinary power, such as the ability to perform miracles, granted to a Christian by the Holy Spirit." The theological dimension of the term is to be noted, especially in Weber's classic use of the concept, as is the idea that charisma is by its very nature "rare." Its nature does not invite analysis; in fact, it discourages it. Even careful analytic writers like Robert Nozick are reduced to such impoverished New Age metaphors as an "aura."[15] It will not do to take the nature of charisma as given, trying only to understand its use and effects.[16] The fact that it is rare (and "blessed") encourages gratitude and reverence rather than critical analysis, and its kinship to "magnetism and charm" tends to foreclose any meaningful investigation. Indeed, James MacGregor Burns warns that the "term is so overused it threatens to collapse under close analysis."[17]

Bernard Bass describes charisma as displayed by leaders "to whom followers form deep emotional attachments and who in turn inspire their followers to transcend their own interests for superordinate goals."[18] This is true, perhaps, but what are these emotional attachments? How do they work? What are their vicissitudes? The mysterious origins of charisma also invite a serious worry: What happens when this "blessing" turns into a curse and serves evil rather than good (the "Hitler Problem" again)? How do we know that the gift is from God rather than from Satan, except by the results?[19] Thus C. Hodgkinson warns, "Beware charisma,"[20] and Michael Keeley, in a powerful essay, attacks "transformational leadership" precisely on the grounds that it gives too much credence to charisma and too little to the Madisonian checks and balances that control or contain charisma.[21] Charisma, according to such authors, is a dangerous genie to let out of the bottle. But few of them pay much if any attention to what charisma actually is, leaving unanalyzed charisma's enviable status as "an extraordinary power" (if not exactly "the ability to perform miracles"), "a rare personal quality" of leaders "who arouse fervent popular devotion and enthusiasm."

WHY CHARISMA IS MISLEADING

I want to argue that charisma is not anything in particular. It is not a distinctive quality of personality or character, and it is not an essential implement of leadership. Rather, it is a misleading even if exciting concept that deflects us from the emotional complexity of leadership, which might better occupy our attention. Charisma is not a single quality, nor is it a single emotion or set of emotions. It is a generalized way of pointing to and emptily explaining an emotional relationship that is too readily characterized as fascination but should more fundamentally be analyzed in terms of trust. Within the range of what is usually identified as "charisma," I would want to distinguish[22]:

What the leader is saying. Is it the message itself that is fascinating? Often a good idea—even sound common sense—will evoke sufficient emotion that the praise goes to the speaker when it is the idea that is really being endorsed.

The rhetorical persuasiveness of how he or she says it. Martin Luther King was a brilliant orator, although that by itself is not what made him a great leader. Rhetorical skills alone do not count as charisma, or many English professors would be leaders. Nevertheless, rhetorical skills certainly play a considerable role in what is called charisma. Such skills may make a mediocre message—and the speaker—much more memorable than the ideas themselves deserve.

The hopes, wishes, fears of the audience. Obviously, what gets said is fascinating not just for its own sake; it speaks to powerful emotions on the part of the audience. But this by itself says more about the receptivity of the audience than the character of the speaker—riling people up is not yet leading them. Yet, insofar as leadership is an emotional relationship that concerns the future, responding to hopes, wishes, and fears may well be interpreted as charisma by an appreciative audience. Paranoia, notably, produces some of the most "charismatic" leaders.

His or her degree of enthusiasm, "infectiousness." What is obviously an aspect of the personality of a leader is his or her ability to excite and transmit emotion, even against the initial resistance or opposition of others. One analysis of Franklin Roosevelt suggests "his remarkable capacity to transmit his internal strength to others."[23] Enthusiasm is certainly high up on the list of ingredients of charisma, and enthusiasm plus infectiousness takes us a long way to understanding what is meant by the term. Motivational speakers are often called "charismatic," but we should note again that this does not imply leadership.

Such personality traits as charm, intelligence, sincerity. Much of what passes for charisma is in fact some combination of much more easily understood character traits. "Charm" may be difficult to define (although literature abounds with some excellent witticisms, such as "charm is getting what you want without asking"). Much of John Kennedy's famous charisma was a combination of his straightforward charm and his good looks. Inevitably, a fascinating or comforting leader is characterized as "attractive," "sexy," "fatherly," or "motherly." (A concept that deserves some rigorous analysis is "presence." Although this term shares many of the problems of "charisma," at least it is rarely confused with magic. It is, for example, highly correlated with such mundane features as height.)

"Celebrity." These days celebrity is often confused with leadership, and it is celebrity, not leadership, that attracts the attribution of "charisma." But celebrity clearly requires no particular virtues or characteristics other than merely being in the news, often on television, the butt of popular jokes and late-night humor, or being readily recognized. (Indeed, the talking heads who do nothing but read the news headlines on television are typically viewed as celebrities.) What does this have to do with leadership?

The nature of the situation or "context." Sometimes an individual who stands up or comes through in terrifying, dangerous, promising, or hate-filled circumstances may thereby get accepted as a leader. This is not charisma; the circumstances, rather than any particular quality of the character in question, supply the aura of seeming greatness, at least for a while.

Change. Many leadership theorists (e.g., Burns, Rost) note presiding over change as an essential ingredient in leadership. Whether this is so, being visibly "in charge" of change is itself often conflated with the dynamism of charisma. But, as in Tolstoy's introduction to *War and Peace*, there is always the question of where the action really is, in the leader or in the change itself. True, there is much to be said about managing change, and much to be debated about the ability of any leader to bring about change without the forces of society already mustered. But my point here is that the dynamics of change itself may be readily confused with the dynamic character of the leader.

Resemblance/continuity. On the other hand, sometimes charisma may be little more than continuity, a carryover or echo of previous leadership or, perhaps, the result of an enduring myth or faulty memory. George Bush had enough seeming charisma to carry him through one presidential election, but some of this was nothing more than the fading continuation of the Reagan "magic." Harry Truman, by contrast, suffered from comparison with his great predecessor. Regardless of whether he had his own degree of charisma, he had to establish his reputation for leadership from a decidedly disadvantaged position.

What is called charisma may be some blend or mixture of all these different ingredients, and no doubt more besides, but that is not the point of this crude dissection. I suggest that charisma doesn't refer to any character trait or "quality" in particular, but is rather a general way of referring to a person who seems to be a dynamic and effective leader. And as a term of analysis in leadership studies, I think that it is more of a distraction than a point of understanding.

THE EMOTIONAL CORE OF LEADERSHIP: TRUST

Charisma distracts us from looking at the relationship between the leader and the led, and, in particular, the relationship of trust. The mistake is not so much that charisma is dangerous in the "wrong" leaders, but rather that it is a distorted perspective on leadership. The word *trust* appears in virtually every current book on leadership, and it is taken as a commonplace that without trust, leadership is impossible. This has not always been the case. Machiavelli, for example, suggests that leaders should strive to be feared, not loved. But trust is hard to analyze, and it is hard to say anything very useful about it. Francis Fukuyama published a 400-page book simply entitled *Trust*,[24] but one is hard put to find any discussion of the subject in those many pages. Fukuyama utterly ignores the dynamics of trust, the ways in which trust is created and cultivated, particularly between cultures and rival subcultural groups. Nevertheless, many of the examples of what Fukuyama calls "spontaneous sociability" are revealing.

Several standard definitions of trust (e.g., N. Luhmann and B. Barber) characterize it primarily in terms of *expectations*,[25] but this is only half the story. It also involves decisions and the dynamics of a relationship. Trust, in other words, is an emotional relationship, as is leadership. Putting it more succinctly, leadership is an emotional relationship of trust.

Niklas Luhmann distinguishes trust from confidence, noting that we trust (or don't trust) people but have (or do not have) confidence in institutions. This points to an important distinction, but it does not yet reach it. The distinction between persons and organizations is convenient and obvious but often, especially in business and organizational ethics, misleading or counter-productive. Organizations and institutions have many features of persons (not least, that in the eye of the law they are persons, with fiduciary obligations, rights and responsibilities). As such, we trust them (or not) much as we would trust a person who had made us a promise or with whom we had agreed on a contract. On the other hand, we sometimes have confidence in people we do not or would not trust; for example, bureaucrats who are known for their fairness and efficiency but are personally unknown to us. We may also have confidence in someone precisely because we do not trust him or her; for instance, when we place our confidence in the double-dealing habits of an old enemy, or "have confidence" that our friend will fail to quit smoking this time as he or she has failed in every one of the last 31 attempts to do so. (This use of "have confidence" is not wholly ironic.)

Laurence Thomas and others make the distinction Luhmann seeks by distinguishing between trust and prediction.[26] We predict that something will happen. We trust that someone will do something.

The distinction is between mechanism and agency, nature and persons. Trust, in other words, is not predicting that something will be the case. This, it seems to me, is fairly obvious, yet it has taken up a substantial portion of the literature (perhaps just because it is so seemingly straightforward). Here, I think, is where Luhmann is aiming us as well, although he mislocates the cleavage. Organizations and institutions are not mechanisms, no matter how efficiently (i.e., "mechanically") they may be constructed. Organizations and institutions are people, working together. Those people, and consequently the organizations and institutions they create, are agents. Thus they have obligations, rights, and responsibilities. What they will do is not simply a matter of probabilities. It is a matter of trust. This is why the commonsensical notion (advocated by Luhmann and adopted by Barber) that trust is first of all a set of expectations is misleading. It is this, of course, but it is much more than this. Trust, as opposed to prediction or confidence, presupposes a relationship. And relationships by their nature involve much more than a calculation of probabilities and outcomes. They involve values and emotions, responsibilities and the possibility of not only disappointment but also betrayal.

Trust is an umbrella term. It is not an emotion as such, although in certain situations it can manifest itself as a very powerful emotion, notably and most dramatically in the case of betrayal, but also in its positive display. One way of describing this feature of trust is to say that, by its very nature, it is part of the "background" of our social activities.[27] To say that trust is not an emotion is does not remove it from the realm of emotion. Quite the contrary, trust is the framework within which emotions appear, their precondition, the structure of the world in which they operate. Without trust, there can be no betrayal, but, more generally, without trust, there can be no cooperation, no community, no commerce, no conversation.[28] And in a context without trust, all sorts of emotions readily surface, starting with suspicion, quickly escalating to contempt, resentment, hatred, and worse. Thus "trust" serves to characterize an entire network of emotions and emotional attitudes, both between individuals and within groups and by way of a psychodynamic profile of entire societies. (This is Fukuyama's theme in *Trust*.) In such large contexts, one might even say that trust is something of an "atmosphere," a shared emotional understanding about who is or who is not to be included, contracted, "trusted."

One reason to argue that trust is not an emotion is to get rid of the uncritical picture of trust as a "warm fuzzy feeling" of the sort so disdained by hardheaded ethicists and leaders of all sorts. Thus I would disagree with John Dunn when he argues that trust is a human passion or sentiment.[29] It is not like compassion. It is not even an attitude. Not that I object to warm, fuzzy feelings. On the contrary, sentimentality can be a powerful (although easily exploited) quality of leadership and one that is often neglected in the more "macho" emphasis on charisma. But to think of trust as a particular feeling—not to mention a mawkish feeling—is to demean it and to give a misleading characterization of what trust entails. Trusting does not indicate a "softness," a gullibility, or a weakness. It is a strength and a precondition of any alliance or mutual understanding. It is not a vulnerability, except insofar as, by the very nature of the case, someone who is trusted is thereby in a position to betray that trust. And trust is, I would argue, necessarily a reciprocal relation. This is not to say that Franklin can only trust Benito if Benito trusts Franklin as well, but it is to say that trust is a relationship and not merely an attitude. If Franklin "trusts" Benito but Benito has no relation to Franklin, I am tempted to say that this cannot be a matter of trust at all, but rather predictability or confidence.

WAYS OF THINKING ABOUT TRUST

One might think of trust in negative terms, as, for example, a suspension of fear or a suspension of certain thoughts. However, although this notion captures an important insight (namely, that trust as such doesn't *feel* like anything in particular), it fails to capture the important positive dimensions of trust, because it fails to appreciate the nature and character of emotion. Put one way, perhaps too starkly, emotions are not feelings, except in the most generic and, for the most part, vacuous sense of that term (as any felt mental state or experience). Even anger, which would seem to be as profoundly "felt" as any emotion, is not just a feeling or even primarily a feeling. It is an attitude toward the world, specifically directed at a person, action, situation, or state of affairs. More accurately, anger is a systematic set of judgments, judgments of blame, especially, which cast their target in a particular role, put him or her on trial, consider him or her for punishment.[30] Trust, by way of this perspective, is a certain *conception* of the world and other people. It is a way of seeing, a way of estimating and valuing. Thus it establishes a framework of expectations and agreements (explicit or not) in which actions conform or fail to conform. A leader, one might surmise, is one who succeeds in establishing or sustaining a framework of trust. Indeed, perhaps the increasingly evasive distinction between attentive leaders and actively participating followers has not to do with the recommendation or initiation of actions but rather with the primary responsibility for such a framework.[31]

Trust can also be a decision. To talk about trust as background brings it dangerously close to something that is taken for granted, something that is either there or not there (Fukuyama's general assumption about "high trust" and "low trust" societies). But as we all know from our own experience, trust can be a very conscientious, extremely difficult, and deliberative decision. We meet someone new, or we find ourselves in a new situation with someone we do not know very well. Something comes up. Something must be done. We have to decide: Do we trust this person? In such cases, we establish a framework that was not in place before. Of course, there will be a more general framework within which this relationship and this situation takes place, and that general framework will influence and may well define the boundaries of the decision. One does not want to be too deterministic about this. Some of the most important trust decisions—in particular, decisions to trust a new leader —are made in defiance of an existing trust or distrust situation. But trust is not always in the background. Sometimes when we have to decide whether or not to trust someone, it may be very much in the foreground. Indeed, it may be the definitive aspect of the situation. In leadership, the establishment of trust by a new president just taking office, for example, may be the most important factor in his or her success or failure.

But then, trust is also dynamic.[32] As such, it can clearly be talked about in terms of emotion, but I think on examination it turns out to be something more than an emotion. It is more of a family of emotions, negotiations, deliberations, and decisions. For example, a woman has all of the evidence imaginable that her husband has been and is still being unfaithful. She refuses to accept that evidence, or, rather, she refuses to accept it *as evidence* and thus refuses to accept the obvious conclusion. One might glibly say that this is self-deception, a blatant attempt to refuse to recognize what she in fact clearly knows.[33] But I would argue that it can also be a conscious decision and not deception at all. It is not that the woman refuses to acknowledge (if only to herself) what she knows. It is rather that she has decided to trust her husband, regardless of his behavior (which can then be conveniently ignored or pushed to the side). So, too, I want to argue, while leaders

may be said to earn the trust of their followers, it is the followers who
have the capacity to give that trust. Trust thus becomes a part of the
dynamics of the relationship between those who would be leaders
and their followers, even when the leadership position is indepen-
dently determined, as it usually is. (CEOs, supervisors, officers, deans,
and college presidents—at least in Texas—are placed in their positions
by such higher authorities as boards of directors and generals, not by
those whom they are to lead.)

One problem in analyzing trust is a certain ambiguity, much of it due
to the previously mentioned background-foreground contrast. But
because trust covers so many situations, one is tempted to try to sharpen
the edges and define trust in terms of its context or content. Thus
Benjamin Barber distinguishes three different meanings of *trust* by virtue
of the object or content of that trust: first, a general meaning regarding
social expectations; second, a "competence" sense of trust, that one has
the skills and knowledge to carry out one's responsibilities (e.g., a doctor,
an explosives expert, a White House economist); and third, a "partnership" or "fiduciary" sense, in which one is trusted to carry out certain
duties or obligations, as a result of a certain relationship, usually by
virtue of some commitment, contract, or agreement.[34] I find such distinctions troubling mainly because I think that it is a problem to distinguish
kinds of trust on the basis of trust's object or content, but also because
one's obligations and one's expected competencies are usually correlated in a logical way ("ought implies can," says Kant in a phrase of
admirable brevity). Furthermore, it is not clear in what sense the two
"specialized" senses of trust are not just that—not different meanings
or senses of trust but only more specific instances of trust in general.
And, as if to underscore the problem of multiplying senses needlessly,
Barber spends much of his book criticizing alternative accounts of trust
on the grounds that they conflate the latter two senses of "trust," which
gets ill the way of some of his genuinely interesting observations about
trust in practice, in the family, in politics, and (in a less obvious sense)
in business.[35] What he does not discuss, unfortunately, is the central role
of trust in leadership (as opposed to politics) as such.

DIMENSIONS OF TRUST

What I am suggesting is that different dimensions (not "senses") of
trust be distinguished not on the basis of the object or content of trust,
but on its social role, its role as an emotion, and its role as background.

In many situations, paradigmatically in the primordial situation in which as infants we trust our parents, trust might best be considered part of the "background." It is present and taken for granted throughout in every transaction. It is not "at issue" and not in question. Often, such trust relationships are unrecognized as such, until the trust is breached. For example, banks have been the target of distrust and abuse by U.S. populists and political activists since the last century. President Andrew Jackson even sought to outlaw them. And yet, the amount of trust taken for granted by anyone who has any business with banking at all is astounding. We trust that the money we deposit will be returned to us as promised. We trust that the bills and most checks we receive are valid and genuine. The fact that we ask for a "bank check" or "cashier's check" for absolute security is further evidence of our trust in banks, however great our distrust may be on some more abstract level.[36] And yet, we all have seen the consequences of even a minor bank scare. Not just that bank, but all banks are suddenly under scrutiny and suspicion.[37] Banking depends on trust—not as an issue, but as background. Trust has already been compromised once it has become an issue, once the question arises: "Is my money really safe in that bank?" So, too, once a leader comes under suspicion, no matter that the charges against him may be, malevolent and/or political, trust in him as a leader is already compromised.

The emotional dimension of trust is more explicit, more dynamic. Here trust is an active relationship and transaction rather than the background of relationships and transactions. This is most evident when it is most in question, for example, at the negotiating table between two bitter and mutually distrustful enemies such as the Israelis and the Palestinians. Trust here involves decisions. One decides to trust the other, however tentatively. It is here that the dynamic of trust gets really interesting, for even the slightest hint of betrayal can be met by the most awesome response. We can also witness the evolution or growth of trust, typically not in a single all-or-nothing decision but rather in incremental increases, although it may be generations before trust is sufficiently established to blend into the background. Sometimes, miraculously, mutual trust can just become a fact. Indeed, what I find most fascinating about trust is the human tendency to trust, despite all of the cynicism and suspicion to the contrary. Most people, in the absence of any clear warning or traumatic past experience, tend to be trusting. Trust in general is not so much an achievement as an assumption. It is the initial state rather than a result. People would rather trust than not (and, obviously, would rather be trusted than not). If this is so, it lends an interesting twist to all of the current questions about a "crisis of trust" in U.S. leadership. Alexander Cockburn sagely suggests that this "crisis" in fact reflects people's resentment and distrust of pollsters and professors rather than of one another.[38] He also adds that the U.S. people have always distrusted their leaders. Based on my own reading, I believe this to be false, and so one is moved to ask what particular and obviously effective obstacles to trust are operative in the current political environment.

We talk a great deal about *earning* trust, but I would suggest that *giving* trust is a more promising avenue of pursuit. Earning trust is, ultimately, encouraging trust to slip into the background. Giving trust is a dynamic decision, the transformation of a relationship of the most basic and sometimes most difficult kind. This, I would suggest, is central to any conception of "transforming" or "transformational leadership," indeed, to any leadership at all. But this places an enormous burden on the led. Their decision to trust or not to trust makes leadership possible, and I believe much of the traditional talk about charisma as "a special quality" might better be viewed as the endowment or the projection of such a quality, by way of the people who then "find" that property worthy of following. When it is not part of the background, trust is something that has to be given. But for most leaders in most situations, certainly today, trust cannot be presumed to be part of the background. Thus they must make considerable effort in the name of earning people's trust, but earning usually entails desert, and the history of politics makes all too clear that life in politics is not fair. Ultimately, perhaps, in politics there is no such thing as deserving the people's trust. One is trustworthy, or one is not. One is trusted, or one is not. But whether or not trust can be earned, it can be wisely or foolishly given. Thus it is those who would follow, not those who would lead, who are the ultimate power in any leadership relationship because they are the ones who can decide to give trust.

CONCLUSION: WHETHER 'TIS BETTER TO BE LOVED OR FEARED

Whether it is "better to be loved or feared" is, of course, one of the more famous questions raised by Machiavelli in *The Prince*, and his answer was unambiguous. Better to be feared, he said, but what should be obvious, even within that grim framework, is that the emotional choices are woefully incomplete. One need not fear a leader to obey, nor love a leader to trust. Indeed, the extremes of emotion all too often tend to provoke the extremes of reaction, which Machiavelli clearly sees, and neither provides a very promising guide to leadership, much less ethical leadership. Charisma is designed to solve the problem by providing an emotional intermediary that salvages the power of fear and love but dispenses with the liabilities of both: the hatred generated by fear; the fickleness invited by love. But charisma serves this purpose only by introducing opacities and misunderstandings of its own. Thus I have suggested, albeit briefly, that trust would be a much better emotional vehicle for the discussion of leadership than charisma.

NOTES

1. See "Leadership Ethics," in Chapter 1 of this edition.

2. One can often choose to be a follower without being chosen, but one cannot be a leader without being chosen, in some sense, to lead (even those who, in Shakespeare's phrase, have leadership "thrust upon them").

3. I have benefited from several excellent books in the field: Heifetz; *Leadership Without Easy Answers* (Cambridge: Harvard University Press, 1994). Jay A. Conger, *The Charismatic Leader* (San Francisco: Jossey-Bass, 1989); and, of course, James MacGregor Burns, *Leadership* (New York: Harper, 1978).

4. E.g., R. Heifetz, Heifetz (1994) who begins *Leadership Without Easy Answers* with "Leadership arouses passions," 13. Conger remarks, "They [charismatic leaders] touch our emotions," xi.

5. Robert C. Solomon, *The Passions* (Indianapolis, IN: Hackett, 1993).

6. The role of emotionality in leadership, as opposed to emotions, is complex. An interesting illustration is crying, an explicit display of becoming emotional. Senator Ed Muskie reputedly lost his bid for the Democratic nomination for the presidency when he cried at a press conference during the primaries. Jimmy Carter cried on losing the 1980 election to Ronald Reagan; his act was treated with considerable disdain. Congresswoman Pat Schroeder cried in public about the same time, but reactions were more mixed, ranging from "just like a woman" to "crying shows strength."

7. See Joseph C. Rost, *Leadership for the Twenty-First Century* (New York: Praeger, 1991).

8. In fact, I would argue that the misguided search for definitions in the social sciences more often paralyzes than clarifies research. Precipitous attempts at definition distort and falsify both hypotheses and data and provoke debates that by the very nature of the case, cannot be resolved before the research is well under way. The hidden model here, I believe is that of Socrates, developed 2,500 years ago. Socrates also searched by definitions, but he believed that a definition would yield a "numenal" (almost mystical) insight into the true nature of reality. But without the fantastic metaphysics

that accompanies this belief, the search for definitions is not much more than the naive sophomoric demand that we "define our terms." The truth is that a proper definition comes at the end, not at the beginning of an intensive research program. Even then, it should be considered no more than a summary account of "work in progress." This applies to wholly technical, stipulative terms, and certainly to loaded historical terms like *leadership*.

9. This language is particularly prominent in the work of James MacGregor Burns, who distinguishes between "transactional" and "transformational" leadership on this basis. There is a political sense in which the term *organizer*, however, operates very much like "leader" and connotes the passionate "transformation" of a cause rather than coldly bureaucratic efficiency. Labor organizers, for example, would be a case in point, as opposed to the purely managerial 1934 E. S. Bogardus definition quoted by Rost: "Leadership is a process in which the activities of many are organized to move in a specific direction by one" (Rost, 47). See also Joanne B. Ciulla, "Leadership Ethics: Mapping the Territory," *Business Ethics Quarterly* 5, no. 1 (January 1995): 11.

10. I have taken the following definitions from Ciulla and Rost.

11. At one point, Burns attacks Rost on the supposed need for consensus and comments that consensus erodes leadership. It is worth speculating why this might be so. Consensus is usually the outcome of negotiation and compromise, typically "cool-headed" rather than enthusiastic. Thus, we encounter a somewhat traditional philosophical question: Can such cool-headed reason motivate action, or does consensus, while it may promote harmony and even efficiency, stifle the passionate urge to do something difficult, even seemingly impossible? In other words, does consensus undermine the emotional appeal of, as well as the need for leadership?

12. Despite decades of denial, that the German people in general were fully knowledgeable participants in Hitler's vision is now generally believed. See, for example, Daniel Goldhagen, *Hitler's Willing Executioners: Ordinary Germans and the Holocaust* (New York: Knopf, 1996).

13. First published in 1904, it appeared in English in 1930 (New York: Scribner).

14. See Hans Gerth and C. Wright Mills (Eds.), "The Sociology of Charismatic Authority," in *From Max Weber: Essays in Sociology* (New York: Oxford University Press, 1946), 245.

15. Robert Nozick, *Philosophical Explanations* (New York: Simon & Schuster, 1990).

16. See Conger.

17. Burns, 243.

18. See Ciulla.

19. Jim Jones and David Koresh are examples. If not for the ultimately lethal consequences, would such figures ever have been considered "leaders"?

20. Quoted by Edwin P. Hollander, "Ethical Challenges in the Leader-Follower Relationship," *Business Ethics Quarterly* 5, no. 1 (January 1995): 57.

21. Michael Keeley, "The Trouble with Transformational Leadership," *Business Ethics Quarterly* 5, no. 1 (January 1995): 67–96.

22. I should say here that I am indebted to Jay Conger's work on charismatic leadership, although my analysis is quite different from his and I do not give "charisma" the centrality that he does.

23. Robert Wilson (Ed.), *Character Above All* (New York: Simon & Schuster, 1996).

24. Francis Fukuyama, *Trust* (New York: Free Press, 1995).

25. Niklas Luhmann, *Trust and Power* (New York: John Wiley, 1980), 80; Bernard Barber, *Logic and Limits of Trust* (New Brunswick: Rutgers University Press, 1983), 2, 71.

26. Laurence Thomas, *Living Morally* (Philadelphia: Temple University Press, 1989); Annette Baier, *Moral Prejudice* (Cambridge, MA: Harvard University Press, 1994).

27. The concept of the "background" comes from Heidegger and his analyses of human practices in general, but John Searle also explains it in a more analytic framework in his book *Intentionality* (Cambridge: Cambridge University Press, 1983).

28. Of course, there can be banter and all kinds of "speech," but the number of "speech acts" that simply break down is mind-boggling, and not only those that depend on trust that the other person is telling the truth.

29. In Diego Gambetta, *Trust* (Oxford: Blackwell, 1988), 73.

30. I have argued this analysis of anger at much greater length in my book, *The Passions* (New York: Doubleday, 1976; Indianapolis, IN: Hackett, 1993), and in numerous articles, for example, "Getting Angry," in *Culture Theory*, edited by Richard Schweder and Robert LeVine (Cambridge: Cambridge University Press, 1984).

31. Burns, January 22, 1996.

32. Thus, Dunn also insists that trust is a "modality" as well as a human passion. See Gambetta.

33. I have discussed this sort of self-deception as an active and necessary ingredient of social relations in "Self, Deception and Self-Deception," in *Self and Deception*, edited by Roger Ames (New York: SUNY Press, 1997).

34. The last definition follows Talcott Parsons, to whom Barber is obviously indebted. See Parsons on trust as a consequence of commitment in his *Politics and Social Structure* (New York: Free Press, 1969), 4.

35. Barber seems to conflate "trust" with "confidence," a distinction he borrows from Luhmann, who talks about trust in "the market."

36. The difference between practical trust and theoretical distrust is a fascinating topic in its own right, especially in leadership studies. It is often noted, for example, that U.S. people now claim to distrust their government at the same time that their demands and expectations of government are at an all-time high. Attitudes toward banks and banking—except for those rare eccentrics who prefer to keep their cash under the mattress—is another case in point. "In God We Trust" is printed on American money. The awkward truth, however, is that "In Government We Trust" is the necessary precondition of the value of any currency.

37. The Bank of New Zealand scare of 1990 threatened to undermine that entire economy, not to mention the current difficulties of the big Tokyo banks.

38. Alexander Cockburn, *The Nation* (February 1996).

Part III

The Morality of Leaders: Motives and Deeds

6

Why Leaders Need Not Be Moral Saints

Terry L. Price

Few would disagree with the claim that we want our leaders to be moral. But just how moral do we want them to be? Here, my focus is not the issue of "dirty hands," which prompts some thinkers to suggest that our leaders must sometimes be willing to do the wrong thing—in effect, to get their hands dirty.[1] Rather, the question I want to address is whether our leaders should be as moral as possible. Do we want them to be, as Susan Wolf famously put it, "moral saints"?[2] There is significant support for this kind of expectation both in our everyday discourse about leadership and in the leadership literature. We frequently hear, in response to bad behavior by leaders, that our standards should be higher for people in power than they are for everyone else. According to this view, we look to our leaders to set the moral example for the rest of us. Leadership theories—from *transforming* and *servant* leadership to *authentic* and *ethical* leadership—point in the same general direction.[3] Leaders who live up to the tenets of these theories stand out morally from followers, as well as from other leaders, especially with respect to how they are motivated. It is no overstatement to say that the current orthodoxy in the leadership literature holds that leaders ought to pursue the good of followers (and others), not their own good.[4]

Such other-regarding commitments are central to Wolf's notion of the moral saint. Wolf defines a moral saint as "a person whose every action is as morally good as possible, a person, that is, who is as morally worthy as can be" (419). What makes the saint's action morally good is its causal origin in a "concern for others" (420). This other-regarding focus similarly characterizes the maximally morally worthy person. According to Wolf, "A necessary condition of moral sainthood would be that one's life be dominated by a commitment to improving the welfare of others or of society as a whole" (420). Wolf's moral saint thus differs from the religious saint, whose "powerful humanitarian concern" must be understood "in the context of a more comprehensive devotion to God."[5] Rather than being driven by religious commitment, the moral saint is motivated by genuine altruism or a sense that it is a person's moral duty to make others better off (420). Wolf gives the names "Loving Saint" to the altruist and "Rational Saint" to the person who acts to advance the well-being of others "out of . . . intellectual appreciation and recognition of moral principles" (420).

As we shall see, Wolf rejects moral sainthood. Her basic point is that it represents a failed ideal in personal life (419). As Vanessa Carbonell describes Wolf's view, "[A] saint is someone we want neither to *be* nor to *be around*."[6] For the purposes of this chapter, I am not primarily interested in whether moral saints can pursue their individual purposes or whether we find them attractive partners in our personal or social relationships. What I want to consider is whether moral sainthood is the right *leadership* ideal.[7] I have elsewhere argued that leaders are not justified in being morally worse than the rest of us.[8] The moral rules apply equally to leaders and followers. Here, I defend a companion claim: we cannot rightly expect leaders to be morally better than the rest of us. So my thesis is in keeping with a more general, fundamental view of leadership ethics—namely, that leaders are not morally exceptional. Ethics is neither easier nor harder on leaders. Because it makes room for leaders to pursue the many and varied ends that the rest of us pursue, they need not be moral saints.

My argument against moral exceptionalism is ultimately a Kantian one. Immanuel Kant's ethics are characterized by their strictness and their minimalism. The *strictness* of the theory means that leaders cannot use consequences (the ends) or considerations of partiality (the good that could be achieved for self or others) to break the moral rules.[9] The theory's *minimalism* is in the fact that it appeals primarily to negative duties (e.g., duties "not to" lie, cheat, break promises, etc.), leaving it to the individual to decide when and how to discharge positive duties (e.g., duties "to" help others, etc.).[10] The strictness of the theory keeps leaders within the moral rules, whereas its minimalism calls for something well short of saintliness. This reading of Kant contrasts with Wolf's reading, which attributes much greater demandingness to Kant's views.[11] Her criticism of the Rational Saint is a serious one, and in the course of this chapter, I defend Kantianism against it.

THE PRACTICE AND CONCEPT OF LEADERSHIP

Wolf presents both "practical" and "logical" reasons for thinking that moral sainthood is ultimately a bad ideal in personal life (421).The practical reasons derive from contingent facts about the world in which we live. Simply put, it is impossible for people to pursue most of the personal endeavors that occupy them and, at the same time, to commit themselves fully to the welfare of other people:

> [I]f the moral saint is devoting all his time to feeding the hungry or healing the sick or raising money for Oxfam, then necessarily he is not reading Victorian novels, playing the oboe, or improving his backhand. ... An interest in something like gourmet cooking will be ... difficult for a moral saint to rest easy with. For it seems to me that no plausible argument can justify the use of human resources involved in producing a *paté de canard en croute* against possible alternative beneficent ends to which these resources might be put. ... Presumably, an interest in high fashion or interior design will fare much the same, as will, very possibly, a cultivation of the finer arts as well. (421, 422)

Wolf's point is that an overriding commitment to the good of others will not leave room even for dabbling in personal hobbies or diversions.

That is to say nothing of becoming captivated by one of these activities, let alone trying to become good at one of them.[12] Just to attain academic, musical, or athletic competence, one must make a significant commitment to the activity in which one wants to become competent—often at the expense of the good that one might do for others. Expertise comes at even greater expense. Malcolm Glad well cites research supporting the claim that being an expert demands ten thousand hours of practice.[13] Of course, if there were more time in the day or more days in a life, more resources, or—even better—fewer problems, we might

save the world and also become Yo-Yo Ma. With all our good work com-
pleted (or at least all that could be done for the time being), we could
dedicate ourselves to perfection at the cello. But the two goals are practically inconsistent. Unfortunately, our world is not one of unlimited time
or resources, and its problems are many. Here, the trade-off is no less
necessary than the trade-off experts ordinarily make between two
equally demanding personal pursuits. We cannot expect Yo-Yo Ma to
be Tiger Wood, or vice versa.

When we combine this condition of necessity with real-world facts
about the business of leadership, the practical reasons against moral
sainthood apply with even greater force in leadership contexts. For
one thing, leadership is closer to a kind of expertise than it is to dilet-
tantism. Typically, the long hours required to get in a position of leadership are surpassed only by the hours of single-minded dedication
required once in the position. Leaders whose lives are "dominated by
a commitment to improving the welfare of others or of society as a
whole" (420) will not have the time and resources necessary for building luxury cars, designing sleek computers, and developing winning
football teams. There is another way in which the contrast between
ordinary project pursuit and efforts to increase the general welfare
is even starker in the leadership case than it is in our personal lives.
If I decide to devote my personal time to serious marathon training,
there are definite opportunity costs. In addition to precluding many
alternative personal hobbies I might take up instead, my training will
also compete with all kinds of efforts to do good for others, which
likely means less overall welfare than there might otherwise be. But
when a person exercising leadership devotes his energies to a project,
we can expect that (some) followers will do so as well. If the project
ultimately has little to do with the good of others, the leader will have
taken up followers' time and directed their resources away from more
beneficent ends that might have been pursued.

This is not to deny the increased welfare often associated with consumer goods and sporting events. Fancy cars and computers give
some people pleasure, perhaps making them happy or happier than
they would have been. So do winning football teams—at least for half
the fans. And it is also true that the production of material goods
means jobs, either here or abroad, thus allowing us to talk about the
contribution these goods make to well-being throughout society.
However, even if we admit that there is a sense in which creators, pro-
ducers, and consumers of nonessential goods may all be better off,

sometimes benefitting indirectly as part of the larger economy, the good of others hardly stands out as a practical motivational driver for leaders. Claims by business leaders that "it's really about the consumer" or by professional coaches that "it's really about the fans" (or even "the players") do not ring true in most cases. It is also worth noting that when leaders decide to step down, it is often to live a more balanced life, to spend more time with their families, or to take up public service. Sometimes these explanations do not ring entirely true either, but no one questions the fact that resigning from a high-profile leadership position is often practically necessary for increased other-regarding activity—even if we doubt whether newfound altruism has anything to do with the departure.

In contrast with the practical reasons against moral sainthood, the logical reasons for thinking it is a poor personal ideal point to a conceptual conflict between the character traits associated with a prioritized concern for others and their feelings, on the one hand, and the rougher, edgier, even *wicked* qualities we sometimes admire in people, on the other (421–422, 426).[14] Wolf writes,

> [A] moral saint must have and cultivate those qualities which are apt to allow him to treat others as justly and kindly as possible. He will have the standard virtues to a nonstandard degree. He will be patient, considerate, even-tempered, hospitable, charitable in thought as well as in deed. He will be very reluctant to make negative judgments of other people. He will be careful not to favor some people over others on the basis of properties they could not help but have. . . . A moral saint will have to be very, very nice. It is important that he not be offensive. (421, 422)

Is there a problem with having this kind of saintly character? According to Wolf, the logical deficiency of moral sainthood is that it does not leave room for "a cynical or sarcastic wit, or a sense of humor that appreciates this kind of wit in others" (422). The person with the *devilish* sense of humor is funny precisely because he is so unsaintly. For him to be a moral saint, he would have to stop being a devil. Wolf concludes, "[A]s a result, he will have to be dull-witted or humorless or bland" (422).

Concerns about sense of humor do not ground the conceptual conflict between leadership and moral saintliness. But there is a related worry about the disposition of the saint. The moral saint simply sounds too nice for what we understand as leadership. Leadership is rarely careful and conservative; it is about risk and change and crea-tion.[15] In fact, the work of leadership scholars such as Ed Hollander gives us reason to think that doing things in new and different ways is central to what leadership is.[16] So there is a logical point here too. An unyielding commitment to innovation and deviation can bring with it the risk of being impatient, judging people, and perhaps offending them. Sometimes, it simply means not caring very much about what others think. In this respect, the behavior of leaders con-trasts sharply with that of people who are merely following. The best way to get along in the system is to stick closely to social expectations. This kind of conformity—nice and inoffensive though it may be—is a real impediment to change. Indeed, because of the high costs of impos-ing social rules from the outside, the internalization of social expec-tations is a necessary—and perhaps the most important—ingredient in a recipe for keeping things just the way they are.

Recognizing the value of unsaintliness in leadership contexts cannot mean that we must give leaders a moral pass and allow them to behave unethically to achieve their ends.[17] Generally accepted moral requirements apply to leaders no less than they apply to the rest of us.[18] For example, getting things done does not give leaders a justifica-tion for mistreating people or intentionally hurting their feelings—whether followers or outsiders. Nor do pressures toward goal achieve-ment that leaders face make it permissible for them to lie, cheat, or break promises. Ethical leadership can take only so much "going against the moral grain" (422) and "develop[ing] . . . traits that are nec-essary to abandon or challenge societal norms and traditions."[19] But people do not have rights to unlimited patience, charity, hospitality, kindness, and consideration. Moreover, they do not have rights never to be judged or offended. Basic morality, then, is a perfectly good eth-ical aspiration for leaders, although it is well short of moral saintliness. Even if we accept that leaders serve as role models, living up to the fundamental standards of morality is all that we can rightly expect of them in their roles. It is certainly all we can expect if we also want them to have any chance of achieving the ends of leadership.

This strategy for adjudicating between leadership and moral saintli-ness suggests that we embrace leadership at the expense of saintliness. An alternative way to reduce the conflict between the two is to take a different view of moral saints—that is, to draw on a different view of what the ethical ideal would look like. Edward Lawry, for example, writes, "I have a sense that [Wolf] is not talking about *real* moral saints."[20] This line of objection draws on the moral theory of virtue ethics.[21] According to the virtue ethicist, we cannot look to a set of moral behaviors that would be good in all circumstances; rather, the right action is the action that would be done by the virtuous person in particular circumstances.[22] Practical wisdom, built on years of experience, makes it possible for this individual to determine what behavior would be fitting for the situation at hand.[23] Drawing on this general approach, Lawry points out that "the inoffensive niceness of a person seems surely to be an objectionable moral trait when righteous indignation is called for."[24] Like traditional understandings of virtue ethics, Lawry's view of moral sainthood prioritizes the good of individual actors. "[T]he best moral life," he writes, "has to be a good human life."[25] Lawry's moral saint therefore avoids some of the unattractiveness of Wolf's moral saint by returning the focus of ethical theory to personal good, not social good. This focus, because of the rich variety it allows, would also make greater room for moral saints in leadership contexts.

Like Lawry, Vanessa Carbonell recommends sensitivity to the situation in her criticism of Wolf: "Patience . . . seems virtuous only when it is warranted."[26] For example, Carbonell's paradigm case of a moral saint, international healthcare leader Paul Farmer, is rightly "an incredibly inpatient person"[27] because he knows firsthand that lives are at stake. Carbonell adds that blind charity is "downright naïve and certainly inimical to the project of benefitting others" and that "making negative judgments *when they are warranted* is an *essential* component in the project of benefitting others."[28] Notice, however, that Carbonell's defense of moral saints maintains Wolf's more common characterization of the saint—at least in modern times—as someone who is primarily concerned about the well-being of others. For Carbonell, acts that do not look nice, when properly understood in terms of social benefit, are nice after all. In this respect, the argument bears significant resemblance to Machiavelli's claim that some acts of apparent cruelty are actually acts of kindness and that some seemingly stingy behaviors prove generous in the end.[29]

To make this kind of contextual approach to moral saintliness work, its advocates would need to show that social benefit is somehow the aim of ethical behavior. As we have seen, this claim is not universally true in virtue ethics. The virtuous person aims not at social benefit but at virtuousness itself. Admittedly, virtuous *leaders* may have special reasons to make the good of others their foremost aim. These reasons would point to the nature of the activity and, in particular, to leaders' relationships with followers. One might say that it is the main job of leaders to look out for their welfare. Such a view would be in keeping with the claims of contemporary virtue theorists, which hold that what is right is determined not only by the situation but also by the role of the person in that situation.[30] However, I think we should be skeptical of the claim that leadership can be understood in terms of a fundamental commitment to well-being, whether the well-being of followers or of society as a whole. Not even a normative conception of leadership can bear the weight of this kind of commitment. To justify my skepticism, I turn to a consideration of the *Loving Saintly Leader.*

THE LOVING SAINTLY LEADER

To ask whether leaders ought to be moral saints is really to ask a question about the ends of leadership. At its heart, this question is normative: what ends *ought* leaders to pursue. As I pointed out in the previous section, it is false that all (or most) leaders *in fact* pursue the good of others. In many cases, when their activities end up benefitting others, the leaders are not actually aiming at this result. But this point is a descriptive one. It says something about the way the world is—specifically, how leaders behave in it. As such, the point is consistent with all kinds of normative claims about how leaders should be motivated. In particular, it is consistent with the claim that leaders should be altruistically motivated—in effect, that they should be moral saints. To challenge this claim, I will develop the argument that this kind of moral sainthood is too narrow to serve as a normative ideal for leadership. By saying that it is *too narrow*, in contrast with Wolf, I am not arguing that it is a bad ideal. I want to leave open the very real possibility that a leader could rightly aim at the good of others. But this end is only one valuable end among many that might justifiably be pursued by leaders.

The Loving Saintly Leader is the leadership equivalent of Wolf's Loving Saint. Like the Loving Saint, the Loving Saintly Leader is genuinely motivated by altruism (420). She thus takes the good of others to be the primary end of her behavior. Historically, the moral theory that has maintained a direct focus on social benefit is utilitarianism, not virtue ethics.[31] In its simplest form, utilitarianism holds that the right action produces the greatest overall well-being. According to utilitarianism, the happiness of one person counts no more or less than that of anyone else in the overall utility calculations that determine right actions. In many ways, the Loving Saintly Leader looks like a utilitarian (428)—indeed, much more like a utilitarian than a virtue theorist. For the utilitarian, there is a clear focus on particular actions as the objects of moral assessment, and there is a distinct sense in which a person's well-being can be set against, and sometimes sacrificed for, the good of others—what we might expect of a saint. In contrast, because of its roots in Ancient Greek society, virtue ethics makes less room for distinguishing personal well-being—a life well lived—and the good of the society and its members. The individual cannot be properly understood outside of his community and place within it.[32]

A leader whose main commitment was overall utility in society would normally qualify as a Loving Saintly Leader. Acting in ways that maximize societal well-being would seem to involve rigorous discrimination among possible choices, and the most straightforward way for a utilitarian to do this would be to incorporate a fundamental concern for others in his decision rule. Earl Spurgin, for example, implicitly suggests that one unattractive feature of moral saints in business is their underlying commitment to utilitarianism. He writes,

> The resources that pharmaceutical companies devote to developing and marketing erectile dysfunction medications could save many thousands of lives if they were devoted to other life-threatening illnesses. No doubt, saintly businesses would be moved by such an argument. It is hard to imagine how saintly businesses could be comfortable using their resources to help older men have sex when those same resources could be used to save lives, often the lives of children. . . . Such saintliness by businesses, however, would come at societal costs, both those of continued silence about erectile dysfunction and those from the loss of sex lives for men so afflicted.[33]

In Spurgin's example, the pharmaceutical company is clearly doing social good by addressing a problem that causes significant reductions in well-being. Yet the company could be doing even greater good by redirecting its efforts toward those with greater need and, perhaps because of their youth, a greater claim on resources generally.[34] Spurgin's complaint against this kind of utilitarian saintliness is that it cannot condone businesses that produce nonoptimal, but nonetheless, very socially beneficial products.

There is intuitive appeal to the utilitarian idea that societal well-being ought to be maximized, especially on the saintly view that the good of others is the central moral value. But notice that the leader who is focused on making particular people better off—or improving the lives of people with particular needs—still lives up to Wolf's main criterion for sainthood. Wolf suggests that saints are "dominated by a commitment to improving the welfare of others *or* of society as a whole" (420, emphasis added). The disjunction is there for good reason. This broad characterization of sainthood reflects the fact the altruism, unlike utilitarianism, is often "more heartfelt than efficient."[35] A person can do good (or aim to do good) without doing the most good (or aiming to do the most good). Another reason to avoid identifying utilitarianism with loving saintliness is that self-focused action can be utilitarian without being altruistic. A person who is able to maximize overall utility by caring for himself—say, because he is in great need—would hardly be acting in a saintly or altruistic matter. Here, utilitarianism requires self-centeredness, not altruism. For both these reasons, we should reject accounts of altruism that understand it in terms of utilitarian considerations about overall well-being. The Loving Saintly Leader must focus on others, not the self, but this focus can be on particular individuals or groups of individuals (e.g., followers)—that is, not necessarily on the collective as a whole.

If the Loving Saintly Leader does not have to be a utilitarian, it largely misses the point to note that moral saints need not "suffer from the obsessive maximizing that makes Wolf's saint so unattractive."[36] The Loving Saintly Leader may be less attractive than the mindless utility maximizer, but he still has what Wolf takes to be the main defect of all moral saints. By tying the ultimate value of our projects to the good of others, the expectation of moral saintliness threatens the notion "of an identifiable, personal self" (424). According to Wolf, that is, sainthood essentially crowds out the desires that characterize us as humans: "The normal person's direct and specific desires for objects, activities, and events that conflict with moral perfection are not simply sacrificed but removed, suppressed, or subsumed" (424). Her critique certainly signals one of the dangers faced by the moral saint, utilitarian or not—namely, that he is probably "too good for his own well-being" (421). But I do not think that the distinction between self-interest and the interests of others is sufficient to capture what is wrong with saintliness in leadership contexts. The main problem with the Loving Saintly Leader is not that the happiness of others overrides the leader's own happiness or even his "personal excellence" (423, 426). It is rather that privileging this kind of leadership—because of its single-minded focus on well-being—ignores the value of other morally worthy leadership pursuits that are neither welfarist nor properly characterized as personal. Or so I shall argue in the remainder of this section.

The ideal of the Loving Saintly Leader rests on a morally impoverished view of motivation. Increasing welfare is not the only ethical reason for leaders to set their projects in motion and to dedicate much of their lives to making these projects successful. Other, equally good ethical reasons for project pursuit include the value leaders see in the activity of creation or in the thing ultimately produced. Great musical conductors, we might assume, justifiably lead concerts because of their commitment to the music itself—or for the value of producing excellent music—not necessarily (or even likely) because of their love for anyone, including orchestral players or audience members. Religious leaders, like religious saints, work primarily for their God.[37] Even political leaders, often thought to be a paradigm case of leadership with an other-oriented focus, need not see the welfare of others as their primary commitment. Plato was wrong to claim that because crafts such as leadership are "complete," leadership cannot be exercised *for* the sake of the craft.[38] Working *for* something does not always mean *helping* that thing. For example, a life devoted to simplicity would not be *completing* or *helping* simplicity but living according to its value. Likewise, a person might pursue political leadership because of the intrinsic value of the craft, or simply an "intellectual appreciation" (420) of the science of effective governance. Love of country or commitments to political ideals such as freedom are also ethically admirable motivations for entering political life. In other words, the great variety of projects to which people attach value makes it normatively implausible to expect leaders always to act only on the welfarist commitments of moral saints.

It is equally hard to see the ends of leadership as being mainly personal or, in many cases, personal at all—in the way that, say, becoming a great guitarist might be a form of personal excellence. Leadership is not a personal activity; it is a group enterprise. People do not lead alone but, rather, work in concert with others to achieve collective goals. Leadership's necessarily collectivist nature may well be the root of our misguided attraction to the Loving Saintly Leader. The word *collective* is ambiguous. To talk about a collective goal can mean either that we are aiming at something good for all of us or, simply, that it is something at which we are collectively aiming. When the ultimate end of a group's effort is the welfare of its members, leadership is collective in the former sense, as when a labor union strikes to get better pay. But collective goals need not focus on the group that has those goals. For example, a group's efforts to dedicate a monument to victims of terrorism can hardly be understood as based on the welfare of group members. Although the goal is *their* goal, it does not mean that goal achievement is ultimately *for them*—or, for that matter, for the victims (instead, it is *to them*), for people outside the group, or for people who make up society as a whole.

Leadership conflicts with moral saintliness, then, not because the leader's self-interest or personal good is in tension with societal good. It is because leaders are rightly driven by all kinds of ends, many of which are not focused on well-being at all, whether personal or societal. Instead, the collective project pursuit that characterizes leadership is sometimes aimed at ends that are considered worthy for their own sake. People rightly work together to achieve ends that are not really *for anyone*. To be sure, leaders and the groups they lead *want* to achieve what they find to be valuable. And when they achieve what they find to be valuable, there is a sense in which they got what they *wanted*. But this does not mean that the value of their ends must be understood in terms of the wants or desires of the group.[39] Determination of value can be based on judgment, which in many cases precedes desire. In other words, people sometimes want things because these things are thought valuable, rather than valuing these things simply because they are desired.

The same goes for leaders who are focused on the good of others. Although humanitarians get what they want when they save lives, the value of what these Loving Saintly Leaders achieve is not derived from their own desires. Hopefully, the Loving Saintly Leader desires what is good for others rather than fooling himself into thinking that something is good for others just because he desires it. In the best cases, he will have his own ethical view of what has supreme value, a view that defines the ends of his leadership in terms of the welfare of followers or society as a whole. My conclusion in this section, however, is that the Loving Saintly Leader's end—namely, the good of others—is only one value among many. Morality certainly makes room for pursuit of this end, but it also makes room for leaders to pursue all kinds of other things that are valuable in themselves: great music or art, religious and political ideals, and so on. Social benefit is therefore *an* end of ethical leadership, but it is not *the only* end.

THE RATIONAL SAINTLY LEADER

The Rational Saintly Leader is the leadership equivalent of Wolf's Rational Saint. Like the Rational Saint, the Rational Saintly Leader is motivated by moral duty, not by altruism (420). He thus takes conformity to the principles of morality to be the primary aim of his behavior. Historically, the moral theory most closely connected to this kind of behavioral conformity is the view of Immanuel Kant.[40] Roughly, Kantianism holds that right actions respect the demands of reason.[41] Actions are unreasonable, first, when they cannot be universalized.[42] It is unreasonable for a person to think that he should be able to use means that he cannot conceive of everyone else similarly using to achieve their ends—behaviors such as lying, cheating, and promise breaking.[43] Other people's ends are just as important in their own eyes. Second, and much more concretely, unethical behaviors disrespect the reason of particular thinking beings by treating these individuals as mere means to an end.[44] We can therefore equally explain why lying, cheating, and promise breaking are wrong by appealing to the fact that these behaviors bypass the reason of autonomous individuals, treating these people as though they were nothing more than "things."[45] Insofar as the Rational Saintly Leader's duties are derived from Kantian moral theory, he would take these principles seriously indeed, making them his predominant source of motivation. In this final section, I consider the extent to which Kantianism demands this kind of saintliness of our leaders. Are the demands of Kantian moral theory so great—in effect, that leaders should aspire to become Rational Saintly Leaders—that the theory is ultimately incompatible with leadership as we know it?

Initially at least, the Kantian does not look all that much like a moral saint. The moral saint has a central "commitment to improving the welfare of others or of society as a whole" (420), whereas the Kantian gives little weight to the value of happiness or well-being.[46] Kant's theory is committed to the value of reason, and—as Wolf concedes—commitments to happiness and reason can come apart: "On one interpretation of Kantian doctrine ... moral perfection would be achieved simply by unerring obedience to a limited set of side constraints. On this interpretation, Kantian theory simply does not yield an ideal conception of a person of any fullness comparable to that of the moral saints I have so far been portraying" (430). Nevertheless, Wolf is able to motivate a Kantian argument for saintliness by highlighting Kant's insistence that we have not only negative duties to refrain from unreasonable behavior but also positive duties (similarly grounded in reason) to advance the ends of others (430–431) or—as Kant puts it—to make their ends, "as far as possible, *my* ends."[47] According to Kant, it is unreasonable to expect others to help us pursue our ends when we are unwilling to help them.[48] In addition, failing to offer assistance contradicts the fact that people in need are themselves rational individuals just like us, each with his or her own plans and projects. So, within Kantianism, there is enough beneficence to get an argument for sainthood off the ground.

Still, we can challenge Wolf's claim that "[positive] duties are unlimited in the degree to which they *may* dominate a life" (430, emphasis in original). For Kant, our negative duties (duties *not* to do things such as lying, cheating, and promise breaking) differ greatly from our positive, other-regarding duties.[49] Negative duties must be discharged at all times and in all circumstances, whereas positive duties—because of their "wider" nature—can be discharged in some circumstances but not in others.[50] There are good practical reasons for this distinction. For one thing, positive duties come with higher costs: discharging them requires positive action (e.g., if I want to help someone, I need to stop typing and engage in an alternative behavior). Unlike negative duties, they cannot be discharged when we are occupied with other things (e.g., I am not lying as I type) or doing nothing at all. Kant's reasoning for this distinction is that making positive duties as demanding as negative duties undermines the basis for the claim that we have positive duties to help in the first place. Our duty to help others in need depends on the fact that we sometimes need (or have needed, or will need) help from others.[51] That is why we cannot reasonably expect others to help us when we are unwilling similarly to help them.

But neither can others expect that we engage in helping behavior all of the time. As Kant puts it, "a maxim of promoting others' happiness at the sacrifice of one's own happiness, one's true needs, would conflict with itself if it were made a universal law."[52] What is the morally correct amount of sacrifice? It will be determined by a person's own "true needs"—the more a person needs from others, the more (on pain of contradiction) others can expect of him.[53] Notice, though, that there must be limits even here and that these limits will ultimately be based on the person's interests, not the interests of others. Ironically, the needier the person is, the less he will be able to do for others without undermining his ability to take care of himself. Of course, leaders are dependent on others in a different way. Their goals can be achieved only by collective action—that is, with the help of others. But, here too, the corresponding duty that leaders have to help followers (or anyone else) will be necessarily limited by leaders' commitments to the goals that undergird their other-regarding duties. This means that the advocate of Kantian ethics simply cannot endorse the Rational Saintly Leader or Wolf's Rational Saint, who "pays little or no attention to his own happiness ... [and] sacrifices his own interests to the interests of others" (420).

Another potential way of tying Kantianism to moral sainthood focuses on the notion of moral worth. Wolf claims that the moral saint is "a person whose every action is as morally good as possible, a person, that is, who is as morally worthy as can be" (419). The closest Kant comes to privileging this kind of commitment to morality is in his claim that only actions done "from duty" have moral worth.[54] The person who does an action from duty does the right thing for the right reason—namely, because it was his duty to do it. In contrast, when a person's action merely "accords with duty," he does the right thing but acts as he does for some reason besides duty—for example, out of desire, natural disposition, or self-interest.[55] Regardless of motive, the person has discharged his duty. However, for purposes of assigning "moral worth" or "esteem," actions that accord with duty come up short:

> I maintain that in such a case an action of this kind, however right and however amiable it may be, has still no genuinely moral worth. It stands on the same footing as other inclinations—for example, the inclination for honour, which if fortunate enough to hit on something beneficial and right and consequently honourable, deserves praise and encouragement, but not esteem; for its maxim lacks moral content, namely, the performance of such actions, not from inclination, but *from duty*.[56]

According to Kant, then, it does not make sense to give people moral credit for what they would have done anyway. It just so happens that what they were bound to do by duty turned about to be what they were already inclined to do, disposed by character to do, or egoistically tempted to do.

The Rational Saintly Leader, it seems, would aim for his actions to be from duty, not merely to be in accord with duty. Because he is "dominated by the motivation to be moral" (431), the actions of this leader, like the actions of Wolf's Rational Saint, would not be determined by desire, natural disposition, or self-interest. Yet it is a mistake to think that Kantian ethics demands this kind of motivational commitment of leaders or anyone else. Kant argues that there are some things that we must not do and some things that we have a duty to do. Between what is prohibited and what is required are actions that we can do or not do as we please. Within these limits, that is, there is a kind of moral *free space*. For example, the leader who has an idea for a new dietary supplement may or may not decide to pursue its development, assuming he is bound by no promises and that the supplement is not harmful. Morality cannot tell him what he ought to do because he has neither a duty to develop the product nor a duty to refrain from doing so. So, in this case, it is impossible for him to act from duty. To expect all of a leader's actions be motivated by duty misses the central Kantian point that we are free to pursue all kinds of projects, as long as they are within the limits of morality. Morality itself need not be a leader's only project.

Kant also overstates the case against giving moral credit for actions motivated by considerations other than morality. If I do an action that only accords with duty and I would have done the action even if I had a duty not to do it, then clearly my action has no moral worth. But if I would not have done the action had it been against duty, then it is unclear why my action—motivated though it is by desire or something else—does not have moral worth. Imagine that the leader who develops the dietary supplement does so out of self-interest. Although the behavior has an egoistic source, if he would not have developed the product were there a duty not to develop it (say, because of associated health risks), then it seems that there is something morally worthy about his behavior after all. He is consciously pursuing his projects—albeit nonmoral ones—within the limits set by morality.

Despite the weakness of efforts to associate the Rational Saintly Leader with Kant's moral theory, I want to concede that there is something to the charge that this moral theory does have its "saintly" features and that these features are in tension with leadership. The tension is not related to the positive duties the theory generates or to the notion of moral worth. Its source is rather that Kantianism seems to bring with it extreme moral caution. Although there is great freedom within the bounds of morality, one has to be very careful not to go outside these bounds, especially when it comes to discharging one's negative duties. As we have seen, these duties—for example, not to cheat or lie—do not have the discretionary nature of our positive duties. We ought never to fail to discharge them. The problem, however, is that the lines between fair play and cheating, as well as between truth and deception, are not always bright for leaders. The most obvious way to deal with this kind of ambiguity, if a leader absolutely wants to avoid immorality, is to stay far away from where the lines might be. Wolf gets close to identifying this feature of Kantianism when she notes the Rational Saint's "pathological fear of damnation" (424). Damnation is not quite what the Kantian fears, but there is a sense in which Kant's theory lends itself to the charge that it engenders a pathological fear of doing the wrong thing (or failing to do the right thing).

Extreme caution can be an impediment to leadership. A paralyzing aversion to doing the wrong thing hardly lends itself to the deviation and innovation expected of many leaders. Across leadership contexts, leaders adopt means that are not explicitly prohibited to be more productive or successful. We see this phenomenon in business (think of the added efficiency of assembly lines and, more recently, outsourcing), and it is true in sports (think of what the Fosbury Flop did for high jumping and how drivers such as Junior Johnson came up with ingenious ways of increasing speed and safety in NASCAR).[57] What might initially look like an unfair competitive advantage (when it truly conduces to success) gets adopted by others within that particular context. Leaders who are overly concerned about maintaining the status quo or an even playing field will be too conservative for this kind of innovation. It will be similarly difficult for leaders who are preoccupied with the rationality of followers to influence them to achieve group goals. Followers are motivated by all kinds of things that fall somewhere between straightforward appeals to their rationality and straight-out deception. Showing complete respect for follower autonomy *lets* them do things, whereas deceiving followers effectively *makes* them do things. However, a lot of leadership is about "*getting people to act*," which is somewhere between the two.[58] We would therefore be rightly skeptical of leadership efforts that indifferently approach followers with claims such as "You might not want to do this, and I want to engage your rational faculties to the fullest extent when I ask." The methods leaders are expected to use—methods that hardly serve an ideal of follower autonomy—do not comport well the extreme moral caution that might seem to characterize Kantianism.

I am not the first to recognize this particular tension between saintliness and leadership. Spurgin writes, "The very concept of moral sainthood discourages the cultivation of [traits that] lead individuals to 'push the envelope' in ways that are beneficial. People with such traits often challenge societal norms and traditions, thereby becoming the vanguard of positive social change."[59] In fact, he goes so far as to say that a good leader sometimes "breaks ethical norms and standards of his profession and society."[60] The Kantian, of course, cannot resolve the tension between ethics and leadership this way. Actions that a leader knows to be wrong—determined not by profession or society but, rather, by reason—ought not be done. Nevertheless, I want to argue that the advocate of Kant's ethics can get around this tension and, thus, avoid embracing the Rational Saintly Leader. The Kantian has at her disposal two lines of argument. First, the "pathological fear" of morality that characterizes the Rational Saintly Leader looks much more like a heteronomous influence, than an autonomous influence, of behavior.[61] But moral behavior, Kant believes, is necessarily autonomous, not heteronomous. Second, a pathological fear of doing the wrong thing would undermine the ability of leaders to will projects that they can rightly pursue on Kant's moral theory.

For Kant, when we use reason to govern ourselves, we act autonomously, as self-determining individuals.[62] Acting on our own reason thus contrasts with acting on influences other than our rational nature. To signify this sense of *otherness*, Kant refers to these nonautonomous influences in terms of "heteronomy."[63] Heteronomous influences include religion, tradition, society, upbringing, or everyday peer pressure. Oddly enough, they also include many things that we would not be initially inclined to consider as being "other"—for example, our own desires and other psychological states. Despite its initial oddness, this Kantian point actually has strong intuitive appeal, especially if we think about the ways in which we can be controlled by our desires (the extreme case being addiction), as well as by other psychological states (our fears and obsessions). In leadership contexts, we might think of a person's unhealthy desire to please a particularly charismatic leader.[64] Even though these psychological states are necessarily internal to the person who has them, it still makes sense to talk about them as motivational sources that move him away from the ideal of autonomy. Addictions and obsessions prevent us from doing what we want and, more importantly, what we think we really ought to do.[65] The follower who has an overpowering desire to please a leader would find it particularly difficult, maybe impossible, to stand up for what he thinks is right, even if that is what he really wants to do.

There is something similarly deficient about a leader who is primarily driven by the fear of doing what may be wrong. Of course, according to Kant, we should all do what our reason tells us is right and avoid engaging in actions that our reason tells us are wrong. That is what it means to be a self-determining individual. Reason does its job of directing the will,[66] and when necessary, leaders should act on its influence rather than on the influence of nonmoral considerations, regardless of whether these considerations have an internal or external source. But the expectation that leaders act on their own reason is importantly weaker than a requirement that they be "dominated by the motivation to be moral" (431). Morality, important as it is, does not require this kind of motivational preoccupation of leaders. In fact, there is a sense in which the person who is "dominated" in this way—motivated, that is, by the chance that he has moved in the direction of the moral line—actually goes against the ideal of autonomy. Autonomous individuals should not be dominated by anything. Their actions derive from their own reason, not from subservience to fears and obsessions, even fears and obsessions about morality. Because the leader with a pathological fear of doing the wrong thing acts from a kind of moral neurosis, he is better described as acting heteronomously.

A pathological fear of doing the wrong thing would also make it very difficult for a leader to carry out his projects, so difficult—I think—that he cannot will extreme moral caution. The leader who wants to guarantee that he never breaks a promise would have to cut himself off from all human interaction and avoid contracting with others. Admittedly, like the hermit or someone banished from society, he would have a failsafe plan for discharging his negative duty never to break a promise. The problem, however, is that social isolation gets the leader moral safety at the expense of all project pursuit, indeed, at the expense of leadership. As we have seen, Kant holds that we depend on others to pursue our projects—whatever these projects are.[67] Our dependence on others is especially important in leadership contexts. Collective effort is a necessary means for leaders to achieve their ends, and to will these ends is to will the means for achieving them.[68] Why, then, are leaders unable to will extreme moral caution? As Kant puts it, "[S]uch a will would contradict itself."[69] All this is to say that moral risk is a necessary part of social life and, so too, of leadership. The only way to eradicate moral risk, to guarantee moral safety, is to avoid leadership altogether.

We should therefore reject the claim that the Rational Saintly Leader, any more than the Loving Saintly Leader, represents the moral ideal for leadership. Whereas the Loving Saintly Leader's single-minded commitment to welfarist ends makes him too morally narrow to serve as the ideal, the Rational Saintly Leader's obsession with moral safety is not consistent with autonomous project pursuit by leaders, which is necessary to get things done in a social world. Properly understood, the demands of Kant's ethics are significantly more minimal than the moral commitments adopted by the Rational Saintly Leader. We can expect leaders to work within the bounds of morality, but we cannot expect them to do all that is within their power never to approach morality's limits. This is not to say that they have a license for "dirty hands." However, we should acknowledge that leaders—as they approach these limits—will sometimes get things wrong. This minimalism is as it should be. It is hard enough to be ethical, which is why it is the most that we expect of ourselves. Being ethical, not saintly, is also all that we should expect of our leaders.

NOTES

1. Michael Walzer, "Political Action and the Problem of Dirty Hands," *Philosophy and Public Affairs* 2 (1973): 160–80. Notice that even these leaders are expected to be moral in some meaningful way. For example, Walzer claims that it is a test of a leader's morality that he feels guilty when he has to do wrong; it shows "both that he is not too good for politics and that he is good enough" (167–8).

2. Susan Wolf, "Moral Saints," *Journal of Philosophy* 79 (1982): 419–39. All internal page references in the remainder of the text are to Wolf's article.

3. See, for example, James MacGregor Burns, *Leadership* (New York: Harper and Row Publishers, 1978); Robert K. Greenleaf, *Servant Leadership: A Journey into the Nature of Legitimate Power and Greatness* (New York: Paulist Press, 1977); Michael E. Brown and Linda K. Triviño, "Ethical Leadership: A Review and Future Directions," *Leadership Quarterly* 17 (2006): 595–616; and Bruce J. Avolio and William L. Gardner, "Authentic Leadership Development: Getting to the Root of Positive Forms of Leadership," *Leadership Quarterly* 16 (2005): 315–38.

4. See Brown and Triviño's catalog of the similarities among various leadership theories ("Ethical Leadership," 598).

5. Robert Merrihew Adams, "Saints," *Journal of Philosophy* 81 (1984): 392–401, at 395.

6. Vanessa Carbonell, "What Moral Saints Look Like?" *Canadian Journal of Philosophy* 39 (2009): 371–98, at 372.

7. Earl Spurgin draws out the implications of Wolf's argument for business contexts in his "Can Businesses Be Too Good? Applying Susan Wolf's 'Moral Saints' to Businesses," *Business and Society Review* 116 (2011): 355–73. I take up Spurgin's view below.

8. Terry L. Price, *Leadership Ethics: An Introduction* (New York: Cambridge University Press, 2008).

9. Immanuel Kant, *Groundwork of the Metaphysic of Morals*, trans. H. J. Paton (New York: Harper & Row Publishers, 1964), 82–4.

10. Ibid., 91.

11. As Wolf points out, "A quick, breezy reading of utilitarian and Kantian writings will suggest the images, respectively, of the Loving Saint and the Rational Saint" (427).

12. See Wolf's discussion of "the dominance an aspiration to become an Olympic swimmer or a [concert] pianist might have" (423).

13. See his discussion of "The 10,000-Hour Rule" in Malcolm Gladwell, *Outliers: The Story of Success* (New York: Little, Brown and Company, 2008), 37–42.

14. Also see Spurgin, "Can Businesses Be Too Good?" 358.

15. In his critique of saintliness in business, Spurgin notes that "[s]ociety often benefits when businesses are at the forefront of challenges to norms and traditions" ("Can Businesses Be Too Good?" 362).

16. See Ed P. Hollander, *Leaders, Groups, and Influence* (New York: Oxford University Press, 1964); and Terry L. Price, *Leadership Ethics*.

17. Spurgin, in "Can Businesses Be Too Good?," sides with Wolf in his defense of "ethical standards and restraints," but—as I shall argue in the section The Rational Saintly Leader—the examples he gives of justified deviance contradict this position.

18. Price, *Leadership Ethics*.

19. Spurgin, "Can Businesses Be Too Good?" 361.

20. Edward Lawry, "In Praise of Moral Saints," *Southwest Philosophy Review* 18 (2002): 1–11, at 1.

21. Ibid., 2.

22. Aristotle, *Nichomachean Ethics*, trans. Terence Irwin (Indianapolis, IN: Hackett Publishing Company, 1985), 44 [1106b20].

23. Ibid., 160 [1142a15].

24. Lawry, "In Praise of Moral Saints," 4.

25. Ibid.

26. Carbonell, "What Moral Saints Look Like?" 381.

27. Ibid.

28. Ibid.

29. Niccolò Machiavelli, *The Prince*, eds. Quentin Skinner and Russell Price (Cambridge: Cambridge University Press, 1988), 55–61.

30. Alasdair MacIntyre, *After Virtue: A Study in Moral Theory*, 2nd edition (Notre Dame, IN: University of Notre Dame Press, 1981).

31. See the works of thinkers such as John Stuart Mill, *Utilitarianism*, ed. George Sher (Indianapolis, IN: Hackett Publishing Company, 1979).

32. See MacIntyre, *After Virtue.*

33. Spurgin, "Can Businesses Be Too Good?" 363–4.

34. Redistributing resources to the young typically means greater impact in terms of overall utility because of the longer expected life span over which to experience well-being. See Robert M. Veatch, "How Age Should Matter: Justice as the Basis for Limiting Care to the Elderly," in Helga Kuhse and Peter Singer, *Bioethics: An Anthology*, 2nd edition (Malden, MA: Blackwell Publishing, 2006), 437–47, for a discussion of these issues.

35. Carbonell, "What Moral Saints Look Like?" 378.

36. Ibid. For this reason, Spurgin's counterexample above also fails.

37. See Adams, "Saints." Whatever concern they have for human well-being is mediated through their conception of God's love or God's commands. Although mediated concern for others sometimes looks very close to the real thing, as when

it draws on language about God being "within" us all, we can expect that the human element is—indeed, for most theologies, has to be—secondary.

38. Plato, *Republic*, trans. G. M. A. Grube and rev. C. D. C. Reeve (Indianapolis, IN: Hackett Publishing Company, 1992), 17ff [341c].

39. See Joel Feinberg, "Psychological Egoism," *Reason and Responsibility: Readings in Some Basic Problems of Philosophy*, eds. Joel Feinberg and Russ Shafer-Landau, 10th edition, 493–505 (Belmont, CA: Wadsworth Publishing Company, 1999), at 504.

40. Wolf, in "Moral Saints," defends connections between the Rational Saint and Kantianism,430ff.

41. Kant, *Groundwork*, 62–64, 88–89.

42. Ibid., 70.

43. Ibid., 91.

44. Ibid., 95–96.

45. Ibid., 96.

46. Ibid., 63, 67.

47. Ibid., 98.

48. Ibid., 91.

49. Ibid.

50. Ibid.

51. Ibid.

52. Kant, "The Metaphysics of Morals," in *Practical Philosophy*, trans. and ed. Mary J. Gregor (Cambridge, UK: Cambridge University Press, 1996), 524.

53. Ibid.

54. Kant, *Groundwork*, 65.

55. Ibid.

56. Ibid., 66.

57. I thank Thomas Hudson, Sandra Peart, and Jeff Pollack for a discussion of this phenomenon and for their suggestions. For an excellent account of innovation in racing, see Nascar Race Hub: The Gray Area, Fox Sports (2013), http://msn.foxsports.com/topics/m/video/79515551/nascar-race-hub-the-gray-area-part-2-2013.htm (accessed September 20, 2013).

58. Joel Feinberg, *Doing and Deserving: Essays in the Theory of Responsibility* (Princeton, NJ: Princeton University Press, 1970), 160, emphasis added.

59. Spurgin, "Can Businesses Be Too Good?" 357.

60. Ibid., 359. Spurgin uses the notoriously deceptive lead character in the television show *House* to make his point.

61. Kant, *Groundwork*, 108ff.

62. Ibid., 108.

63. Ibid.

64. See, for example, Andrew Young, *The Politician: An Insider's Account of John Edwards's Pursuit of the Presidency and the Scandal That Brought Him Down* (New York: St. Martin's Press, 2010).

65. Harry Frankfurt, "Freedom of the Will and the Concept of a Person," *Journal of Philosophy* 68 (1971): 5–20.

66. Kant, *Groundwork*, 62.

67. Ibid., 91.

68. Ibid., 90.

69. Ibid., 91.

7

Democratic Leadership and Dirty Hands

Nannerl O. Keohane

Must a political leader who wants to govern effectively be prepared to behave immorally? And does it make a difference if the leader is chosen by and governs on behalf of other citizens?

These questions are often discussed under the rubric "dirty hands," from Jean-Paul Sartre's play *Les Mains sales*, evoked by Michael Walzer in a particularly influential essay.[1] We sometimes associate the issue specifically with authoritarian leaders, power-holders who have few constraints on their behavior. But the ethical problems that may face democratically elected leaders are intriguing and pressing, too.

This chapter makes several points. First, I claim that the phrase *dirty hands* captures a significant problem in ethics and governance. This

This chapter is a revised version of a paper by the same name presented at the American Political Science Association meetings in September 2010; a second version, "The Responsibilities of Leadership and the Problem of Dirty Hands," was delivered as the Cal Turner Lecture at Vanderbilt University on October 6, 2011. I am grateful to Chuck Beitz, Corey Brettschneider, Bob Keohane, Melissa Lane, Steve Macedo, James Stoner, and Lucas Swaine for comments on earlier drafts.

point is not obvious; several thoughtful philosophers have concluded that the notion of dirty hands names an illusory problem.[2] I argue that this concept identifies a significant dilemma that cannot be resolved by a simple yes/no answer. Instead, we are better served by the more complex and nuanced approach exemplified by Max Weber's "ethic of responsibility." To clarify the issue, I ask why dirty hands questions are most frequently associated with political life, even though analogous dilemmas sometimes arise in other contexts.

Next I explore the concept of *responsibility* by identifying a number of different types of situations in which persons may be held to be responsible for or to some other persons, institutions, or causes. Then I turn to the distinctive dimensions of ethical leadership in a democracy, asking how the *ethic of responsibility* applies in this kind of governance. I show how the answers must differ for participatory and representative democracy, and emphasize the importance of institutions of accountability. Representative democracies rest on a set of reciprocal responsibilities between leaders and citizens; nonetheless, I argue that, in the last analysis, the decision-making leader must bear the primary responsibility for her actions and their consequences.

In discussing this topic, it is important to be clear what we mean by the word *leader*. This term is often used without definition, which can lead to obscurities and misunderstandings. In an earlier discussion I offered this definition, which I will follow in this chapter: "Leaders determine or clarify goals for a group of individuals and bring together the energies of members of that group to accomplish those goals."[3]

Another point to keep in mind is that, as C. A. J. Coady puts it, "[t]he idealized conditions invoked by the philosophers of dirty hands are often comically remote from the reasoning and psychology of the spooks and politicians that actually get their hands, arms and shoulders dirty."[4] The characters in Sartre's play display some of this distasteful reasoning and psychology. They engage in violence routinely in the service of their ideological beliefs and goals. Consideration of the possible implications of moral impurity attendant on their actions is one background theme, but conflicting strategic choices, desire for personal advancement, potential dangers to one's person, and the irony of unforeseen outcomes are much more prominent in the play than the tragic struggles over moral dilemmas discussed by those of us who philosophize about dirty hands.

Against this background, it is easy to see how the problem of dirty hands is related to the potentially corrupting effects of power, most famously captured in Lord Acton's maxim.[5] But the topics are not the same, and it is important to distinguish them. Lord Acton claimed that power *always* tends to corrupt, no matter what the context. The dirty hands dilemma refers to a *specific situation* in which any leader confronts a choice of policy or strategy in performing her duties, a choice that inescapably includes courses of action that will harm others. Dennis Thompson puts it this way: "The problem of dirty hands concerns the political leader who for the sake of public purposes violates moral principles."[6] This is a more complex situation, fraught with far tougher choices, than the straightforward claim that power tends to corrupt.

TWO ANSWERS TO OUR BASIC QUESTION

One direct answer to the question, Must political leaders behave immorally to govern effectively?, is no. On this account, political leaders are just as much bound by moral precepts as ordinary citizens or subjects—perhaps more so, because leaders have broader duties and larger responsibilities. Leaders are also in positions where their behavior will be taken as exemplary, and thus their ethical decisions have widespread implications. The negative answer sometimes rests on the conviction that even if immoral behavior brings short-term political advantages, in the long run it will inevitably damage the community as well as the individual leader.

This was the position taken by Cicero, who held that honorable behavior is always beneficial for a leader and dishonorable behavior never pays off.[7] A parallel but somewhat different version of this response was given by Renaissance humanists and incorporated in the mirror of princes literature. On this account, a leader who violates moral principles by abusing his power, particularly if he attends primarily to his own advancement or the narrow interests of a few, does not deserve the office. Erasmus firmly stated: "Only those who dedicate themselves to the state, and not the state to themselves, deserve the title 'prince'. For if someone rules to suit himself and assesses everything by how it affects his own convenience, then it does not matters what titles he bears: in practice he is certainly a tyrant, not a prince."[8] This assertion echoes Aristotle's familiar distinction between monarchy and tyranny in Book IV of the *Politics*. The same claim has been put forward more recently by James MacGregor Burns. He argues that someone who harms or diminishes his followers does not deserve to be called a leader, but a dictator or power-wielder.[9]

Yet however well intentioned and conscientious leaders may be, most of them will at some point confront moral dilemmas to which there is no right or easy answer, and whatever they do will be immoral by someone's definition. The awareness of these pressing and complex dilemmas has prompted the opposite reaction to our basic question: the widespread conviction that a political leader cannot succeed unless he is willing to engage in shady or even downright immoral behavior. Because of the power a political leader wields, his scope of unconstrained action is generally broader than that of private actors, and most leaders will at some point be tempted to choose measures of dubious morality. Indeed, such measures may at times be the only ones that make it possible to achieve worthy goals. Thus, the second answer to the question "Must leaders be willing to behave immorally to govern effectively?" is yes.

In his treatise *The Prince*, Machiavelli was the primary proponent in the history of political thought for this response. He was famously clear in that treatise that princes who wish to be successful cannot always behave according to the moral standards that govern private behavior, including integrity, truth-telling, and compassion. He asserted bluntly that leaders sometimes have to act wickedly to maintain their power and accomplish their goals. This is because "how men live is so different from how they should live that a ruler who does not do what is generally done, but persists in doing what ought to be done, will undermine his power rather than maintain it. If a ruler who wants always to act honorably is surrounded by many unscrupulous men, his downfall is inevitable. Therefore, a ruler who wishes to maintain his power must be prepared to act immorally when this becomes necessary."[10] A more familiar translation of this passage is the prince must "learn how not to be good."[11]

Machiavelli defends his counsel of immorality in this context by the observation that because everybody else is acting badly, if you want to succeed you have to behave similarly or be outrun by those who are less scrupulous. Politicians may be shady, but all the people they work with and rule over are also shady, so why single the leaders out for blame? This is a cynical statement about human nature rather than a particular insight about politics. However, Machiavelli goes on to assert in that same brief chapter of *The Prince* that princes must sometimes behave immorally even if most or all of their subjects are placidly doing the right thing. He acknowledges that it would be "praiseworthy" for rulers to be loyal, sober, pious, generous, and merciful. But because no leader can actually have all these virtues and hope to succeed, "one should not be troubled about becoming notorious for those vices without which it is difficult to preserve one's power because . . . doing some things that seem virtuous may result in one's ruin, whereas doing other things that seem vicious may strengthen one's position and cause one to flourish."

Machiavelli focuses on the prince's goals rather than the character of the measures he chooses to pursue them. To found a state, maintain his power, and bring security to his people, the prince must be prepared to do what is necessary. As Machiavelli says in *The Discourses*: "A wise mind will never censure any one for having employed any extraordinary means for the purpose of establishing a kingdom or constituting a republic. It is well that, when the act accuses him, the result will excuse him; and when the result is good, as in the case of Romulus, it will always absolve him from blame."[12]

ETHICAL DILEMMAS IN OTHER CONTEXTS

Machiavelli voiced with some relish a position that has been held, often less explicitly, by many others across the centuries. For some observers, including several in the Christian tradition, this supposedly inexorable connection between politics and immorality is grounds for distancing oneself from political action, eschewing positions of worldly authority. Before we link politics inexorably with dirty hands, however, we should note that thorny ethical dilemmas are not faced only by political leaders in official positions of power. We can find analogues for many aspects of the dirty hands challenges in private life or in dilemmas faced by leaders in other areas.

The need to deceive in pursuit of a worthy political goal is often used as a prime example of dirty hands. Leaders may feel compelled to lie to allies and even their subjects about diplomatic or military strategy to keep that information from their adversaries. But recall the familiar story of the German citizen giving shelter to a Jewish family who lies to the Nazi inspectors who have come to search his home. "Jews?" he says. "No, I haven't seen any Jews." A Kantian perspective that gives a very high priority to truth-telling would have dictated a different outcome. Most observers today would be more likely to condemn this man's *immorality* if he had lost his courage and surrendered his guests to the Nazis. My point is this: whatever he does will be regarded by some observers as immoral. We generally pose such questions as paradigmatic ethical dilemmas rather than invoking the concept of dirty hands, but there are similarities nonetheless.

Even more salient to our question, disadvantaging or harming some individuals in pursuit of a collective purpose is a familiar challenge for leaders in many fields. Yet we do not usually encompass all kinds of leaders in the sweeping charge of dirty hands. Corporate executives make decisions to downsize a company or outsource work to a subsidiary abroad for financial reasons, thus weakening a community dependent on this industry and creating grave hardship for many families. Cathy Davidson has written a thought-provoking book about plant closings and how they can eviscerate a hitherto healthy community.[13] The "business case" may be quite clear, in terms of the bottom line, but what about the men and women who have worked for a company for generations? How will they reassemble their shattered lives? In the long run, people will move somewhere else or a new industry will come in or the town will become a ghost town. But there are serious hardships in the "short run," which may last for decades. There are real ethical dilemmas here, even though they rarely come to the fore in such decisions.

Academic leaders must address campus protests calling for divestment from certain kinds of industries or protesting the use of sweatshop labor in some distant country to make baseball caps or sweatshirts that say "Duke" or "Harvard" or "Wisconsin." These are thorny ethical issues on which different members of the campus community are bound to hold quite disparate views. University leaders must also deal with issues about fair wages on campus and labor negotiations that have a strong ethical dimension for some constituents.

These examples are intended to show that leaders in many different fields, including corporate life and higher education, face complex moral dilemmas. Nonetheless, we usually think of the problem of dirty hands as particularly relevant to political leaders. Dennis Thompson notes: "Although similar conflicts arise in other activities, they are likely to be more intense or more frequent in politics."[14] Why should this be true? How is the political leader's situation different from that of any of us facing complicated moral dilemmas in ordinary life? And how might we frame a response to our initial basic question that responds helpfully to the situation of honorable men and women in politics?

As we approach this question, we should keep in mind the importance of distinguishing among several types of actions by political leaders: actions that are undertaken by an ethically insensitive leader without significant political purpose and are clearly immoral by any definition (e.g., genocide); decisions that have unfortunate consequences but are simply obtuse or unthinking, and were not undertaken as the result of any moral decision-making process; and unavoidable but morally unpalatable outcomes that are thoughtfully weighed to advance an important political goal for the community one leads. Only the latter situation invokes the particular challenges of dirty hands.[15]

WEBER'S POLITICAL ETHIC

Machiavelli's *The Prince* has had countless followers across the centuries, both acknowledged and hidden under professions of conventional morality. The cold clarity of his answer, however, belies the actual experiences of many morally sensitive and thoughtful persons in positions of political power. To those men and women, behaving as ethically as possible while nonetheless accomplishing the pressing purposes of governance is a sustained and important goal. "You are going to have to behave immorally, so get used to it and don't let it bother you" does not ring true to their own values or to reality as they experience it.

In his essay "Politics as a Vocation," Max Weber provides a third answer to our basic question, an answer that is likely to be more relevant to such conscientious leaders than a simple yes or no.[16] On this account, if a political leader wants to fulfill his responsibilities, he will sometimes have to use measures of "dubious morality" with "evil ramifications," and be aware of the "diabolic forces" that lurk within some of the choices he may have to make. But Weber does not just say, "[Y]ou are going to have to get your hands dirty, so be prepared to live with that."Instead, he explores a distinctive political ethic that he calls the "ethic of responsibility" that should govern the behavior of political leaders, which he distinguishes from an "ethic of ultimate ends" that guides some individuals in their personal moral choices.[17]

Like Machiavelli, Weber emphasized the deployment of violence as the factor that makes ethical issues facing political leaders especially complex and thorny. In Weber's view, "[I]t is the *specific means of legitimate violence as such* in the hand of human associations which determines the peculiarity of all ethical problems of politics."[18] Because Weber defines the state as having a monopoly on the legitimate use of violence, he sees controlling instruments of violence as part of a leader's job. Here we have one compelling explanation for the particular connections between *political* leadership and dirty hands. And for this reason, as Stephen Garrett points out, leadership in times of war "may rightly be regarded as the most severe and complicated test of the political morality of powerful individuals."[19]

In the passage cited just above, Weber also notes:"Whosoever contracts with violent means for whatever ends—and every politician does—is exposed to its specific consequences."Using violence often involves ethical as well as strategic choices with implications that can reverberate well down the line, for the leader's character as well as for the organization that he leads.[20] The saint who follows the "ethic of ultimate ends" is concerned only with the purity of the goal: saving his own soul. The purity of the end must not be sullied by the use of dubious means, including harm to other individuals. Truthfulness is also an absolute requirement for the saint, whereas the political leader must consider the consequences of revealing sensitive information that may endanger the community. Such leaders may sometimes have to withhold information or deceive others. Anyone primarily concerned with saving his soul should go in for some other line of work.

Weber's "ethic of responsibility" presents its own difficult demands, and brings little comfort for the politician. Weber notes that "no ethics in the world can dodge the fact that in numerous instances the attainment of 'good' ends is bound to the fact that one must be willing to pay the price of using morally dubious means or at least dangerous ones—and facing the possibility or even the probability of evil ramifications."[21] But "using morally dubious means" or dangerous ones and risking "evil ramifications" is not the same as asserting (as Machiavelli does) that leaders must be prepared, regularly and somewhat blithely, to behave "immorally." Weber's point is that behaving according to the saintly standard of strict morality would be inappropriate and ineffective, so that relying on the "ethic of responsibility," even though it may sometimes involve dubious measures, is the *most moral course* a leader can follow.

In the essay I cited at the outset, Walzer asserts that "a particular act of government . . . may be exactly the right thing to do in utilitarian terms and yet leave the man who does it guilty of a moral wrong. . . . If, on the other hand he remains innocent . . . he not only fails to do the right thing (in utilitarian terms) but he may also fail to measure up to the duties of his office (which imposes on him a considerable responsibility for consequences and outcomes)." Walzer notes that adhering to a rigorous standard of morality can have disastrous consequences for the community; in fact, "we would not want to be governed by men who consistently adopted that position." Yet he believes that politicians who use these dubious means incur inescapable moral guilt, even though the achievement of good political ends will sometimes require such an accommodation.[22] There is a catch-22 here that seems inescapable; Walzer's politician is condemned either to feckless dereliction of duty or to serious moral culpability.

Unlike Walzer, Weber makes no reference to the "guilt" of a leader who attempts to follow the ethic he has outlined. The ethic of responsibility does not excuse anything a leader may choose to do. Weber never says we should refrain from blaming or criticizing a leader who cavalierly violates moral dictates to advance her own career, savors cruelty or humiliating others, or obtusely ignores less dubious ways to achieve her goals. A leader who lacks either passion for a cause or a thoughtful, conscientious perspective on the situation she confronts should certainly be condemned. But a leader who scrupulously follows the ethic of responsibility has done the best she can, and that is where the matter ends. There is no sense that people who do not have to face such terrible dilemmas should condemn her for her choices on the grounds of immorality. As Kai Nielsen puts it, in choosing the lesser of two evils in a dirty hands dilemma, "we do what, everything considered, is the right thing to do: the thing we ought—through and through ought—in this circumstance, to do."[23]

This does not mean that the political leader blithely accepts wrongdoing without a second thought. A conscientious leader who follows the precepts of the ethic of responsibility wrestles with the ambiguity of the dilemmas she faces within her own soul. In language that has no parallel in *The Prince*, Weber says that "whoever wants to engage in politics at all, and especially in politics as a vocation . . . must know that he is responsible for what may become of himself under the impact of these [ethical] paradoxes. I repeat, he lets himself in for the diabolic forces lurking in all violence." A thoughtful, ethical human being must recognize that engaging in morally dubious measures is likely to have some impact on her character, and do the best she can to maintain her moral compass. Remorse about harm done to other individuals is a reaction that we would usually praise in a leader who has made a difficult decision on our behalf. But remorse is not the same as guilt. There is tragic dimension here that has quite a different tone from Machiavelli's *Prince*.[24]

The Ethic of Responsibility

In explaining the "ethic of responsibility" especially appropriate to political leadership, Weber asserts that "three pre-eminent qualities are decisive for the politician," to ensure that he can do his job well and protect himself against some of the consequences of using violence: "passion, a feeling of responsibility, and a sense of proportion." Passion is defined not as "sterile excitation" but as a matter-of-fact devotion to a cause, a steady commitment to some higher end, not just one's own advancement. Weber insists that "the serving of a cause must not be absent if action is to have inner strength." A number of types of causes can do the work here. But there must be something of this kind; otherwise, "the curse of the creature's worthlessness overshadows even the externally strongest political success."[25]

This commitment to a worthy cause is the main factor that legitimates a leader's behavior. As with Machiavelli, the end is more important than the means, but for Weber, not just any *end* will do. Neither advancing your personal glory nor maintaining your power for its own sake is consistent with this ethic. There must be some kind of "cause" beyond your own direct interests. Weber also insists that leaders need a sense of proportion or perspective, a "distance to things and men," including distance from oneself. This distance enables a leader to consider matters coolly and thoughtfully rather than being moved by narrow self-interest, empathy for the individual circumstances of some followers, or other factors irrelevant to the cause she serves. And this unlikely conjunction of passion for a cause and a distance from oneself helps explain why great leaders are so rare.[26]

Max Weber is not the only theorist who has focused on *responsibility* as the most salient dimension of the ethical issues that confront political leaders. Discussions of dirty hands often invoke the concept of *responsibility*, either casually or as a more prominent feature of the argument. John Parrish is particularly clear about the centrality of the concept in discussions of this sort. "To refuse to get one's hands dirty on grounds of absolute principle," he says, "is to abandon the central place that the notion of *responsibility* for others must invariably hold at the heart of our moral conceptions."[27]

Stuart Hampshire makes a claim similar to Weber's in his essay entitled "Public and Private Morality."Although Hampshire insists that he is not developing an alternative kind of ethic specific to politics, he asserts that the person who moves from private to public life crosses "a moral threshold," on the other side of which "a new responsibility, and even a new kind of responsibility, and new moral conflicts, present themselves." In his view, this "new kind of responsibility . . . entails, first, accountability to one's followers, secondly, policies that are to be justified principally by their eventual consequences, and thirdly, a withholding of some of the scruples that in private life would prohibit one from using people as a means to an end and also from using force and deceit."[28]

It is illuminating to ponder examples of the *new kind of responsibility* that arises when one takes on the duties of political leadership. When France was defeated in June 1940, Winston Churchill was concerned about the French fleet (one of the finest in the world) falling into German or Italian hands. A large contingent of that fleet was stationed in Oran, Algiers. Churchill instructed the British admiral in the Mediterranean to offer the French naval commander four choices for immediate action: continue to fight against the Axis powers; sail to a British port, so that the ships could be commandeered by the British and the sailors could return home; sail to a French port in the West Indies not yet under Nazi control, where the ships could be disarmed and perhaps entrusted to U.S. care; or scuttle the ships. Otherwise, the ships (and their men, who had been Britain's staunch allies only a week before) would be destroyed by the British. And, in the end, that was what happened. Almost 3,000 French sailors were killed in the bombardment and 350 wounded. Despite the difficulty of this choice, Churchill never wavered.[29]

Churchill's decision can be condemned or praised, but avoiding the issue would have been as vulnerable to criticism as the course he chose to pursue, in terms of its consequences for the war, for the British people for whom Churchill was responsible, and indeed for the people of all the world's democracies. As the leader of Great Britain, the only major power standing up to the Fascists at that point, Churchill could not just decide to ignore the problem and retreat to his country house until everything blew over.

In concluding "Politics as a Vocation," Weber notes that a political leader following the "ethic of responsibility" may somewhere reach the point where he says, with Martin Luther: "Here I stand; I can do no other." And "insofar as this is true, an ethic of ultimate ends and an ethic of responsibility are not absolute contrasts but rather supplements, which only in unison constitute a genuine man—a man who *can* have a 'calling for politics.' "[30] Weber thus allows for the possibility that a political leader may reach a point where he is unwilling to engage in a particular form of dubiously moral behavior. One thinks of political leaders who have resigned their offices rather than undertake assignments they regarded as beyond the pale. It is not true that "anything goes" according to the ethic of responsibility.

WHAT DO WE MEAN BY *RESPONSIBILITY*?

To understand the particular responsibilities of the political leader, it is helpful to distinguish among four different kinds of moral situations, involving purely individual action, having personal responsibilities for other individuals, having institutional responsibilities, and having the special kinds of institutional responsibilities associated with political leadership.

First, consider individuals making decisions about their own behavior *as individuals*. Morals and ethics by definition are about how we relate to other human beings (or, for some philosophers, to all sentient beings). When I travel on the subway I am morally obliged not to steal from other passengers, or assault or lie to them, but I have no further connection with any of them. We might, using the term loosely, speak of my having the *responsibility* to behave morally in this situation, but this is a very broad usage. I have no special responsibility to or for any of these individuals. I am responsible only for myself.

The second category involves persons who have responsibilities for other individuals. Suppose there is an electrical outage on the subway and the train stops in the dark tunnel. If I am traveling with a small child, I have a responsibility to help that child to safety, and it would clearly be immoral for me to abandon the child to make sure I got out myself. If I am traveling alone, I am not formally responsible for any of my fellow passengers, but I might decide, on moral or intuitively empathetic grounds, to help a fellow passenger to safety—an older person with a cane, or a child who has lost her mother in the dark. By embarking on such a course I assume new obligations to the person for whom I have temporarily made myself responsible. I would face a moral dilemma if, to honor a pressing obligation to someone else outside the subway, I needed to leave quickly and this meant abandoning the other person, given that I had initially offered help and taken on a new responsibility.

Parents or caretakers confront moral dilemmas that would not arise if we were each responsible only for ourselves. The mother of several children may have to determine how to allocate scarce resources, treating each child fairly but not identically. A husband whose wife is dying for want of a drug they cannot afford may decide to steal the drug for her although he would not do so for himself.[31] *Having responsibilities for other human beings creates moral dilemmas more complex than those that involve only our individual behavior.* This complexity is at the core of the *ethic of responsibility,* which in this way is applicable not only to politicians but to anyone who has responsibility for other people.

The third category includes leaders in other walks of life, apart from politics, whether in business, universities, religious institutions, or volunteer activities. If the leadership is institutionalized in a formal group or organization, the leader is *responsible to* other individuals (followers, employees, colleagues) to do the best job he can to further the joint purposes of members of the group. In some situations the leader is also responsible *for* these persons. Leadership of any kind may present ethical dilemmas more complex than those that confront an individual acting for himself alone, or one who holds no institutional office and is responsible for a smaller number of other persons.

When we move from leaders in general to members of our fourth category—*political leaders*—a number of factors make the dirty hands dilemma particularly salient. We immediately see the relevance of control of the legitimate means of violence, which both Weber and Machiavelli emphasize. Decisions about the morally appropriate use of violence occasionally come up for private individuals, including issues of self-defense, a teacher protecting students against a gunman in a school or a parent shielding a family against a violent intruder. But such occasions are much less frequent in private life than they are for those who control "the legitimate means of violence," which includes political leaders from mayors of cities and military officers to heads of nation-states.

Psychologist Amos Tversky described his experience as the commander of an Israeli mobile army unit moving through a desert when his troop captured some enemy soldiers. The laws of war dictated that these soldiers should be taken prisoner, fed and sheltered, and safely delivered to justice. But the enemy soldiers had a clear interest in undermining or killing the capturers and thus had to be watched and guarded closely. All this required time, attention, and scarce resources. Diverting some of these resources to the supervision and provisioning of the prisoners endangered Tversky's own troops in this situation of great scarcity. Tversky's decision to take care of the prisoners rather than shooting or abandoning them was resented by some of his own men, and could even be criticized as immoral in this context because it endangered those for whom he was most directly responsible. Nonetheless, it was clearly required by international conventions governing treatment of prisoners, and mandated also, I would argue, by the precepts of human dignity.[32]

In addition to needing to grapple with the ethical implications of the legitimate control of violence, most political leaders are also responsible for (and to) more people than a private actor. This creates unique layers of complexity that enhance the kinds of moral dilemmas leaders face. One's responsibilities as a political leader are not to one homogeneous set of constituents. The interests of citizens in different circumstances, opponents in various kinds of competitions, even parts of one's own government, can create ethical dilemmas that have no counterpart for those who are responsible only for themselves or a small number of family members and friends.

The political leader also has a larger scope of responsibility than leaders in other walks of life because of the distinctiveness of political life in human experience. Aristotle argued that politics is the "central organizing principle of any community," the grounding of everything else. Social, domestic, and economic life have as their framework the political system that people share, and other dimensions of a community take on characteristics that the political system embodies and represents.[33] In this same vein, in delineating the "moral threshold" between public and private life, Hampshire says: "public policy is a greater thing, as Aristotle remarked, and an agent in the public domain normally has responsibility for greater and more enduring consequences and consequences that change more men's lives."[34]

We can sum up these points by noting that political leaders generally occupy an *office*, in the specialized meaning of this term having to do with the structures and purposes of government. They fulfill a designated *role* that sets them apart from *private individuals* as well as other leaders, a role that brings with it significant opportunities—and also the distinctive ethical dilemmas that we associate with dirty hands.[35]

DISTINCTIVE FEATURES OF RESPONSIBILITY IN A DEMOCRACY

So far I have discussed ethical dilemmas confronting political leaders as though their situations—the political systems in which they work—were all the same. What difference does it make if the leader works within a democracy rather than a monarchy, autocracy, or oligarchy? What are the implications for a leader's responsibilities if he or she is chosen by and governs on behalf of other citizens? As Parrish reminds us, "we need to ask not only what it is to have dirty hands, but also precisely whose hands we think are dirty."[36]

It may seem that (to use Stuart Hampshire's term) the "moral threshold" democratic leaders face should be higher than that for other leaders, so that acts of "dubious morality" that might be excused in an absolutist monarch are off-limits for a democratic leader. Bernard Williams asserts that "democracy has a tendency to impose higher expectations with regard even to means, since under democracy control of politicians is supposed to be a function of the expectations of the electorate."[37] But the expectations of electorates may sometimes be as low as those of subjects in any other form of government—think of the Athenian citizens in the worst stages of the Peloponnesian War. One can find occasional parallels to this in the behavior and expectations of citizens in most democracies today. As Garrett puts it, only an exceptionally optimistic or foolhardy person "would assume that the morals of the 'people' are always such that they constitute pressure on their leaders to behave in exemplary ways."[38]

Most discussions of this issue focus not on the leader per se but instead on the *citizens* in a democracy, exploring the ways in which we may (or may not) share in responsibility for dubious moral outcomes. Dennis Thompson has posed this issue in a particularly compelling way. He refuses to allow democratic citizens to stand back and judge their leaders as though the citizens were not implicated in the leaders' decisions and policies. Such distancing, he says, ignores the fact "that the bad that the official does, he does not only for us, but with our consent—not only in our name, but on our principles. It is not clear, therefore that we as citizens have any grounds" for blaming him.[39] Michael Walzer makes a different point when he asserts that the fact that our leader "acts on our behalf, even in our name" means that when he "hustles, lies or intrigues" he is doing so *for us*, and that this heightens the moral dimensions of the action taken.[40] Walzer makes this point without in any way suggesting that we as citizens are therefore partially responsible for these actions.

In a *direct participatory democracy*, a group of citizens who have collectively decided on a dubiously moral policy all have dirty hands, not just those who proposed or who have been charged with implementing the decision. Responsibility in this situation is clearly shared by all the citizens, or at least by those who have voted for or been willing to implement the chosen course of action. In representative democracies, on the other hand, the most salient function of the citizens is choosing among potential leaders and deciding when to replace them. Although citizens hold ultimate sovereignty, in a representative system citizens collectively do not often make major policy decisions for the whole political system. This makes the question of the responsibility of the democratic citizen in such systems especially complex.

Eric Beerbohm's thought-provoking book *In Our Name* makes the strong claim that "the office of citizenship" in a representative democracy engages us in the activities of our government regardless of our attitudes toward the policies of our leaders."Public officials claim to govern, act, and speak in our name. Because our primary mode of political agency is mediated, we are vulnerable to the charge of participating in the wrongdoing of another."[41] Beerbohm is quite clear that electors in a representative system cannot simply offload responsibility on others and, like a collective Pilot, wash their hands.

Discussions of what it means to act "in our name" sometimes focus on the question of differential responsibility for a decision depending on whether a citizen has actually voted for the representative who made that decision and whether the citizen knew (or could have known) that such a policy was likely to be chosen. In recent comments on Beerbohm's book, Anna Stilz has raised some thoughtful questions about this issue. She distinguished among three hypothetical citizens: Amy, who voted for George Bush in 2000 as a supporter of his "compassionate conservatism," could not have known how he would respond to 9/11 and strongly opposed the decision to invade Iraq; Bob, who voted for Gore and made his choice on purely economic grounds; and Carmen, who was out of the country and did not vote in the election but was a vigorous supporter of the Iraq War. How, asked Stilz, would we decide among these citizens in terms of degrees of responsibility for the war in Iraq?[42] Political issues involving complex moral decisions often come up unforeseen and no one, including the leader, could have known in advance that such a decision would have to be made. In such conditions, holding individual voters in a representative democracy responsible for a specific policy involves a number of argumentative steps that can each be questioned along the way.

Taking a firm position in this debate, Thomas Nagel distinguishes between two forms of democratic legitimation relevant for dirty hands: first, the "periodic answerability" of the leader to the electorate, and second, the specific consent of the citizens. For Nagel, consent cannot be assumed just because the leader has been duly elected.[43] On this account, the devices of election and representation cannot create a form of responsibility in which the citizens must share some of the burden. The pathways of assigning blame or credit are too diffuse to make such a relationship meaningful.

INSTITUTIONS OF ACCOUNTABILITY

Given the complexity of assigning responsibility for specific policy decisions to individual voters in a representative democracy, I would argue that a better way to approach this question is to ask about the vibrancy and strength of the political institutions of the representative polity being discussed, and especially the quality of its institutions of democratic accountability. Accountability, as defined by Ruth Grant and Robert O. Keohane, "implies that some actors have the right to hold other actors to a set of standards, to judge whether they have fulfilled their responsibilities in light of these standards, and to impose sanctions if they determine that these responsibilities have not been met."[44]

Effective accountability in this sense depends on effective monitoring. Citizens must take this obligation seriously, and leaders must recognize the legitimate interest and ultimate control of the citizens and provide regular reports on their performance. Thompson notes that responsibility to citizens "requires that legislators explain their actions to the citizens they represent. Giving reasons is part of what being responsible means, and part of what being reelected requires."He goes on to point out that publicity is essential to this giving of reasons.[45] If the institutions that give force to this accountability in any polity— including elections, the court system, freedom of speech and press, and well-crafted systems of administrative law—are effective and resilient, then it could make sense to assert that the citizens of that democracy share some responsibility with their leaders.

However, in complex nation-states the institutions of accountability are often diffuse, unwieldy, or corrupted. Elections are about many different things, and rarely yield a clear mandate on any particular vexed question. Events move quickly, and dilemmas arise that could not have been foreseen either by electors or by their representatives. In such situations, it is hard to argue that citizens share responsibility for choices they could not have foreseen from information previously available to them. For example, critics of the current electoral process in the United States often zero in on the muddling effect of "negative campaigns" dedicated solely to impugning the intelligence or character or loyalties of the opposing candidate rather than defining and defending one's own record or proposals. Such campaigns may be effective in garnering votes, but they do nothing to advance meaningful responsibility by the leaders to the citizens for their decisions. These kinds of strategies make it harder to connect the election of representatives and the policies that they pursue and implement, so democratic accountability is significantly undermined.

There is also the problem of multiple leaders having dirty hands. Dennis Thompson notes: "The portrait that dominates discussions of the moral dilemmas of officials presents a solitary figure, agonizing alone when making moral choices, and acting alone when executing them." But this portrait does not jibe with the way in which many decisions are made in government.[46] Not just democratic citizens, but democratic leaders in any hierarchical government face the question of how to determine responsibility for joint decisions. It is not always clear exactly whom we should hold accountable, unless one assumes that the chief executive is always responsible for whatever may happen in his administration.[47]

Democratic accountability sometimes involves seeking specific consent in advance. As Thompson points out, if a democratic leader gains the consent of the citizens for his course of action, he is "not uniquely guilty in the way that the problem [of dirty hands] in its traditional form presumes." If he does not gain that consent, he commits a further wrong, by violating the democratic process.[48] Yet the kinds of actions that we normally think of in connection with dirty hands are rarely aired in advance. They often involve secrecy or deception, and securing advance consent would be impossible. Citizens may be asked to approve a vague general policy in advance, even if they are not made aware of specific actions, or they may delegate responsibility for oversight to another representative. But such measures are often quite ineffective in allowing citizens to have meaningful awareness of decisions being made "in our name."

An obvious example is the controversy in the United States about the National Security Agency gaining access to the phone and e-mail messages of millions of U.S. citizens and foreign nationals to forestall terrorist attacks, or spying on allies around the world to gain an advantage in negotiations. The outrage expressed by many citizens when these matters became public was not assuaged by the fact that the National Security Agency was acting on its interpretation of the Patriot Act, which was passed by Congress in the wake of 9/11 and renewed under President Obama. Nor were concerned citizens reassured that some members of Congress (as our representatives) had been privy to these developments, especially when it became clear that several of these representatives strongly opposed the activities but were precluded by laws governing secrecy from making their opposition public. This situation makes clear that the concepts of *prior authorization* and *representative oversight* are clumsy tools for enforcing accountability in a complex modern democracy.

Institutions designed to assure accountability of elected officials in a democracy most frequently involve the responsibility of a democratic leader to explain and justify her actions after the fact. As Nielsen puts it, the political leader must be prepared "to publicly justify" what he has done, "at least in the fullness of time."[49] The "fullness of time" may be quite an extended period, however, and the damage involved will long ago have already been done. In such a situation, the concept of shared responsibility becomes rather hollow.

EFFECTIVE ACCOUNTABILITY

Alex Zakaras refers to "the central normative premise of modern democracy: that citizens are themselves responsible for their government."[50] With this in mind, we can agree that if the mechanisms for accountability and oversight are in good working order, and if citizens either deliberately approve of the actions that raise ethical dilemmas or fail to avail themselves of these mechanisms for monitoring their representatives, it makes sense that the citizens should share some of the responsibility for actions that they have explicitly or implicitly condoned. In that situation, it is plausible to claim that the dirty hands are partly theirs.

However, as we have seen, it is difficult to trace a causal pathway for this responsibility through the circuitous workings of governance in large nation-states. And if the mechanisms for monitoring and accountability are not in good order, it seems unfair to blame the citizens alone for actions by their leaders. In that same passage, Zakaras argues that "if our institutions have grown corrupt, democracy's logic says that *we* are the ones responsible for their reform." But surely our leaders share some responsibility for allowing the mechanisms of accountability to become dysfunctional. At most, one could blame the citizens and their leaders together for not taking more vigorous steps to improve and repair their institutions of accountability.

Responsibility—ethical and otherwise—is more broadly shared in an effectively functioning democracy than in monarchies or oligarchies, which to some extent alleviates the burden on the democratic leader. But the principal attribution of responsibility is nonetheless to the elected leaders. Even in the healthiest representative democratic system, the leader is ultimately responsible for her decisions and their consequences. She must be held accountable for those decisions, but enforcing accountability is not the same as making the crucial judgment call. Citizens in general are seldom in a position to make and implement such choices. This is the job of the leader. Therefore, on a daily basis, the issue comes back to the potentially dirty hands of those individuals who hold positions of leadership in the polity. In Harry Truman's immortal words, the buck stops somewhere, and with the buck comes final ethical responsibility for the activities of political leadership.

WEBER ON RESPONSIBILITY AND DEMOCRATIC LEADERSHIP

This final ethical responsibility of the leader is very clear in Weber's "Politics as a Vocation."Although the essay is not focused specifically on democratic leadership, Weber's examples from contemporary politics are almost all drawn from democratic political systems, referring to elections, associations, political parties, parliaments, and other aspects of democratic governance. It is in that context that Weber insists that, in contrast to bureaucrats or civil servants, "the honor of the political leader, of the leading statesman ... lies precisely in an exclusive *personal* responsibility for what he does, a responsibility he cannot and must not reject or transfer."[51] This makes the essay a particularly useful source for democratic politicians considering how to fulfill their individual responsibilities as leaders.

One might question this claim given, as Nick O'Donovan has recently pointed out, that Weber's emphasis on the politician's primary devotion to a *cause* about which he is passionate may get in the way of a democratic leader's responsibility to those who have elected him. It is true that Weber's essay does not deal directly with the desires and aspirations of the citizens, and his conception of democracy was hardly participatory. O'Donovan quotes a passage from the biography of Weber written by his wife, Marianne, in which Weber discusses the subject of democracy in a conversation with former German general Ludendorff. In response to Ludendorff's question, "What do you mean by democracy?," Weber replies: "In a democracy, the people selects a leader in whom they trust. Then the chosen leader says: 'now shut up and obey me'. People and parties are no longer allowed to interfere. ... Afterwards the people can sit in judgment—if the leader has made mistakes, to the gallows with him!"[52]

Yet despite this rather undemocratic conception of democratic government, Weber's clear focus on the individual leader allows us to think more deeply about what it means for any leader, including leaders in democracies, to exercise *responsibility*. Weber's definition of "an ethic of responsibility" entails specifically that "one has to give an account of the foreseeable results of one's actions."[53] This emphasis on outcomes, in the sense of *responsibility for the foreseeable results of one's actions*, has important implications for a system of accountability. As democratic citizens, we should expect our leaders to take thought for the future and consider *the foreseeable results* of their actions, rather than going off half-cocked or focusing only on the short-term challenges they face.

One of the reasons John F. Kennedy's stance in dealing with the Cuban Missile Crisis was both exemplary and successful was that he deliberately considered the hugely important *foreseeable results* of his decision for the nation and the world. Richard Neustadt and Ernest May's account of the decision-making process in this crisis makes clear that although the initial reactions of those involved in the debates were focused on the immediate situation, by the end of the first day some of these men had "lifted their sights." McGeorge Bundy noted that "our principal problem is to try and imaginatively to think what the world would be like if we do this and what it will be like if we don't." Kennedy himself, referring to Barbara Tuchman's book *Guns of August*, said to his brother Bobby: "I am not going to follow a course which will allow anyone to write a comparable book about this time, *The Missiles of October*. If anybody is around to write after this, they are going to understand that we made every effort to find peace and every effort to give our adversary room to move."[54]

Such insights are particularly poignant in light of Weber's further insight that "the final result of political action often, no, even regularly, stands in completely inadequate and often even paradoxical relation to its original meaning."[55] Even the most thoughtful leader, conscientiously attempting to fulfill his responsibilities in light of foreseeable outcomes, must recognize that the end result depends on multiple factors and will very probably turn out to be quite different from anything he could have planned or foreseen. In the Cuban Missile Crisis, as Neustadt and May point out, even though the decision-making in the White House was as deep and careful as it could have been in the urgent situation our leaders faced, the outcome could well have been very different. Decisions made in Moscow independent of those made in Washington, the timing of the discovery of the missiles, and the willingness of the press to maintain secrecy even when some reporters got wind of the situation, all these factors and many more were not within Kennedy's control, and small changes in any of them could have skewed the outcome in a very negative direction.

In his discussion of Weber's ethical theory, Nicholas Gane notes that politics is "a sphere of human conduct that retains an element of irrationality. This is demonstrated by the fact that political means, ends, and consequences very often do not either correspond as intended or ethically justify one another."[56] With this in mind, one can understand why Weber asserts that ethical decision-making in political contexts has tragic dimensions, and why he calls politics "the strong and slow boring of hard boards." He concludes his essay by saying that "only he has the calling for politics who is sure that he shall not crumble when the world from his point of view is too stupid or too base for what he wants to offer. Only he who in the face of all this can say 'In spite of all!' has the calling for politics."[57]

CONCLUSION

As this chapter has attempted to demonstrate, the questions involved in the specific issue of *dirty hands* are complex and subtle. The question whether a political leader must behave immorally to do her job cannot be answered with a simple yes or no. The answer rests on a particular understanding of the responsibilities political leaders must face, the systems of accountability within which they work, and the factors that may be held to justify their decisions. And this, in turn, requires that we explore the concept of *responsibility* more fully than is often the case in discussions of this sort.

Despite the complex challenges leaders and citizens face, successful democratic governance, governance that is both ethical and productive of healthful consequences for a community, is one of the finest achievements of the human spirit. We should be grateful for leaders who manage to navigate successfully through the shoals of ethical dilemmas that the rest of us do not have to face, and sympathetic to the distinctive complexities these dilemmas may entail. We should not be too quick to call them morally guilty for undertaking a course of action chosen in good faith to advance the goals of the polity they lead. But as democratic citizens, we should also hold leaders rigorously accountable when they engage in morally dubious behavior that involves ducking their responsibilities, advancing their own narrow selfish purposes, or choosing a course of action that undermines the integrity of the political system they are charged with helping to preserve.

NOTES

1. Michael Walzer, "The Problem of Dirty Hands," *Philosophy and Public Affairs* II:2 (Winter 1973), 160–80. Jean Paul Sartre, *Dirty Hands*, included in *No Exit and Three Other Plays* (New York: Vintage, 1989).

2. In his entry on "Dirty Hands" for Blackwell's *Companion to Applied Ethics*, ed. R. G. Frey and Christopher Heath Wellman (2005) #13 (online), Gerald F. Gaus explores "five different conceptions of dirty hands" and concludes that "none of these formulations presents an analysis of morality and rationality that is both compelling and establishes an interesting moral problem of dirty hands."

3. This definition is taken from N. Keohane, *Thinking about Leadership* (Princeton: Princeton University Press, 2010), 23.

4. C. A. J. Coady, *Messy Morality: The Challenge of Politics* (Oxford: Oxford University Press, 2008), 78.

5. Lord Acton, *Essays on Freedom and Power*, ed. Gertrude Himmelfarb (Boston: Beacon Press, 1948), 364, from a letter to Mandell Creighton in 1887. Keohane, *Thinking about Leadership*, 208–11, discusses some of the implications of Acton's claim.

6. Dennis Thompson, *Political Ethics and Public Office* (Cambridge, MA: Harvard University Press, 1987), 11.

7. Marcus Tullius Cicero, *On Duties*, ed. M. T. Griffin and E. M. Atkins (Cambridge, MA: Cambridge University Press, 1991), book III: sections 17–19, 46.

8. Desiderio Erasmus, *The Education of a Christian Prince*, ed. Lisa Jardine (Cambridge, MA: Cambridge University Press, 1997), 25.

9. James MacGregor Burns, *Leadership* (New York: Harper & Row, 1978), 2–4.

10. Niccolò Machiavelli, *The Prince*, ed. Quentin Skinner and Russell Price (Cambridge, MA: Cambridge University Press), XV, 54.

11. This choice is made by Max Lerner in *The Prince and the Discourses* (New York, NY: Modern Library edition, 1940) , XV, 56.

12. Machiavelli, *The Discourses*, Max Lerner, ed. *The Prince and the Discourses*, IX, 139.

13. Cathy Davidson, *Closing: The Life and Death of an American Factory* (Boston: W. W. Norton, 1998).

14. Thompson, *Political Ethics and Public Office*, 2.

15. I am indebted to Corey Brettschneider for clarifying this point.

16. Paul Rynard and David Shugarman's edited volume entitled *Cruelty and Deception: The Controversy over Dirty Hands in Politics* (Toronto: Broadview Press, 2000) focuses specifically on the "third view" type of answer to our basic dilemma; see especially Shugarman's thoughtful introductory essay. Max Weber is only an occasional focus of the discussion in that book, but the goal of offering an alternative to simple yes/no answers to the dilemma of *dirty hands* is similar to the purpose of my chapter.

17. Max Weber, "Politics as a Vocation," *From Max Weber: Essays in Sociology*, translated and edited by H. H. Gerth and C. Wright Mills (Oxford: Oxford University Press, 1958), 120.

18. Ibid., 124–5. Emphasis added.

19. Stephen A. Garrett, *Conscience and Power: An Examination of Dirty Hands and Political Leadership* (New York: St. Martin's, 1996), v.

20. In his essay "Politics and Moral Character," Bernard Williams explores a number of ways in which making political decisions can affect the character of a leader; he is particularly interested in the question of what "sorts of persons" would be likely to be willing to engage in such behavior, what moral dispositions they may have (or lack). Stuart Hampshire, ed., *Public and Private Morality* (Cambridge, MA: Cambridge University Press, 1979), 160–80.

21. Weber, 121.

22. Walzer, 161, 167–68.

23. Kai Nielsen, "There Is No Dilemma of Dirty Hands," in P. Rynard and D. Shugarman, *Cruelty and Deception*, 140–41.

24. In this discussion, Weber, 117, specifically draws on the concept of "tragedy" when he makes clear his disdain for a "mere 'power politician' " whose "shoddy and superficially blasé attitude towards the meaning of human conduct ... has no relation whatsoever to the knowledge of tragedy with which all action, but especially political action, is truly interwoven."

25. Weber, 115–17.

26. As Weber puts it, "the problem is simply how can warm passion and a cool sense of proportion be forged together in one and the same soul?" 115.

27. John Parrish, *Paradoxes of Political Ethics: From Dirty Hands to the Invisible Hand* (Cambridge, MA: Cambridge University Press, 2007), 8. Emphasis in the original.

28. Stuart Hampshire, "Foreword" to *Public and Private Morality*, ix; Hampshire, "Public and Private Morality," essay in the same volume by this name, 52.

29. Roy Jenkins, *Churchill: A Biography* (New York: Plume, 2002), 623–24.

30. Weber, 127. Emphasis in the original.

31. Lawrence Kohlberg (following Piaget), "The Development of Children's Orientation toward a Moral Order," *Human Development* 51, no. 1 (February 2008): 12.

32. Personal conversation, Amos Tversky, Stanford, California.

33. Aristotle, *Politics*, ed. Ernest Barker (Oxford: Oxford University Press, 1995), I:1, 1252a. On this same point, see Keohane, *Thinking about Leadership*, ch. 5.

34. Hampshire, "Public and Private Morality," 49.

35. Thomas Nagel, "Ruthlessness in Public Life," explores the relevance of the concept of "office" in discussing this topic. Hampshire, *Public and Private Morality,* 75–91.

36. Parrish, *Paradoxes of Political Ethics,* 15–16.

37. Williams, "Politics and Moral Character," 62.

38. Garrett, *Conscience and Power,* 10.

39. Thompson, *Political Ethics and Public Policy,* 18.

40. Walzer, 162–63.

41. Eric Beerbohm, *In Our Name: The Ethics of Democracy* (Princeton: Princeton University Press, 2012), 1–2.

42. American Political Science Association, August 31, 2013, panel on Eric Beerbohm's *In Our Name,* comments by Anna Stilz.

43. Nagel, "Ruthlessness in Public Life," 87.

44. Ruth W. Grant and Robert O. Keohane, "Accountability and Abuses of Power in World Politics," *American Political Science Review* 99(1) (February 2005): 29.

45. Dennis Thompson, *Restoring Responsibility: Ethics in Government, Business and Healthcare* (Cambridge, MA: Cambridge University Press, 2005), 99, 117.

46. Thompson, *Political Ethics and Public Office,* 40; this sentence introduces Thompson's chapter "The Moral Responsibility of Many Hands."

47. Garrett, *Conscience and Power,* 13–17, has a particularly good discussion of this problem, which he calls "the imprint of many hands."

48. Thompson, *Political Ethics and Public Office,* 11.

49. Nielsen, "There Is No Dilemma of Dirty Hands," 149.

50. Alex Zakaras, *Individuality and Mass Democracy: Mill, Emerson, and the Burdens of Citizenship* (Oxford: Oxford University Press, 2009), 4.

51. Weber, 95.

52. Nick O'Donovan, "Causes and Consequences: Responsibility in the Political Thought of Max Weber," *Polity* 43, no. 1 (January 2011), 84–105.

53. Weber, 120.

54. Richard E. Neustadt and Ernest R. May, *Thinking in Time: The Uses of History for Decision Makers* (New York: Simon and Schuster, The Free Press, 1986), 14–15.

55. Weber, 117.

56. Nicholas Gane, "Max Weber on the Ethical Irrationality of Political Leadership," *Sociology* 31, no. 3 (August 1997), 550.

57. Weber, 128.

Part IV

The Ethical Influence of Leaders

8

The Trouble with Transformational Leadership: Toward a Federalist Ethic for Organizations

Michael Keeley

Following the American War of Independence, a variety of local conflicts broke out within the loosely united states. New York taxed ships bound for New Jersey, which retaliated by levying lighthouse fees. Maryland fishermen fought Virginians over oysters taken from the Chesapeake Bay. Moneyless farmers in Massachusetts banded together to stop courts from convening and sending debtors to prison. Such events brought state delegates to Philadelphia in the summer of 1787 to plan a new organization: a federal government to coordinate their joint affairs and protect their individual rights. The resulting plan, the Constitution of the United States, was shaped in large part by James Madison, who set the stage for the Philadelphia convention with a speech about a classic organizational problem.

Madison told the delegates that all societies were divided into different interest groups, or factions: "rich and poor, debtors and creditors, the landed, the manufacturing, the commercial interests, the inhabitants of this district, or that district, the followers of this political leader or that political leader, the disciples of this religious sect or that religious sect (June 6, 1787)."[1] He went on to observe that throughout history different factions have tried to take advantage of one another: "In Greece and Rome the rich and poor, the creditors and debtors, as well as the patricians and plebeians alternately oppressed each other with equal unmercifulness. ... We have seen the mere distinction of color made in the most enlightened period of time, a ground of the most oppressive dominion ever exercised by man over man." Madison concluded that a key problem in designing a system of government was how to manage factional tensions, given the readiness of groups to pursue their own interests at others' expense.

Over 200 years later, this is still a key problem in the management of governments, corporations, and organizations of all sorts. The general issue is how to deal with the diverse interests that are prevalent in any complex social system: How, for example, to reconcile the expectations of various lobbies, lawmakers, taxpayers, and other constituents of public agencies; how to satisfy the frequently competing claims of investors, employees, customers, dealers, and other stakeholders of private firms; how, more specifically, to control in-fighting among corporate divisions, to gain union cooperation in meeting foreign competition, to contain executive salaries and perks, to keep insiders from exploiting privileged information, and so on.

Lately, management writers have voiced real concern about such things. In both popular and academic reports, a common complaint is that many of our organizations are going to ruin because those in charge have let private interests (their own included) run amok. Zaleznik, for instance, contends that "business in America has lost its way" because of mediocre management whose major fault has been complicity in self-serving organizational politics as opposed to productive work.[2] John Gardner adopts a Madisonian perspective and sees "the mischiefs of faction" throughout the fabric of American society, which is at best "loosely knit, at worst completely unraveled"; to Gardner, "it is a mystery that [this society] works at all," as group after group pursues parochial aims and grievances in a "war of the parts against the whole."[3] From a global standpoint, Bennis and Nanus argue "a chronic crisis of governance—that is, the pervasive incapacity of organizations to cope with the expectations of their constituents—is now an overwhelming factor worldwide."[4]

What is interesting about recent attempts to deal with the problem of faction is that these writers, and many others, offer a cure that Madison in 1787 considered worse than the disease. The suggested remedy is a type of *leadership* that transforms self-interest and unites social systems around common purposes (often termed *transformational* leadership). So opposed was Madison to this prescription that he insisted on constitutional devices to counteract it in the American system of government. The American experiment was to be a government of *laws*, not of men or women or charismatic leaders.

Perhaps Madison was shortsighted; perhaps his concerns have little applicability to nongovernmental organizations; perhaps they are no longer relevant at all. But possibly he recognized something important that has been overlooked by modern leadership theorists. The purpose of this chapter is to compare Madison's views and emerging theories of leadership, especially as these bear on the problem of controlling self-interested organizational behavior.

TRANSFORMATIONAL VERSUS TRANSACTIONAL LEADERSHIP

Much of the current interest in transformational leadership stems from a study of governmental leaders by political scientist-historian James MacGregor Burns.[5] Burns differentiates two sorts of leadership: *transactional* and *transforming*. The more common, he notes, is transactional leadership. This involves the exchange of incentives by leaders for support from followers—in politics, for instance, jobs for votes or subsidies for campaign contributions. The object of such leadership is agreement on a course of action that satisfies the immediate, separate purposes of both leaders and followers.

Transforming leadership, in contrast, aims beyond the satisfaction of immediate needs. According to Burns, "the transforming leader looks for potential motives in followers, seeks to satisfy higher needs, and engages the full person of the follower."[6] Here, the object is to turn individuals' attention toward larger causes (political reform, revolution, national defense, etc.), thereby converting self-interest into collective concerns. The distinguishing feature of transforming leadership is a common goal; the purposes of the leader and followers, "which might have started out as separate but related, as in the case of transactional leadership, become fused."[7]

Burns goes on to develop the basic normative theme of the paradigm: Transforming leadership is generally superior to transactional—indeed, the latter is hardly leadership at all. For Burns, transforming leadership is motivating, uplifting, and ultimately "*moral* in that it raises the level of human conduct and ethical aspiration of both leader and led."[8] A textbook example is Gandhi's elevation of the aspirations and life chances of millions of Indians who followed him toward independence. Transactional leadership, on the other hand, is characterized as immobilizing, self-absorbing, and eventually manipulative in that it seeks control over followers by catering to their lowest needs. Burns's examples of transactional figures include Tammany Hall bosses bent on trading political favors for preservation of the status quo. In Burns's view, transactional politicians are questionable *leaders* because they focus on mutually tolerable behavior, rather than jointly held goals—on means, rather than ends—and "leadership is nothing if not linked to collective purpose."[9]

This line of analysis has been extended to organizations by a number of theorists. Bass finds elements of transactional leadership at the root of popular organizational theories (such as exchange, expectancy, and path-goal models) and common management practices (such as contingent reinforcement and management-by-exception).[10] These theories and practices imply that organizations consist of agreements between managers and subordinates to fulfill specific obligations for mutual advantage; they further imply that leaders should make these agreements even more specific to increase subordinates' satisfaction and performance. Bass argues, however, that any satisfaction or performance gains from transactional leadership are apt to be small. He claims that *transformational* leaders produce much larger effects on followers.

THE VISION THING

Bass builds on Burns's framework by identifying three main components of transformational leadership. The first and most important component, *charisma*, is displayed by leaders "to whom followers form deep emotional attachments and who in turn inspire their followers to transcend their own interests for superordinate goals."[11] The second component, *individualized consideration*, is shown by leaders who mentor and enhance the confidence of followers. The final component, *intellectual stimulation*, occurs as leaders arouse awareness of shared problems and foster visions of new possibilities.

Bass associates these three aspects of transforming leadership with extraordinary levels of effort and high degrees of organizational effectiveness. Although he stops short of insisting that transformational administrators are always more moral than transactional types, he follows Burns in portraying the former as true *leaders* who raise attitudes and behavior to a "higher plane" of maturity, and the latter as mere *managers* mired in "compromise, intrigue, and control." According to Bass, transactional managers act like "everyone has a price; it is just a matter of establishing it," whereas transformational leaders motivate individuals to put aside selfish aims for the sake of some greater, common good.[12]

Other theorists have concentrated on particular features of transformational leadership. Conger and Kanungo, for instance, try to give a more precise account of charisma as a dimension of leader behavior.[13] The authors describe charismatic transformation as a three-stage process in which leaders, first, identify deficiencies in the status quo; second, formulate and articulate a vision of ideal goals that highlight present deficiencies; and third, devise innovative means of achieving the vision. Throughout this process, charismatic leaders exhibit a variety of distinctive behaviors: They actively search out existing or potential needs for change, set bold (even utopian) goals, and employ unconventional or countercultural tactics. They build enthusiasm for their vision through symbols, rhetoric, and other forms of impression management. Finally, they set examples by performing heroic deeds involving self-sacrifice and personal risk. Conger and Kanungo hypothesize that these charismatic behaviors result in high emotional attachment of followers to leaders, high commitment to shared goals, and high task performance.

ADMINISTRATIVE IMPLICATIONS

Among students of transformational leadership, there is hardly consensus on all issues, but there does seem to be broad agreement on the following basic ideas: It is a fact of organizational life that participants get preoccupied with their own aims and interests. This has certain negative consequences, such as unproductive conflict and depletion of resources. To avoid these consequences, it is necessary to unify organizational members by refocusing their attention on collective goals. This is no job for the faint of heart. Extraordinary leaders are required to transform members' self-interested tendencies—leaders who can create exciting visions, communicate these in compelling ways, and energize others to achieve them, despite personal costs. Bass summarizes the administrative ideal:

> Superior leadership performance—transformational leadership—occurs when leaders broaden and elevate the interests of their employees, when they generate awareness and acceptance of the purposes and mission of the group, and when they stir their employees to look beyond their own self-interest for the good of the group.[14]

The policy implication is that "transformational leadership should be encouraged."[15] Bass supplies examples. At the individual level, factors associated with transformational leadership "should be incorporated into managerial assessment, selection, placement, and guidance programs." At the organizational level, institutional constraints on managerial behavior should be reduced to allow transformational leaders more freedom of action: "Organizational policy needs to support an understanding and appreciation of the maverick who is willing to take unpopular positions, who knows when to reject the conventional wisdom, and who takes reasonable risks."[16]

Proponents of transformational leadership suggest that, without it, organizations are just marketplaces for self-serving transactions, subject to drift and disintegration. With no leaders to transform them, corporations become disabled by bureaucracy and mediocrity, since positions of authority fall to transactional managers who simply *muddle through*, much like their governmental counterparts described by Burns:

> [They] grope along, operating "by feel and by feedback." They concentrate on method, technique, and mechanisms rather than on broader ends or purposes. They protect, sometimes at heavy cost to overall goals, the maintenance and survival of their organization because they are exposed daily to the claims of persons immediately sheltered by that organization. They extrude red tape even as they struggle with it. They transact more than they administer, compromise more than they command, institutionalize more than they initiate. They fragment and morselize policy issues in order to better cope with them, seeking to limit their alternatives, to delegate thorny problems "down the line," to accept vague and inconsistent goals, to adapt and survive. Thus they exemplify the "satisficing" model, as economists call it, far more than the "maximizing" one.[17]

Who would want to settle for leaders of this type? Who would *not* find transformational leadership more interesting to study and more deserving of encouragement? Possibly, James Madison.

THE FRAMERS' VISION AND THE CHIEF EXECUTIVE OF THE CONVENTION

Many of the governmental practices that bother leadership theorists such as James MacGregor Burns are the legacy of Madison and the other framers of the U.S. Constitution. Burns, in particular, has very grudging respect for this legacy. In an earlier work, he characterized the American political process as *The Deadlock of Democracy,* an allusion to "the system of checks and balances and interlocked gears of government that requires the consensus of many groups and leaders before the nation can act."[18] Burns states that this system exacts a "heavy price of delay and devitalization" and that it was "designed for deadlock and inaction" from the start—by Madison and those delegates to the Constitutional Convention who shared his fear of strong leadership.

The framers' implicit theories of leadership, however, were far from naïve, and their explicit plan of government, with all its interlocking checks and balances, was not irrational. The framers were people of practical affairs—planters, lawyers, traders, above all politicians—and so, perhaps, transactional leaders in Burns's terms. Yet they were also educated people, who were aware of the heights to which leaders could aspire in the ideal world of political theory. They obviously never read John Gardner, or used the jargon of transformational leadership. But they read similarly inclined writers, like Plato; they knew of related protagonists, like philosopher-kings. And they rejected the lot.

What's more, the framers shied away from transformational leadership knowing, firsthand, maybe the finest example of it. At their meeting in Philadelphia, they drafted their plan of divided government under the supervision of one of the most revered leaders in history. Look for a moment at the background of the convention's chief executive.

The unanimous choice to preside over the Constitutional Convention was George Washington—father of the country, symbol of virtue, and a larger-than-life monument even in 1787.[19] Much of Washington's fame stemmed from his ability to transform a fractious lot of rebels into a victorious army in the American War of Independence. No small feat: Rank-and-file U.S. citizens were not eager to risk *their* lives and fortunes fighting for the sacred honor of Congress. Volunteers from some states wanted nothing to do with militia from others. Farmers and merchants were reluctant to take Continental currency and provide food or supplies to Washington's forces. Washington's staff included quarrelsome, treasonous, and just useless officers. (While short of good officers, for instance, Washington had a surplus of unemployed European officers sent by friends abroad; Morison notes that "since Americans disliked serving under foreigners, there was nothing for most of them to do except serve on Washington's staff, and tell him in French, German, or Polish as the case might be, that his army was lousy.")[20]

Washington's army lost most of the battles, yet somehow won the war. Flexner's account of Washington's behavior as commander in chief describes a transformational leader in every sense of the term.[21] From the outset, Washington displayed heroic acts. Upon accepting command of the Continental Army, he informed Congress that he would take no salary, a selfless and inspiring gesture in an age when it was customary for military officers to enrich themselves at public expense. Throughout the war, shortages of money and equipment drove Washington to devise unconventional means of motivating his troops. British and other professional soldiers of the time were paid to carry out orders without concern for what the struggle was all about. European kings and generals did not want their armies thinking about which way to point their weapons! Lacking the funds to employ such compliant professionals, Washington united and motivated a bunch of rugged individualists by refocusing their attention on higher ends: "Washington labored to inspire his soldiery with confidence in the value and the nobility of the cause."[22] This military innovation—encouragement of combat by appeals to nationalism—transformed not only the Continental Army but also the very nature of modern warfare.[23]

Such was the man selected to serve as president of the Constitutional Convention. If ever there existed a role model of transformational leadership, here it was right in the midst of the delegates as they went about designing a system of government.

What is interesting is that the framers recognized and appreciated individual greatness—but they refused to count on it. Despite the pressing social problems that brought them together, they decided *not* to bet their future, and ours, on model leaders like George Washington. Rather, they chose to protect us from the misdeeds of scoundrels and the frailties of ordinary men and women. The fates of nations whose political systems are more open to strong leadership (say, China or the former Soviet Union) suggest that the choice was a fortunate one. The historical record suggests it was also an *informed* choice.

MADISON'S PLAN

Madison's analysis of the issues is the most famous. Recall his opening point that all societies are divided into different interest groups or factions: rich and poor, debtors and creditors, inhabitants of various regions, disciples of one religion or another, followers of this leader or that, and parties to all sorts of commercial dealings. These factions tend to pursue their own welfare at others' expense, resulting in conflict. Unless managed in some way, conflicts get settled by force: Policies are made by those with the most power at the time. This leads, ultimately, to injustice and instability. How, then, to manage factional conflict and minimize its potential for harm?

In *Federalist* No. 10, Madison examines alternative strategies. According to Madison, there are two ways of curing the mischiefs of faction: one, by removing its causes; the other, by controlling its effects. There are, in turn, two ways of removing the causes of faction: the first, by suppressing the freedom of persons to advance their own interests; the second, by persuading persons to share the same interests.

Madison questions both methods of avoiding the causes of faction. He considers the first, denying personal freedom, unwise. It stifles initiative, destroys political life, and is even worse for individuals than the condition it is meant to remedy. Madison considers the second, inducing common interests, impractical. Although some people may share some interests for some time (for instance, the coalition of militants who waged the American War of Independence), commonality of purpose is fragile at best (as shown after the war, when those who fought and wound up impoverished turned against those who profited). Madison argues that, if nothing else, the varying abilities and fortunes of individuals will divide them into haves and have-nots, whose interests diverge in matters of social policy. He adds that "different leaders ambitiously contending for pre-eminence and power" will be more apt to inflame and exploit such societal divisions than to reconcile them. Madison, therefore, opts to control the effects of faction, instead of its causes. He proposes to use government to help factions check and balance one another, thus limiting the capacity of the strong to take advantage of the weak.

In sum, the framers' task was to "enable the government to control the governed; and in the next place oblige it to control itself."[24] The trick was to preclude tyranny, which Madison equates with the accumulation of power in the same hands—whether few or many, whether self-designated or elected. Consolidation of power or tyranny, he says, cannot be prevented by formal, legal restrictions, by mere "parchment barriers," but only by "rival and opposite interests." So the framers set about dividing power, devising checks and balances. Power was first divided between "two distinct governments," state and federal, which vie to control each other. Within each government, power was then subdivided among "distinct and separate departments," which have wills of their own, stemming from the desires of member-officials to maintain or enlarge their personal authority. Madison comments,

> Ambition must be made to counteract ambition. The interest of the man must be connected with the constitutional rights of the place. It may be a reflection on human nature that such devices should be necessary to control the abuses of government. But what is government itself but the greatest of all reflections on human nature? If men were angels, no government would be necessary.[25]

Further divisions were created, Madison continues, since "it is not possible to give each department an equal power of self-defense" against encroachments by others. (Because Congress was considered likely to dominate, for example, federal legislative power was divided again between two houses.) Still other checks and balances, such as an executive veto, were added as backup devices for preserving, in practice, the departmental independence prescribed on paper.

This compounding of separations has seemed excessive to some critics, who complain that it weakens national resolve, hampers unified action, or thwarts majority wishes.[26] But Madison and the framers accepted consequences of this sort to avoid more serious ones. Their constitutional system was arranged to protect individuals in minority factions from being bulldozed by members of majority factions bent on pursuing some alleged common goal. In this regard, the framers and Madison especially showed insights into social behavior and ethics that elude modern advocates of transformational leadership.

MADISONIAN AND TRANSFORMATIONAL LEADERSHIP MODELS COMPARED

To better appreciate Madison's approach, compare his views of human nature with the motivational assumptions of transformational leadership as outlined by Burns. Like Madison, Burns begins with conflict, which provides the *seedbed* of leadership: "Every person, group, and society has latent tension and hostility. ... Leadership acts as an inciting and triggering force in the conversion of conflicting demands, values, and goals into significant behavior."[27] In this process, leaders can appeal to a variety of motives for cooperation. The type of motive triggered is critical, argues Burns. Here he invokes a theory of psychological development borrowed, in part, from Freud, Maslow, Kohlberg, and others—which, all together, looks a lot like Herzberg's two-factor theory of motivation.[28]

Burns differentiates *lower* needs, such as physical survival and economic security (similar to Herzberg's hygiene factors), from *higher* needs, such as moral purpose and "participation in a collective life larger than one's personal existence" (similar to Herzberg's motivators). The lower needs are addressed by transactional leaders, who may at best defuse conflict by meeting the parochial demands of their different constituents. The higher, more *authentic* needs are engaged by transforming leaders who can refocus attention—with much greater effect—on common goals that have transcendent value. The greater the goal, the greater the energizing force: "the leader who commands compelling causes has an extraordinary potential influence over followers. Followers armed by moral inspiration, mobilized and purposeful, become zealots and leaders in their own right.[29]"

Madison could have accepted most of this; he was certainly not ignorant of the transforming potential of leadership. But he thought beyond it, to the problems that zealots—armed by moral inspiration, mobilized and purposeful—might create for persons who disagreed with them. Madison concentrated on a fact about human motivation that proves troublesome for transformational-leadership theories: Not everyone is attracted to the same goals or leaders. This fact has been well established by research on both motivation and leadership. Not all workers, for example, are motivated as Herzberg and Burns suggest; some (especially academics and other professionals) do appear to be driven by *higher* needs and transcendent goals, but others seem to prefer fulfillment of the bread-and-butter flavor.[30] With respect to leadership, even champions of the transformational approach acknowledge the fact of individual differences; "some employees may not react well to a leader even though most view the leader in a positive way and as transformational."[31] To Madison, such individual differences make all the difference in the world.

Madison reminds us that, because people differ, minority ideas about the value of particular goals and interests are likely to exist within large social groups—even where leaders are able to transform many individual views into a majority vision. In a letter to Thomas Jefferson dated October 24, 1787, soon after the Constitutional Convention, Madison wrote that popular theories supposed "that the people composing the Society enjoy not only an equality of political rights; but that they have all precisely the same interests, and the same feelings in every respect." Were this really the case, Madison noted, "[T]he interest of the majority would be that of the minority also; [public policy] decisions could only turn on mere opinion concerning the good of the whole, of which the major voice would be the safest criterion." But, he points out to Jefferson, "no society ever did or can consist of so homogeneous a mass of Citizens." Madison cites his famous examples of different economic interests (rich and poor, farmers and merchants, etc.) and differences of belief (political, religious, etc.), emphasizing that these persistent distinctions matter very much to ordinary people if not to social theorists. "However erroneous or ridiculous these grounds of dissension and faction may appear to the enlightened Statesman or the benevolent philosopher," Madison says, "the bulk of mankind who are neither Statesmen nor Philosophers, will continue to view them in a different light. It remains then to be enquired whether a majority having any common interest, or feeling any common passion, will find sufficient motives to restrain them from oppressing the minority."[32]

Here we come to the crux of things. If not all social participants have the same goals, if transformational leaders are not able to persuade *everyone* to voluntarily accept a common vision, what is the likely status of people who prefer their own goals and visions? Judging from the rhetoric of management experts like Bennis—who complain of individuals marching stubbornly to their own drummers—or communitarian writers like Etzioni—who sound alarms about persons selfishly asserting their rights against society—it may be perilous indeed.[33] Leadership theorists have been targeted nonconformists for criticism since Plato (see his *Republic*), and historical leaders with single-minded majorities on their side subjected minorities to *real* injury. (A brutal illustration is the persecution of Chinese dissidents in the Cultural Revolution inspired by Mao Zedong, one of James MacGregor Burns's transforming heroes.)

Madison posed the question to Jefferson: What if two persons share an interest that is disagreeable to a third; would the rights of the third be secure if decisions were left to a majority of the group? "Will two thousand individuals be less apt to oppress one thousand or two hundred thousand one hundred thousand?" (October 24, 1787).[34] What, after all, will stop majorities from taking advantage of anyone who opposes them? Madison considers possible restraints, such as concern for the public good, fear of negative public opinion, and personal moral standards. He rejects each as ineffective: The public good is no use, because majorities (and their leaders) define it for themselves. Similarly, public opinion supports their actions, by definition. And personal morality falls victim to groupthink.

> The conduct of every popular Assembly, acting on oath, the strongest of religious ties, shews that individuals join without remorse in acts against which their consciences would revolt, if proposed to them separately in their closets.[35]

The conclusion drawn by Madison is a flat-out repudiation of transformational leadership. He reasons that, if differences in individual interests exist within society, and if a majority united by a common interest cannot be restrained from harming minorities, then the only way to prevent harm is to keep majorities from uniting around common interests—the *reverse* of what transformational leaders are supposed to do. In other words, unless leaders are able to transform everyone and create absolute unanimity of interests (a very special case), transformational leadership produces simply a majority will that represents the interests of the strongest faction. Sometimes this will is on the side of good—as in Gandhi's case. Sometimes it is on the side of evil—as in Hitler's case. In any case, might is an arbitrary guide to right, as Madison clearly understood.

This, then, is why the Madisonian system of government divides power and purpose, why it frustrates majority wishes, and why it checks leadership in the pursuit of *collective* goals. It was designed to work this way to protect the basic interests of the weak from the self-interest of the strong. Without such protection, any response to the problem of faction is no solution: Social life can remain as imagined by Burns and others who would transform it—dog-eat-dog.

ORGANIZATIONAL IMPLICATIONS

Warren Bennis, a veteran observer of organizational leadership, sounds a familiar theme. Asking *Why Leaders Can't Lead*, Bennis points to increasing selfishness in American society and organizations. He notes that "everyone insists on having his or her own way now," from young urban professionals, to corporate executives, to the president of the United States. The trouble is that there is no agreement or commitment to the public good, no common vision, no mutual purpose:

> As the world has divided into factions, so has America, and so consensus is harder and harder to come by. Each faction marches stubbornly to its own drummer, has its own priorities and agenda, and has nothing in common with any other faction—except the unbridled desire to triumph over all the others. The Peruvians call this *arribismo*. It means, "You've got yours, Jack, and now I'm going to get mine." It means "making it," carried to the nth power. This fragmentation and fracturing of the common accord occurred for good reason, because, in America, those on top have traditionally tried to keep everyone else down, but it makes leadership a chancy undertaking at any level.[36]

Bennis's solution: "People in authority must develop the vision and authority to call the shots."[37]

Huh? Entrust those greedy individuals on top with even greater power to pursue "the common good" as they envision it? In fairness to Bennis, there's a bit more to his argument, but it is difficult, in theory, to get from selfish public and corporate officials to selfless transformational leadership—perhaps even harder, in practice. Madison foresaw this. Moreover, his view is just as applicable to *private* organizations as to governmental ones, since the same problems arise in their design. Among the most fundamental are problems of controlling factions and ambitious leaders.

THREATS POSED BY LEADERS

Madison suggests to us that, in any kind of social system, inspired leadership can do as much harm as good. Lately, journalists and insiders have documented ample damage done by corporate folk-heroes once hailed as transformational leaders. Some advocates of transformational leadership allow that there is *dark side*, that the risks can be as large as the promises.[38] Yukl remarks that history is full of charismatic leaders who caused death, destruction, and misery or who ruled over firms like tyrants and egomaniacs.[39] However, Madison remains exceptional in taking the matter seriously.

In proposing social structures that would impact people's daily lives, Madison recognized a responsibility to build in protections against abuses of power. Contemporary leadership theorists are more inclined to shrug off the issue—and to depict protective devices (i.e., checks and balances and right-conferring rules) as bureaucratic hindrances that reduce the autonomy and transforming potential of leaders. Bass, for example, grants that some transformational leaders have "authoritarian tendencies," that "some fulfill grandiose dreams at the expense of their followers," yet he still prescribes more "flexible" organizational structures to encourage determined leadership.[40] Others offer timid advice to treat transformational leadership with caution. Roberts and Bradley compare charisma to an unpredictable genie in a bottle; they ask whether it should be set free to transform organizations; then, they leave the question hanging.[41] Howell and Avolio go a bit further and urge top managers to screen corporate leaders more carefully to weed out unethical charismatics, but they fail to indicate just what to screen for, how to control those doing the screening, or what to do about opportunists who slip through the net. Howell and Avolio hold out a lot of hope for voluntary ethical codes and executives who function as positive role models.[42] Although such things are not necessarily worthless, Madison knew enough not to rely on them. He felt that flesh-and-blood persons who might suffer from misconduct by public officials deserved better than parchment barriers and hypothetical defenses. Persons vulnerable to corporate officials do, too.

But Madison's challenge goes far beyond showing the dangers of charismatic leaders or the moral obligation to control them. It cuts to the very heart of transformational leadership theories, to the value of collective goals. Individuals are at risk, Madison argues, not only from self-interested leaders but also from self-interested majorities acting in the name of some "common purpose." In modern organizations, no less than in the colonial assemblies of Madison's experiences, focused groups can act in ways that their members would not dream of, alone in their closets.

THREATS POSED BY FACTIONS

Grenier tells a relevant story of a company named (*really*) Ethicon. A suture-making subsidiary of Johnson & Johnson, Ethicon built an innovative plant in New Mexico that was designed to *de-bureaucratize* the work environment: Jobs were organized around teams—quality circles—in a flexible, participative organizational structure. "The designers of the Ethicon work environment were trying to present a new vision of work in contemporary America, a vision of unity, cooperation, purpose, and inspiration."[43]

Grenier studied teams in operation and found some grim facts behind the vision. In Ethicon's explanation of quality circles to employees, "the concept was likened to a sports team, where all participants worked together for a common goal and had a voice in how that goal would be reached."[44] In theory, company supervisors (the team coaches) served as *facilitators* of communication, whereas workers discussed means of achieving production goals, including decisions about hiring, firing, evaluating, and disciplining other team members. In reality, "many workers referred to the team system as the 'rat system,'" because it pitted workers against one another to root out "counterproductive behavior." Counterproductive behavior turned out to be any expression of discontent with Ethicon or support for the Amalgamated Clothing and Textile Workers Union, which began an organizing campaign soon after the plant opened. A key issue among union supporters was their low wage in New Mexico, compared to company workers elsewhere. For Ethicon, the lower wage was a reason for locating in New Mexico in the first place, and a reason for trying to stay nonunion.

From the start, Grenier reports, management carefully screened employees to select "team players" and exclude union sympathizers. A subsequent strategy used teams to control workers who developed pro-union attitudes. The team strategy relied on peer pressure, in the words of the Ethicon psychologist, "to deprive the pro-union employees of status and identify them as losers."[45] Facilitators were trained not only to bring "negative attitudes" to the group's attention in team meetings but also to encourage the anti-union majority to denounce their pro-union colleagues (with remarks like "If you're not happy with the company, why don't you resign? If it were up to me I'd fire you").[46] Workers singled out for public censure compared the feeling to being attacked by a pack of wolves, and some union activists were, indeed, fired. According to Grenier, such things went on because facilitators won approval from management, team members in turn won recognition from facilitators, and new hires won acceptance from the group by showing support for the company. Seeing the fate of "losers," the majority of workers just conformed. "The issue was who had the power to do more for the workers, and management had convinced most of the workers that management could do more, good and bad, than the union."[47]

In the end, the pro-union minority lost the election (141 to 71). The victors gloated. And their opponents filed unfair-labor-practice charges (some of which were later settled in favor of union supporters discharged or denied jobs during the campaign).

The moral of the story is that Ethicon's efforts to achieve unity of purpose produced, instead, a sharply divided workforce motivated by fear. Ethicon's approach was to eliminate the causes of faction (1) by enlisting persons to share the same interests and (2) by suppressing dissent among those who failed to go along—the very cures that Madison said were worse than the disease. And the result, as Madison might have predicted, was not the peaceful absence of conflict, but a bitter truce between the victorious majority and a resentful, powerless minority.

RIGHTS VERSUS GOALS IN ORGANIZATIONAL THEORY

Many ordinary people might agree wholeheartedly with proposals to secure basic individual interests and freedoms against infringement in the workplace. Many might welcome, for example, guarantees of rights to due process in termination decisions (rights that tenured faculty members, of both public and private institutions, take for granted). Leadership theorists, on the other hand, express much less enthusiasm about protecting individual rights that could conflict with organizational goals. Things like freedom in the factory, unions, and constitutional checks on corporate policies are not generally what theorists have in mind when speaking of worker *empowerment*. In the leadership literature, the meaning of the term is more like the interpretation at Ethicon-New Mexico: a Hegelian notion of freedom to serve the goals of the organization.[48] Charles A. Reich's idea of empowering workers to seek their own goals in organizations is apt to seem a little too, well, *free*.[49] In such ethical matters, however, the opinions of Reich, Madison, and ordinary people may be better guides than traditional theories of organization.

Organizational theorists have historically found individual rights and freedoms less appealing than collective goals, not only in organizations but in society at large. On the heels of the American and French Revolutions, a pioneering organizational theorist, Henri de Saint-Simon, criticized Madisonian tendencies in the French Constitution:

[Lack of collective purpose] is the great gap in the Charter. It begins, as do all the constitutions dreamed up since 1789, by putting forward the rights of Frenchmen, which can only be clearly determined when the purpose of society is established in a positive way, since the rights of every associate can only be based upon the abilities which he possesses and which contribute toward the common goal.[50]

It cannot too often be repeated that society needs an active goal, for without this there would be no political system. ... The maintenance of individual freedom cannot be the goal. ... People do not band together to be free. Savages join together to hunt, to wage war, but certainly not to win liberty.[51]

Saint-Simon was wrong—and Madisonian thinking prevailed in the reformation of many Western governments. More than 200 years of political history have shown that people *do* join together in societies to advance personal freedom and individual rights. People have joined organizations (especially labor organizations) for similar reasons.

Social theorists have remained uncomfortable about all this. Auguste Comte, Saint-Simon's disciple and the founder of modern sociology, challenged workers to consider themselves servants of society and its goals rather than "insisting on the possession of what metaphysicians call political rights, and engaging in useless discussions about the distribution of power."[52] Later, Henri Fayol, who laid much of the groundwork for a theory of management, expressed dismay that individuals refused to subordinate their interests to a common goal, either of business or of nation: "ignorance, ambition, selfishness, laziness, weakness and all human passions tend to cause the general interest to be lost sight of in favor of individual interest and a perpetual struggle has to be waged against them."[53] More recently, Henry Mintzberg, a prominent organizational theorist, has likened organizations without common goals to "a bucket of crabs, each clawing at the others to come out on top," just as in society at large, where pulling toward private ends (a pluralist "political arena") "will be found in the breakdown of any form of government, under conditions typically described as anarchy or revolution."[54]

Some have tried to argue that "organization[s] would not exist if it were not for some common purpose."[55] Since they do exist, organizations must have the glue—or goals. This "goal paradigm" is still found in mainstream textbooks on organization,[56] but it has prompted growing criticism in more analytical works.[57] The main objection is that it is easy to talk about common, organizational goals in the abstract, yet difficult to find them in the real world. Certainly, organizations produce real, objective *consequences* (e.g., profits, deficits, wages, pollutants, all kinds of goods and costs). However, participants frequently disagree about the value of these consequences, about which of them are actual *goals* of the organization. In a firm, for instance, owners might view profits as goals, and wages as costs; workers might view wages as goals, and profits as costs; others might view both profits and wages as goals (say, top managers) or costs (say, consumers). It seems that people participate in organizations for a variety of purposes. It seems arbitrary to take some participants' purposes, or goals *for* an organization, to represent goals *of* the organization as a whole. And, for the most part, it seems that organizations look little like the organic, goal-seeking entities of management folklore.

Operational difficulties in identifying organizational goals are disappointing but not quite fatal for the goal paradigm. Theorists have developed a second line of defense, which interprets goal diversity not as evidence of a bad paradigm but bad organizations. In other words, if organizations do not, in fact, have common goals, then they lack the glue that holds social systems together. And thus, *of course*, they do not resemble functionally integrated organisms but, rather, *disintegrating* "buckets of crabs" or "houses divided against themselves,"[58] wars of parts against the whole,[59] fragmented and fractured communities of you've-got-yours-now-where's-mine egoists,[60] and so forth. As we have seen, the implication of these images is that social systems without common goals are falling apart and need something, like a transformational leader or spirit of community, to supply the missing glue of collective purpose.

What we can learn from Madison, on the other hand, is that no such purpose or glue is necessary. For two centuries, his system of competitive federalism has held together, as a system of *laws* not of leaders or public purposes. To this day, it works better than suggested by the disparaging images of transformational-leadership theorists. For instance, Burns's depiction of pluralist public agencies as pork barrels tended by transactional bureaucrats—who muddle along, spewing red tape, passing the buck, and dragging the system down with them—just does not square with the facts.[61] Despite sensational reports of government waste, public bureaucracies such as the Social Security Administration have served clients with fairness and efficiency relative to its resources.[62] Despite media criticism of governmental gridlock, divided government has enacted decent legislation, such as the Americans with Disabilities Act of 1990 and the Civil

Rights Act of 1991. As Charles E. Lindblom has stressed, Madisonian government works not because participants agree on goals, but because they can agree on specific activities (as in acts of legislation) that address their different goals.[63] So, too, in *private* organizations, like corporations, the glue that holds them together need not be consensus on ends but can be simply consent to means—agreement on rules, rights, and responsibilities that serve the separate interests of their participants.

Some organizational theorists have appreciated the point and concluded that organizations generally look like neither social organisms nor asocial free-for-alls, but more like political coalitions[64] or markets,[65] sets of contracts,[66] or stakeholders.[67] Empirically, models of this sort more fairly reflect the possibility that in organizations, as in society, participants may be less concerned with collective goals than with individual rights (e.g., contractual rights to a paycheck or return on investment, legal rights to equal opportunity or workers' compensation, moral rights to information about the risks of products or services). Madison's model indicates why these participant concerns are appropriate ethically.

The fundamental issue is that notions of a *common goal, general interest, public good*, and so forth are *theoretical* concepts (every bit as metaphysical as natural rights). Any *real* social consequence used to operationalize these theoretical terms is apt to impact persons in different, often arbitrary, ways. That is why participants find it hard to agree on *organizational goals*. Collective consequences like profits, wages, even organizational survival may greatly benefit some participants (say, employees of tobacco firms) but ultimately disadvantage others (say, tobacco customers who develop smoking-related illnesses). Even participants who share an interest in a particular organizational consequence may be affected very differently by it: Employees with a joint interest in higher wages may care less about an organization's overall salary pool—which could be distributed capriciously—than about *who gets what?*

Organizations and their leaders can deal with distributional concerns either by seeking fairness of outcomes to individuals (a Madisonian strategy) or by changing the subject. In the tradition of Saint-Simon, transformational leadership aims to get people's thoughts *off* distributional questions and refocus them on common goals, or communal interests. This may sound moral to James MacGregor Burns and like-minded theorists as well as some critics such as Joseph Rost.[68] But the ethical justification for diverting attention from individual to communal interests is unclear, given the hypothetical nature of the latter. If the operational consequences taken to represent collective ends are, in fact, weighted in favor of *some persons'* interests, it seems deceptive to win other persons' support by calling these weighted—perhaps biased—consequences *common goals, goods, interests,* and so on. Many people are quick to perceive such deception (as demonstrated in public ridicule of trickle-down economics). Other people are more trusting and vulnerable (as shown by supporters of televangelists' visions). In any event, reliance on extraordinary leaders to define collective purposes just papers over the problem of faction and, as Madison saw, puts participants at risk of manipulation, or worse.

In sum, contrary to the claims of theorists like Burns, common goals are no more imperative ethically than they are empirically. As Madison realized, people can still care for one another, if not for some alleged common good. As he explained in *Federalist* No. 10, factional mischief does not follow directly from diversity of interests; rather, it occurs when some people try to impose their interests on others. In other words, the problem of faction is not that individuals pursue separate interests, but that some are stronger, smarter, or richer than the rest and may use their power to take unfair advantage of other persons. Thus, Madison proposed a safer way to prevent factional mischief than transforming individuals and eliminating diversity of interests. His solution was to deter advantage-taking: to devise an impartial system of rules, checks, and balances that can accommodate personal ambitions while protecting each person's basic interests from impairment by others—especially leaders who function in the name of the community.

CONCLUSION

Let me conclude by illustrating what difference a Madisonian perspective might make in a familiar kind of organization. The views of Saint-Simon, Mintzberg, Burns, and later leadership theorists are typified by Bennis in a classic article about his experiences as president of the University of Cincinnati. Wondering "Where have all the leaders gone?" Bennis sees factional misbehavior all about him. The university, he writes, "has blunted and diffused its main purposes" through a proliferation of interest groups.[69] It is besieged by "external" constituencies such as alumni, parents, and lawmakers. It is "fragmented" by internal pressure groups of all sorts:

> We have a coalition of women's groups, a gay society, black organiza-
> tions for both students and faculty, a veterans' group, a continuing edu-
> cation group for women, a handicapped group, a faculty council on
> Jewish affairs, a faculty union organized by the American Association
> of University Professors, an organization for those staff members who
> are neither faculty nor administrators, an organization of middle-
> management staff members, an association of women administrators, a
> small, elite group of graduate fellows.[70]

These groups, Bennis complains, go their own separate ways—
marking the end of community.

Like Bennis, many of us work in complex universities with diverse
aims, interest groups, and external dependencies. However, unlike
Bennis, few might find such diversity objectionable. What, exactly, is
wrong with women's groups or black groups or disabled groups or
staff associations or other groups that flourish on our campuses?

Why do differences among these groups—in viewpoints, interests,
and goals *for* the university—make us less a community, or just a
bucket of crabs?

By invoking the ritual formula that organizations *should* have
common purposes—and by painting organizations without them as
snake pits—theorists perpetuate the illusion that there is something per-
verse about people who behave differently. Bennis, for example, por-
trays participants who assert their legal rights in universities as "belly-
achers" who take advantage of the system, waste the organization's time
and money in court, and prevent the proper authorities (especially presidents, like himself) from exercising real leadership. He is critical of persons who bring suits for injuries, malpractice, civil rights violations, or
who are just "fed up with being ignored, neglected, excluded, denied,
subordinated."[71] To counter those who might be tempted to file
complaints under consumer protection laws, he adds:

> At my own and many other universities ..., we are now in the process of
> rewriting our catalogs so carefully that it will be virtually impossible for
> any student (read: consumer) to claim that we haven't fulfilled our end
> of the bargain. At the same time, because we have to be so careful, we
> can never express our hopes, our dreams, and our bold ideas of what a
> university could provide for the prospective student.[72]

This is the rub, then. Leaders cannot do what they want, because constituents have bold ideas of their own about what the organization

should provide in return for their cooperation, and because "the courts are substituting their judgments for the expertise of the institution."[73] "Time was," Bennis says wistfully, "when the leader could decide— period. A Henry Ford, an Andrew Carnegie, a Nicholas Murray Butler, could issue a ukase—and all would automatically obey."[74] (But no longer. Thanks to government, unions, lawyers, and their recalcitrant clients.)

Thanks, also, to Madison and the framers. Were it not for the system of law they set in motion, individuals in harm's way of organizations might have little recourse at all. Bennis evokes a timeless undercurrent of leadership theory that Madison struggled against in 1787: a longing for "the philosophical race of kings wished for by Plato."[75] Leaders, in this view, are to fabricate a vision of collective purpose—if necessary, a unifying myth. Followers are to put aside personal interests in its pursuit. (Madison, no doubt, read Plato's parable of the poor carpenter who fell ill and was advised by a doctor to look after himself for a time before carrying out his assigned duties to the community; Plato remarks that the worker must be inspired to ignore such advice, to "go back to his normal routine, and either regain his health and get on with his job, or, if his constitution won't stand it, die and be rid of his troubles.")[76] Modern theorists are more sensitive to personal entitlements than the ancient Greeks, but the very concept of transformational leadership implies that individual interests are less legitimate than collective ends. Why else would they require transformation? Accordingly, participants who do not subordinate their interests to *organizational* goals—as envisioned by leaders or majorities—are disparaged, even when their expectations seem quite reasonable. In a university, for instance, what is so *unreasonable* about students expecting to be treated like consumers? Or expecting accurate information in a college catalog? Or expecting the university to fulfill *its* end of the bargain? It is nonsense to suggest that leaders cannot meet such basic expectations and still express *their* hopes and dreams. And it is presumptuous to suppose that these expectations are less valid than the visions of people in power.

In a recent study of academic leadership, Birnbaum responds appropriately to Bennis's plaintive question, Where have all the great leaders of the past gone? "They are dead," says Birnbaum, "along with the simpler times in which formal leaders could wield unbridled power to get what they wanted. In today's world of greater participation, shared influence, conflicting constituencies, and assorted other complexities, heeding the current vogue of calls for charismatic presidents who can transform their institutions would be more likely to lead to campus disruption than to constructive change."[77] Birnbaum's conclusions are based on a five-year longitudinal study of how college and university presidents exercise leadership. His research challenges a number of myths about effective leaders.

Myth 1—Presidents need to create a vision for their organization that transcends individual interests. Birnbaum found otherwise. Successful leaders and acceptable visions reflected the diverse interests of constituents rather than the leader's goals for the institution. One effective president advised: "[D]o a lot of listening. And when you do that, solicit the dreams and hopes from the people. Tell the people the good things you are finding. And in three to six months, take these things and report them as the things you would like to see happen."[78]

Myth 2—Presidents should be transformational leaders. Birnbaum discovered that transformational leadership, which changes participants' values and goals for the organization, is abnormal in universities. "Good leaders," he reports, "help change their institutions, not through transformation and the articulation of new goals or values, but through transactions that emphasize values already in place and move the institution toward attaining them."[79] Transformational efforts to initiate grand schemes "inflict leadership" on constituencies and cause more factional strife than they resolve.

Myth 3—Charisma is an important aspect of leadership. Birnbaum found only a few institutions where presidential charisma helped rather than hindered the organization. He proposes that charisma has more to do with impression management than the hard work of running an institution. It allows presidents to substitute glitz for substance, and it encourages both leaders and followers to act on faith, as opposed to an understanding of the situation. Most importantly, reliance on presidential charisma tends to diminish the authority of other decision-makers and weakens the formal administrative structure of the university. The focus on a leader's persona diverts attention from the long-term job of building an "institutional infrastructure" of mutually accepted practices, rights, and responsibilities.

Birnbaum (a former college president himself) views the support of multiple constituencies as central to presidential effectiveness. His data indicate that the kind of imperial presidency suggested by Bennis is *not* effective. Among institutions studied, a primary cause of presidential failure was unilateral action that furthered presidential goals but was perceived to violate constituents' (particularly faculty) rights. In contrast, effective academic leaders in Birnbaum's sample seem downright Madisonian. The president of one successful institution described his college as "a political system: a 'pluralistic democracy,' with himself as a 'governor,' " which meant treating faculty, union leaders, and other administrators as colleagues, instead of subordinates.[80] In general, successful academic leaders respected diversity (appreciating, not deprecating, different values). They respected participants' own goals for the institution (building on them, versus correcting them). They respected individuals' right-claims (placing the needs of people before system requirements). And they respected shared leadership (dispersing power, not just decentralizing it)—all clearly Madisonian priorities.

There is a final point. I suspect that most of us work in universities with *some* Madisonian characteristics, whether top administrators encourage them or not. It is interesting that academic professionals create and seek employment in organizations with such institutionalized checks and balances as self-supporting departments, faculty senates, unions, tenure policies, grievance processes, and committees representing every interest imaginable. If this sort of federalist system is what we choose for ourselves, if we claim academic freedom as our right, why should we prescribe any less freedom for others.

NOTES

1. Saul K. Padover, ed., *The Complete Madison* (New York: Harper & Brothers, 1953), 17–18.

2. Abraham Zaleznik, *The Managerial Mystique* (New York: Harper & Row, 1989), 11.

3. John W. Gardner, *On Leadership* (New York: Free Press, 1990), 94–93.

4. Warren Bennis and Burt Nanus, *Leaders: The Strategies for Taking Charge* (New York: Harper & Row, 1985), 2.

5. James MacGregor Burns, *Leadership* (New York: Harper & Row, 1978).

6. Ibid., 4.

7. Ibid., 20.

8. Ibid.

9. Ibid., 3.

10. Bernard M. Bass, *Leadership and Performance Beyond Expectations* (New York: Free Press, 1985).

11. Ibid., 31.

12. Ibid., 187.

13. Jay A. Conger and Rabindra N. Kanungo, "Behavioral Dimensions of Charismatic Leadership," *Charismatic Leadership*, edited by Jay A. Conger, Rabindra N. Kanungo, and Associates (San Francisco: Jossey-Bass, 1988), 78–97.

14. Bernard M. Bass, "From Transactional to Transformational Leadership: Learning to Share the Vision," *Organizational Dynamics* 18, no. 19–31 (1990), 20.

15. Ibid., 25.

16. Ibid., 26.

17. Burns, *Leadership*, 405.

18. James MacGregor Burns, *The Deadlock of Democracy* (Englewood Cliffs, NJ: Prentice-Hall, 1963), 6.

19. Marcus Cunliffe, *George Washington: Man and Monument* (New York: New American Library, 1982).

20. Samuel Eliot Morison, *The Oxford History of the American People* (New York: Oxford University Press, 1965), 230.

21. James Thomas Flexner, *George Washington in the American Revolution* (Boston: Little, Brown and Company, 1967).

22. Ibid., 542–43.

23. Washington's inspirational effect on his compatriots is well illustrated by an incident at the close of the war. As hostilities with Britain diminished, so did cooperation between the states with regard to honoring war debts. American soldiers were owed years of back pay; officers had been promised pensions if they served for the duration; and now state representatives were reluctant to pay the bill, hoping the army would just go home. The army instead grew resentful at the lack of public gratitude for members' sacrifices in the cause of independence. A mass meeting of officers was called to discuss ways of securing their rights. Proposed actions included refusing to lay down arms or disband, marching on Congress, and even forming a military community in unsettled land. Some officers wanted Washington to lead the movement against civil authorities, but he appeared at their meeting and argued for restraint. His audience remained unpersuaded—until Washington pulled from his pocket a piece of paper, a conciliatory letter from Congress. Flexner (1967: 507) describes the scene:

> The officers stirred impatiently in their seats, and then suddenly every heart missed a beat. Something was the matter with His Excellency. He seemed unable to read the paper. He paused in bewilderment. He fumbled in his waistcoat pocket. And then he pulled out something that only his intimates had seen him wear. A pair of glasses. With infinite sweetness and melancholy, he explained, "Gentlemen, you will permit me to put on my spectacles, for I have not only grown grey but almost blind in the service of my country."

With tough veterans moved to tears, Washington read the letter and left. Passions cooled, officers drifted off, and plans for insurrection were abandoned.

24. James Madison, *Federalist* No. 10, *Federalist* No. 49, *Federalist* No. 51, *The Federalist Papers*, edited by Clinton Rossiter (New York: Mentor, 1961), 77–84, 313–17, 320–25.

25. Ibid., No. 51, 322.

26. See Robert A. Dahl, *A Preface to Democratic Theory* (Chicago: University of Chicago Press, 1956); Burns, *Deadlock*; and James L. Sundquist, *Constitutional Reform and Effective Government* (Washington, DC: Brookings Institution, 1986).

27. Burns, *Leadership*, 38.

28. Frederick Herzberg, *Work and the Nature of Man* (New York: Crowell, 1966).

29. Burns, *Leadership*, 34.

30. Edgar H. Schein, *Organizational Psychology*, 3rd edition (Englewood Cliffs, NJ: Prentice-Hall, 1980). Richard M. Steers and Lyman W. Porter (Eds.), *Motivation and Work Behavior*, 4th edition (New York: McGraw-Hill, 1987).

31. Bruce J. Avolio, David A. Waldman, and Francis J. Yammarino, "Leading in the 1990s: The Four I's of Transformational Leadership," *Journal of European Industrial Training* 15, no. 9–16 (1991), 15.

32. Padover, *Complete Madison*, 40–1.

33. Warren Bennis, *Why Leaders Can't Lead* (San Francisco: Jossey-Bass, 1989). Amitai Etzioni, *The Moral Dimension* (New York: Free Press, 1988).

34. Padover, *Complete Madison*, 41.

35. Ibid., 42.

36. Bennis, *Why Leaders Can't Lead*, 144.

37. Ibid., 154.

38. Jane M. Howell and Bruce J. Avolio, "The Ethics of Charismatic Leadership: Submission or Liberation?" *Academy of Management Executive* 6 (1992): 43–54.

39. Gary A. Yukl, *Leadership in Organizations*, 2nd edition (Englewood Cliffs, NJ: Prentice-Hall, 1989).

40. Bass, "From Transactional to Transformational Leadership," 24–5.

41. Nancy C. Roberts and Raymond Trevor Bradley, "Limits of Charisma," *Charismatic Leadership*, edited by Jay A. Conger, Rabindra N. Kanungo, and Associates (San Francisco: Jossey-Bass, 1988), 253–75.

42. Howell and Avolio, "The Ethics of Charismatic Leadership."

43. Guillermo J. Grenier, *Inhuman Relations* (Philadelphia: Temple University Press, 1988), xiii.

44. Ibid., 26.

45. Ibid., 90.

46. Ibid., 77.

47. Ibid., 147.

48. Selznick believes that leaders should motivate followers to think for themselves—so long as this contributes to institutional survival and integrity. Similarly, Kanungo tends to equate empowerment with motivation. He rejects notions of empowerment as sharing power or resources. He prefers a view of empowerment as "enabling," which "heightens the motivation for task accomplishment" (418). So conceived, "the behavioral effects of empowerment . . . results [*sic*] in workers both initiating and persevering in

work behavior." See Philip Selznick, *Leadership in Administration* (Evanston, IL: Row Peterson, 1957).

49. Charles A. Reich, "The Individual Sector," *Yale Law Journal* 100 (1991), 1409–448.

50. Claude-Henri de Saint-Simon, "On the Industrial System," *The Political Thought of Saint-Simon*, edited by Ghita Ionescu (London: Oxford University Press, 1976) (Original, 1821), 153–81.

51. Ibid., 158.

52. Auguste Comte, "System of Positive Polity," translated by J. H. Bridges, *Auguste Comte and Positivism*, edited by Gertrud Lenzer (New York: Harper & Row, 1975) (Original, 1851–54), 307–476.

53. Henri Fayol, *General and Industrial Management*, translated by Constance Storrs (London: Pitman, 1949) (Original, 1916), 60.

54. Henry Mintzberg, *Power in and Around Organizations* (Englewood Cliffs, NJ: Prentice-Hall, 1983), 461, 462.

55. Richard H. Hall, *Organizations*, 2nd edition (Englewood Cliffs, NJ: Prentice-Hall, 1977), 83.

56. Richard L. Daft, *Organization Theory and Design*, 2nd edition (St. Paul, MN: West, 1986).

57. For example, see Richard M. Cyert and James G. March, *A Behavioral Theory of the Firm* (Englewood Cliffs, NJ: Prentice-Hall, 1963). David Silverman, *The Theory of Organizations* (London: Heinemann, 1970). Petro Georgiou, "The Goal Paradigm and Notes Towards a Counter Paradigm," *Administrative Science Quarterly* 18 (1973): 291–310. Michael Keeley, *A Social-Contract Theory of Organizations* (Notre Dame, IN: University of Notre Dame Press, 1988). Karl E. Weick, "Sources of Order in Underorganized Systems: Themes in Recent Organizational Theory," *Organizational Theory and Inquiry*, edited by Yvonna S. Lincoln (Beverly Hills, CA: Sage, 1985), 106–36.

58. Mintzberg, *Power in and Around Organizations*.

59. Ibid.

60. Bennis, *Why Leaders Can't Lead*.

61. James Q. Wilson, *Bureaucracy* (New York: Basic Books, 1989).

62. See Charles T. Goodsell, *The Case for Bureaucracy* (Chatham, NJ: Chatham House, 1983). Jerry L. Mashaw, *Bureaucratic Justice* (New Haven, CT: Yale University Press, 1983).

63. Charles E. Lindblom, *The Intelligence of Democracy* (New York: Free Press, 1965).

64. Cyert and March, *Behavioral Theory of the Firm*.

65. Jeffrey Pfeffer and Gerald R. Salancik, *The External Control of Organizations* (New York: Harper & Row, 1978).

66. Keeley, *Social-Contract Theory of Organizations*.

67. R. Edward Freeman and Daniel R. Gilbert, Jr., *Corporate Strategy and the Search for Ethics* (Englewood Cliffs, NJ: Prentice-Hall, 1988).

68. Joseph C. Rost, *Leadership for the Twenty-First Century* (New York: Praeger, 1991).

69. Warren Bennis, "Where Have All the Leaders Gone?" *Technology Review* 79 (1977): 3–12. Reprinted in *Contemporary Issues in Leadership*, 2nd edition, edited by William E. Rosenbach and Robert L. Taylor (Boulder, CO: Westview Press, 1989), 5–23.

70. Ibid., 8.

71. Ibid.

72. Ibid., 13–14.

73. Ibid., 10.

74. Ibid., 7.

75. *Federalist* No. 49, 315.

76. Plato, *The Republic*, translated by Desmond Lee, 2nd edition (Harmondsworth, England: Penguin, 1974), 406.

77. Robert Birnbaum, *How Academic Leadership Works* (San Francisco: Jossey-Bass, 1992), xii–xiii.

78. Ibid., 26.

79. Ibid., 30.

80. Ibid., 127.

9

What Is Ethical Foreign Policy Leadership?

Joseph S. Nye, Jr.

In the book *Just War*, Charles Guthrie and Michael Quinlan write, "[M]oral accountability is a central part of what it means to be a human being."[1] While this description applies to everyone no matter what role the person plays in life, it takes on a special poignancy when we examine the ethics of how leaders formulate and implement foreign policy. Their decisions and behavior potentially influence the well-being of people at home and abroad. Leaders may draw nations into war, establish peace, create famine, or ensure survival of people. That is why ethical leaders and leadership are fundamental to the conduct of foreign policy.

ETHICAL STANDARDS FOR JUDGING LEADERS

In practice, we usually judge ethics in three dimensions: ends, means, and consequences. By *ends* I refer to intentions (as in *his ends were just*). Good goals have to meet our moral standards, as well as a feasibility

This chapter was originally delivered as The Sir Michael Quinlan Lecture, London, May 23, 2012. It is derived from my book *Presidential Leadership and the Creation of the American Era*, Princeton University Press, 2013.

test. Effective means are those that achieve the goals, but ethical means depend on the quality, not just the efficacy, of the approaches employed. When it comes to means, leaders must decide whether they will use hard power—inducements or threats—or soft power—values, culture, and policies that attract people to their goals.[2] Using hard power when soft power will do or using soft power when hard power is necessary raises serious ethical questions about a leader's approach to a foreign policy issue. As for consequences, a leader's effectiveness involves achieving the group's goals, but ethical consequences mean good results not just for the in-group but for outsiders as well. Of course in practice, effectiveness and ethics are often closely related. A leader who pursues unrealistic goals or uses ineffective means can produce terrible moral consequences for followers. For example, even if we attribute good intentions to George W. Bush's invasion of Iraq, unrealistic goals and inadequate means had immoral consequences. Thus, inadequate contextual intelligence and reckless reality-testing that produced bad consequences can result in ethical failure. Conversely, a leader's good intentions are not the only proof of what is sometimes misleadingly called *moral clarity*.

Should leaders be judged by the same moral standard as ordinary citizens? Take the Biblical injunction "thou shalt not kill." In choosing a roommate or a spouse, that commandment would rank high on the list of desired moral values. At the same time, most people would not vote for an absolute pacifist to become president of their country. Presidents and prime ministers have a fiduciary obligation to protect the people who elected them, and under certain circumstances, that may involve ordering troops into battle to take lives. Sometimes leaders must have *dirty hands*, meaning that they must take actions they would otherwise regard as immoral.

Max Weber famously distinguished an ethic of ultimate ends from an ethic of responsibility. In the former, absolute moral imperatives must not be violated for the sake of good consequences, but an ethic of responsibility must focus on the results. Weber warns that "[w]hoever seeks the salvation of his own soul and the rescue of souls, does not do so by means of politics."[3] In the philosophical traditions of the Western Enlightenment, ethicists distinguish a deontological or rule-based approach associated with Immanuel Kant from a consequentialist approach associated with utilitarians such as Jeremy Bentham and John Stuart Mill.[4] The two traditions provide important strands of contemporary moral reasoning in the West today, but they are often difficult to reconcile.

Take Harry Truman's decision to drop the atomic bomb on Hiroshima in an effort to end World War II. Although millions of lives had already been lost in the war, Truman was told that he could save hundreds of thousands of American and Japanese lives by avoiding a land invasion of the Japanese home islands. Moreover, the numbers killed at Hiroshima (and Nagasaki) were fewer than those who had been killed in the conventional firebombing of Tokyo or Dresden. Was Truman's act morally justified? Strict deontologists and just war theorists would answer that two wrongs do not make a right and that the deliberate destruction of so many innocent civilians can never be justified. Some consequentialists could reply that nuclear deterrence helped prevent World War III and that Truman later redeemed himself by refusing to use nuclear weapons when General McArthur urged him to do so in the Korean War. That taboo against nuclear use has lasted for nearly seven decades.

Moreover, if Truman had refused to drop the bomb because of his personal moral beliefs, at what price does a leader's concern about personal integrity translate into selfishness and a violation of followers' trust? There are no easy answers to such problems, and recent scientific discoveries suggest that evolution may have hardwired the dilemma into the human brain. Kenneth Winston argues that in daily practice, people's sense of moral obligation tends to come from three sources. One is a sense of conscience that is personally or religiously informed and leads individuals to try to achieve a sense of moral integrity. A second involves rules of common morality that society treats as obligations for all individuals, and a third includes codes of professional ethics and conventional expectations that might be considered the duties of one's role.[5] Leaders are subject to all three, and these different sources of moral obligation are frequently in tension with each other. Often there is no single solution. As Isaiah Berlin once noted, since "the ends of men are many, and not all of them are in principle compatible with each other, then the possibility of conflict—and tragedy—can never wholly be eliminated from human life, either personal or social."[6]

Many societies have ethical systems that stress impartiality and have an analogue to *the golden rule*—"do unto others as you would have them do unto you." Your interests and my interests should be treated the same way. John Rawls used the wonderful metaphor of an imaginary veil of ignorance about our initial relative positions to illustrate justice as fairness.[7] However, appealing to an intuitive sense of fairness—treating others as you would want to be treated, not playing favorites, and being sensible to individual needs—does not always provide a solution. Amartya Sen invites us to imagine a parent with a flute and three children, each of whom wants it. The first child says, "I made it"; the second says, "I am the only one who can play it"; and the third says, "I have no other toys."[8] Even with a thought experiment about deciding behind a veil of ignorance in which none of the children knows which one is which, the principle of justice as fairness remains unclear in some cases. In such instances, the parent (or leader) may find it more appropriate to turn to a procedural or institutional solution in which the children bargain with each other or agree on a lottery or on a neutral figure to decide how time with the flute will be allocated or shared. The parent can also teach or coach the children about sharing, which is a different image of leadership as persuasion and education rather than exercise of command authority. Teaching followers about processes and institutions—helping a group decide *how* to decide—is often one of the most important moral roles that leaders (and parents) play.

ETHICAL DESIGN AND MAINTENANCE OF INSTITUTIONS

One of the most important skills of good leaders is to design and maintain systems and institutions. This relates both to effectiveness and to ethics. Poorly designed institutions are those that fail to achieve a group's purpose not in each particular instance, but over the long term. Well-designed institutions include means for self-correction as well as ways of constraining the failures of leaders. Poorly designed or led institutions can also lead people astray. Obedience to institutional authority can be bad at times. In 1963 Yale professor Stanley Milgram devised a now famous experiment to test obedience to authority. The experiment encouraged students to administer what they thought were brutal electric shocks to their colleagues.[9] Stanford psychologist Philip Zimbardo conducted a simulated prison experiment in 1971 that also demonstrated the capacity of intelligent people to blindly submit to authority.[10] Both experiments and the violence and humiliation of prisoners at the Abu Ghraib prison in Iraq remind us of both the importance and the danger of poorly designed institutions. The Abu Ghraib guards were reservists without special training who lacked supervision and were given the task of softening up detainees. It is not surprising that the result was various forms of torture. The moral flaws were not simply in the prison guards but also in the higher level leaders who created and failed to monitor a flawed institutional framework. Good leadership is not merely inspiring people with a noble vision, but involves creating and maintaining the systems and institutions that allow effective and moral implementation.

DUTIES BEYOND BORDERS

Not only are ethical standards for judging leaders more complicated than those we use for judging fellow citizens in daily life, but the domain of foreign policy adds an additional level of complexity. To what extent should leaders pay attention to the rights, institutions, and welfare of those who are not their fellow citizens? Skeptics argue that where there is no sense of community, there are no moral rights and duties, and that the classic statement about ethics in international politics was the Athenians' response to the conquered Melians' plea for mercy "that the weak must give in to the strong."[11]

If international relations were simply the realm of *kill or be killed*, then presumably there is no choice, and there would be no role for morality. But international politics consists of more than mere survival, and pretending choices do not exist is merely a disguised form of choice. A degree of international human community does exist, although it is weak. The leader who says, "I had no choice," often did have a choice, albeit not a pleasant one.

International politics is often called anarchic. Anarchy means *without government*, but international anarchy does not necessarily mean chaos or total disorder. International affairs lack the discipline of a domestic leviathan, but there are rudimentary practices and institutions that provide enough order to allow some important choices: balance of power, international law and norms, and international organizations. Even in the extreme circumstances of war, law and morality sometimes play a role. The just war doctrine originated in the early Christian church as Augustine and others wrestled with the dilemma that if the good did not fight back, they would perish and only the bad would survive. It became secularized after the seventeenth century, and today provides a broad normative structure that considers all three dimensions of good ends, discriminating proportional means, and the probability of successful consequences.

Nonetheless, different perceptions affect the way leaders and followers frame their moral choices. Realists see a world composed primarily of states; liberals see a world of peoples with rights, and cosmopolitans stress the importance of individuals. However, these simple categories are not exclusive, and in practice, leaders sometimes mix these views in inconsistent ways when they formulate foreign policies. As a result there is no single view on what duties citizens owe to foreigners, or when and what types of intervention are moral or not. An insular leader thinks only of the concerns of his own group, but a moral leader also considers the types and degree of consequences for those who are not members of the group. The image of a community of humankind may be a weak outer circle in a set of concentric circles of identity, but it still involves some degree of moral duties beyond borders.

The leadership theorist Barbara Kellerman accuses Bill Clinton of insular leadership in failing to respond to the genocide in Rwanda in 1994, and Clinton himself has criticized his reactions.[12] Yet had Clinton tried to send American troops, he would have encountered stiff resistance in parts of his administration, the Congress, and public opinion. Particularly after the death of American soldiers in an earlier humanitarian intervention in Somalia, his followers were not ready for another intervention. Clinton has acknowledged that he could have done more to help the United Nations and other nations to save some of the lives that were lost in Rwanda, but good leaders today are often caught between their cosmopolitan inclinations and their more traditional obligations to the followers who elected them. We may admire leaders who make efforts to increase their followers' concern for the consequences of their actions on the out-group, but it does little good to hold them to an impossible standard whose pursuit could undercut their capacity to remain leaders.

PRUDENCE AS A VIRTUE

How then should we judge the ethics of leaders in foreign policy? They act not in an amoral world but clearly in Max Weber's world of non-perfectionist ethics. Arnold Wolfers has argued that in international affairs, where presidents and prime ministers can have such destructive effects, leaders cannot always follow moral rules. The best one can hope for in judging the ethics of leaders in foreign policy is that they made "the best moral choices that circumstances permit."[13] This is a necessary standard but certainly not a sufficient one.

Such a broad rule of prudence can easily be abused. At the same time, it does not imply amorality. What are some of the ways we can reason about whether leaders did indeed make *the best moral choices* under the circumstances? When we look at the goals that leaders seek, we do not expect them to pursue justice similar to their domestic policies. After all, John Rawls believed that the conditions for his theory of justice applied only to domestic society.[14] Nonetheless, he argued that duties beyond borders for a liberal society should include mutual aid, and respect for rights and institutions that insure basic human rights while allowing people in a diverse world to determine their own affairs as much as possible. Thus, the criteria I suggest for judging leaders' goals include a vision that expresses widely attractive values at home and abroad, but prudently balances those values and assesses risks so that there is a reasonable prospect of their success. This means we judge a leader not only on his or her character and intentions but also on his or her contextual intelligence when it comes to assessing ends and goals.

Regarding ethical means, I include criteria borrowed from Just War theory, such as proportional and discriminate use of force as well as Rawls's liberal concern for minimal degrees of intervention to respect the rights and institutions of others. As for ethical consequences, I would judge whether leaders succeeded in promoting long-term national interests, whether they respected cosmopolitan values by avoiding extreme insularity, and whether they educated their followers to try to create and broaden moral standards at home and abroad. While such a list is modest and by no means complete, it at least provides some basic guidance that goes beyond simple generalities about prudence when we look for answers case by case. Let me illustrate with two recent American presidents: Ronald Reagan and George H. W. Bush.

Ronald Reagan

Ronald Reagan is often cited as the exemplar of a moral foreign policy leader par excellence. A movement conservative, he is remembered for speeches that issued a strong call for moral clarity. As the *Economist* put it, his appeal rested on "knowing that mere reason, essential though it is, is only half of the business of reaching momentous decisions. You also need solid-based instincts, feelings, whatever the word is for the other part of the mind. 'I have a gut feeling', Reagan said over and over again, when he was working out what to do and say."[15]

Like Franklin D. Roosevelt, Reagan lacked a first-class intellect, but made up for it with a first-class temperament. He radiated optimism, and illustrated the point that style can influence substance. As my colleague David Gergen observes, Reagan changed how we think about ourselves. At the same time, he could be "so dreamy and inattentive to detail that he allowed dramatic mistakes to occur."[16] When people today call for a *Reaganite foreign policy*, they tend to mean the moral clarity that went with Reagan's simplification of complex issues and his effective rhetoric in presentation of values. Not only is this inadequate moral reasoning for reasons explained earlier, but it also mistakes the success of Reagan's moral leadership, which included the ability to bargain and compromise as he pursued his policy.

Nonetheless, clear and clearly stated objectives can educate and motivate the public. The key question is whether Reagan was prudent in balancing aspirations and risks of his goals and objectives. Some people have argued that his initial rhetoric in his first term not only created a dangerous degree of tension and distrust in U.S.-Soviet relations that increased the prospect of a miscalculation or an accident leading to war, but also created incentives to bargain, which Reagan put to good advantage when Gorbachev came to power in Reagan's second term. As for insularity, Reagan expressed his values in universal terms, though he was sometimes accused of hypocrisy for focusing on Soviet violations of human rights while ignoring the violations perpetrated by a number of American Third World client regimes. He was quite prepared to live with apartheid in South Africa, and it took two years after the first protests before he reduced his support for the Marcos regime in the Philippines.

With regard to means, Reagan had a mixed record. The circumvention of legal means during the Iran/Contra affair set a bad precedent in terms of domestic as well as international norms and institutions. And the Reagan Doctrine of using covert action to fight wars against leftist regimes in Central America not only raised legal issues with Congress, but also included the mining of harbors in Nicaragua, a country with which the United States was officially at peace. Whether these transgressions of autonomy and institutional restraints were justified by realist necessity is debatable, but the damage was real.

In terms of consequences, Reagan undoubtedly advanced the national interests of the United States, though most of the credit for ending the Cold War and the Soviet Union belongs to Gorbachev. In any event, Reagan took good advantage of the opportunity in a manner that was not limited just to insular American interests. Reagan's rhetoric broadened moral discourse at home and abroad, but it was sometimes subverted by actions (such as support for apartheid in South Africa) that appeared hypocritical in terms of the values that Reagan proclaimed for himself and for his country. By and large, he had an ethical foreign policy in the goals he set and most of the larger consequences to which he contributed, but not always in terms of the means he used.

George H. W. Bush

George H. W. Bush's long career in various government positions equipped him with the best contextual intelligence about international affairs since Eisenhower. As Nicholas Burns, who served under Bush, argued, "Bush's accomplishments in ending the Cold War, unifying Germany, amassing the Gulf War coalition that defeated Saddam Hussein in that same year, and in then pivoting to start Israeli-Palestinian negotiations at Madrid make him arguably the most success-ful foreign policy presidents of the last 50 years."[17] Or as Bush himself summed it up (with Brent Scowcroft), "[w]hat Harry Truman's contain-ment policy and succeeding administrations had cultivated, we were able to bring to final fruition. Did we see what was coming when we entered office? No, we did not, nor could we have planned it. ... The long-run framework of Bush foreign policy was very deliber-ate: encouraging, guiding, and managing change without provoking backlash and crackdown. In the short run, the practical effort inclu-ded as well a certain amount of seat of the pants planning and diplomacy. ... We eluded the shadow of another Versailles."[18]

As his own account describes, Bush did not have transformational objectives (with some exceptions like the unification of Germany). Instead, he was interested in avoiding disaster in a world that was changing dramatically. As he and his team responded to the forces that were largely outside of his control, he set goals and objectives that bal-anced opportunities and realism in a prudent manner. For example, some critics have faulted him for not being more forthcoming in sup-porting the national aspiration of Soviet republics like Ukraine in 1990, or for failing to go all the way to Baghdad to unseat Saddam Hussein in the Gulf War, or for sending Brent Scowcroft to Beijing to maintain relations with China after the Tiananmen massacre of 1989, but in each instance, Bush was limiting his short-run objectives to pur-sue long-term stability as a goal. Critics have complained that Bush did not set more transformational objectives in relation to Russian democracy, or the Middle East, or nuclear nonproliferation at a time when world politics seemed fluid, but again he remained focused on questions of stability more than of new visions. In ethical terms, although Bush did not express a strong moral vision, it is difficult to make the case that he should have been less prudent and taken more risks.

As for means, Bush was respectful of institutions and norms at home and abroad, going to Congress for authorization of the Gulf War and to the United Nations for a resolution under Chapter 7 of the Charter. Although a realist in his thinking, he could be Wilsonian in his tactics. In terms of proportionate and discriminate use of force, Bush's termination of the ground war in Iraq after only four days was motivated in part by humanitarian reactions to the slaughter of Iraqi troops as well as the concern that Iraq not be so weakened that it could not balance the threatening power of its neighbor Iran. While his invasion of Panama to capture (and later try) Manuel Noriega may have violated Panamanian sovereignty, it had a degree of de facto legitimacy given Noriega's notorious behavior. And when Bush organized his coalition to prosecute the Gulf War, he not only worked with the United Nations but also included a number of Arab countries who were needed, not for military purposes, but for the legitimacy that they added to the coalition. With his careful combination of hard and soft power, Bush established a policy that raised moral standards at home and abroad and was capable of being sustainable in the future.

In terms of consequences, Bush was a worthy fiduciary in accomplishing national goals and managed to do so in a manner that was not unduly insular and that caused minimal damage to the interests of foreigners. He was careful not to humiliate Gorbachev and to manage the transition to Yeltsin in Russia. At the same time, not all foreigners were adequately protected, for example, when Bush assigned a lower priority to Kurds in northern Iraq, to dissidents in China, or to Bosnians who were embroiled in a civil war in the former Yugoslavia. In that sense, Bush's realism set limits to his cosmopolitanism.

Could Bush have done more under the circumstances? Possibly, or perhaps, he might have done more in the second term, and losing that opportunity was an instance of bad moral luck. And with a better set of communications skills, Bush might have been able to do more to educate the American public about the changing nature of world they faced after the Cold War. But given the uncertainties of history, I am tempted to agree with Nicholas Burns that Bush had one of the best foreign policies of the past century in both the effective and the ethical meaning of the term.

WHAT IS *GOOD* FOREIGN POLICY?

Contrary to the assumptions of leadership theory, there is little evidence to conclude that leaders with transformational objectives or inspirational styles are better in the sense of more effective, or *better* in its ethical meaning. The best record goes to the incremental and transactional George H. W. Bush (Bush 41), and the poorest records belong to the transformational and inspirational leaders like his son, George W. Bush (Bush 43).

September 11, 2001, led to a transformation in American foreign policy. George W. Bush started as a limited realist with little interest in foreign policy, but his objectives became transformational after the crisis. Like Wilson, FDR, and Truman, Bush 43 turned to the rhetoric of democracy to rally his followers in a time of crisis. Bush's 2002 National Security Strategy, which came to be called the Bush Doctrine, proclaimed that the United States would "identify and eliminate terrorists wherever they are, together with the regimes that sustain them." In this new game there were no rules. The solution to the roots of terrorism was to spread democracy everywhere. In the words of historian John Gaddis, "[i]t is 'Fukuyama plus force', and designed to make terrorism as obsolete as slavery or piracy. Iraq was the most feasible place to strike the next blow."[19]

Bush invaded Iraq ostensibly to change the regime and to remove Saddam Hussein's capacity to use weapons of mass destruction. Bush cannot be blamed for the intelligence failure that attributed such weapons to Saddam, since such estimates were widely shared by many other countries. While no weapons were found, American forces quickly overthrew Saddam. But the removal of Saddam did not accomplish the mission, and inadequate understanding of the context plus poor planning and management undercut Bush's transformational objectives. While some Bush administration apologists try to trace the causes of the 2011 Tunisian, Egyptian, and other Arab revolutions to American policies in Iraq, such arguments are not convincing and are denied by the primary Arab participants. While it is still too early for a definitive historical judgment on the Iraq War, what is clear at this point is that the twenty-first century opened with a crisis that led to a very costly transformational policy.

Despite the shared genes, the policy of George W. Bush could not have been more different from that of his father. Members of the younger Bush's administration often compared him to Ronald Reagan or Harry Truman. But the twentieth-century president he most resembled was Woodrow Wilson. There are uncanny similarities between Wilson and George W. Bush. Both were highly religious and moralistic men who were elected with less than a majority of the popular vote, and initially focused on domestic issues without any vision of foreign policy. Both were initially successful with their transformational domestic agendas in the Congress. Both tended to portray the world in black and white rather than shades of gray. Both projected self-confidence, responded to a crisis with a bold vision, and stuck to it.

Although George W. Bush possessed a master's degree in business administration, he displayed some of the same organizational deficiencies as Wilson in managing the government and sorting out the conflicting information he received in making his decisions. Again this was in contrast to the successful management style of his father. But strength of character is not an adequate substitute for organizational competence (that which Bush's father possessed). Information flows were limited. The younger Bush was decisive and persistent, but like Wilson not very receptive to new information once his mind was made up.

Though Wilson started as an idealist and Bush as a realist, both wound up stressing the promotion of democracy and freedom in the rest of the world as their transformative vision. And both defined visions that had a large gap between expressed ideals and national capacities. Many of Bush's speeches, particularly his second inaugural address about a freedom agenda, sounded like they could have been uttered by Wilson, though Wilson was the better rhetorician. Fortunately for Bush, there were also important differences between the two men. Bush had an emotional intelligence and self-mastery that failed Wilson at crucial moments. He was also more personable, whereas Wilson was often stiff and aloof.

Both Wilson and Bush tried to educate the public to accept their transformational visions. But good teachers need to be good learners, and Bush's impatience hindered his learning. The impatient temperament also contributed to the organizational process Bush put in place that discouraged learning. In his second term, Bush made some efforts to change the debate on Iraq by publicly acknowledging new facts, and he successfully pressed for a surge of additional troops in 2006 that helped to prevent a total defeat. Wilson succeeded initially in educating a majority of the American people about his League of Nations, but he failed because he refused to make compromises with the Senate. Similarly, Bush was initially able to persuade the American people of his proposed transformation of American strategy, and he was reelected in 2004, but he lost support (and the Congress) by 2006. The comparison illustrates that the prospects for transformational leadership in foreign policy are greatest in the context of a crisis, because people see the need for change and the potential costs of not doing so. But even then, success requires a combination of soft power skills to attract people at home and abroad with a feasible vision and hard organizational and political skills to implement the vision. Presidents like Franklin Roosevelt and Harry Truman had the combination. Woodrow Wilson did not. Similarly, George W. Bush articulated transformational objectives, but did not develop a successful strategy to accomplish them.

THE COMPLEXITY OF CONTEXT

As I said earlier, there is little evidence to support the general assumptions of leadership theory and public discourse that transformational foreign policy leaders are better in either ethics or effectiveness. For one thing, the concept of transformational leadership is too ambiguously defined to be useful unless it is more carefully specified. But even with objectives distinguished from style, the evidence does not support the view that leaders with transformational objectives or inspirational style are better. Other leadership skills outlined in my book *The Powers to Lead* are more important than the usual distinction between transformational and transactional leaders. Here it is useful to compare Woodrow Wilson with the first Bush. In the long term, Wilson's vision was partially vindicated, but he lacked the leadership skills needed for its execution and implementation in his own time. With Bush 41, the *vision thing* and his educational impact were very limited, but his execution and management were very good. Perhaps the facetious moral of the story is that at some mythical day in the future, genetic engineering will be able to produce leaders equally endowed with both sets of skills. Comparing the two Bushes, who shared half their genes, makes it is clear that nature has not yet solved the problem. This is not an argument against transformational leaders. Nor is this an argument against transformational leaders in foreign policy. But in judging leaders we need to pay attention to both acts of omission and acts of commission, both things that happened and things that did not happen, dogs that barked and those that did not.

A big problem in foreign policy is the complexity of the context. We live in a world of diverse cultures and still know very little about social engineering and how to *build nations*. When we cannot be sure how to improve the world, prudence becomes an important virtue, and hubristic visions can pose a grave danger. In foreign policy as in medicine, it is important to remember the Hippocratic oath: First, do no harm. For these reasons, the virtues of transactional leaders with good contextual intelligence are very important. A Bush 41 without the ability to articulate a vision but who is able to steer successfully through crises turns out to be a better leader than a Bush 43 with a powerful vision but little contextual intelligence. In trying to explain the role of secretary of state, George Shultz once compared it to gardening: "the constant nurturing of a complex array of actors, interests and goals." But Derek Chollet points out that Shultz's Stanford colleague Condoleezza Rice wanted a more transformational diplomacy "not accepting the world as it is, but trying to change it. Rice's ambition is not just to be a gardener—she wants to be a landscape architect."[20]

There is a role for both, depending on the context, but we should avoid the common mistake of automatically thinking that the transformational landscape architect is a better foreign policy leader—in terms of both effectiveness and ethics—than the careful gardener. For leaders, prudence is often the key virtue necessary for good foreign policy.

NOTES

1. Charles Guthrie and Michael Quinlan, *Just War: The Just War Tradition: Ethics in Modern Warfare* (New York: Walker & Company, 2007), 1.

2. Joseph Nye, Jr., *Soft Power* (New York: Public Affairs, 2004).

3. Max Weber, "Politics as a Vocation," *Max Weber: Essays in Sociology*, edited by H. H. Gerth and C. Wright Mills (New York, NY: Oxford University Press, 1958), 126.

4. See Immanuel Kant, translated by Robert Paul Wolff, *Foundations of the Metaphysics of Morals* (Indianapolis: Bobbs-Merrill, 1969); John Stuart Mill, *Utilitarianism* (Indianapolis: Bobbs-Merrill, 1957).

5. Kenneth Winston, "Necessity and Choice in Political Ethics: Varieties of Dirty Hands," *Political Ethics and Social Responsibility*, edited by Daniel E. Weuste (Lanham, MD: Rowman and Littlefeld, 1994).

6. Isaiah Berlin, *Liberty: Incorporating Four Essays on Liberty* (New York: Oxford University Press, 2002), 214.

7. John Rawls, "Distributive Justice," *Philosophy, Politics, and Society*, edited by Peter Laslett and W. G. Runciman (London: Blackwell; New York: Barnes & Noble, 1967), 58–82.

8. Amartya Sen, *The Idea of Justice* (Cambridge, MA: Belknap Press, 2011), 12–13.

9. Stanley Milgram, "Obedience to Authority," *Journal of Abnormal and Social Psychology* 67, no. 4 (October 1963): 371–78.

10. See Philip Zimbardo, *The Lucifer Effect: Understanding How Good People Turn Evil* (New York: Random House, 2007).

11. Thucydides, translated by Rex Warner, *History of the Peloponnesian War* (New York: Penguin Classics, 1954), 81.

12. Barbara Kellerman, *Bad Leadership* (Boston: Harvard Business School Press, 2004).

13. Arnold Wolfers, *Discord and Collaboration: Essays on International Politics* (Baltimore: Johns Hopkins University Press, 1962), 50.

14. John Rawls, *A Theory of Justice* (Cambridge, MA: Harvard University Press, 1971).

15. *The Economist*, "The Man Who Beat Communism" and "The Reagan Legacy," June 24, 2004, 13, 24–25.

16. David Gergen, *Eyewitness to Power* (New York: Touchtone, 2000), 154.

17. Nicholas Burns, "Our Best Foreign Policy President," *Boston Globe*, December 9, 2011, A.1.

18. George H. W. Bush and Brent Scowcroft, *A World Transformed* (New York: Vintage Books, 1998), xiii.

19. John L. Gaddis, *Surprise, Security and the American Experience* (Cambridge, MA: Harvard University Press, 2004), 93.

20. Derek Chollet, "Altered State: Rice Aims to Put Foggy Bottom Back on the Map," *Washington Post*, April 7, 2005, B.1.

Index

About the Editor and Contributors

JOANNE B. CIULLA is Coston Family Chair in Leadership and Ethics at the Jepson School of Leadership Studies, University of Richmond, where she is one of the founders of the school. She is a visiting professor at Nyenrode Universiteit. Ciulla has held the UNESCO Chair in Leadership Studies at the United Nations International Leadership Academy and academic appointments at La Salle University, the Harvard Business School, and The Wharton School. A PhD in philosophy, some of her publications include *The Working Life: The Promise and Betrayal of Modern Work*, *The Ethics of Leadership*, *Leadership at the Crossroads*, *Honest Work: A Business Ethics Reader*, and *Leadership Ethics*. Ciulla is on the editorial boards of *The Leadership Quarterly*, *The Business Ethics Quarterly*, *Leadership and the Humanities*, and *Leadership*. She is the president of the International Society for Business, Economics, and Ethics.

AL GINI is Professor of Business Ethics and Chair of the Department of Management in the Quinlan School of Business at Loyola University Chicago. He is also the co-founder and long-time Associate Editor of *Business Ethics Quarterly*, the journal of the Society for Business Ethics. For over 27 years he has been the Resident Philosopher on National

Public Radio's Chicago affiliate, WBEZ-FM. His books include *My Job My Self: Work and the Creation of the Modern Individual* (Routledge, 2000), *The Importance of Being Lazy: In Praise of Play, Leisure and Vacations* (Routledge, 2003), *Why It's Hard to Be Good* (Routledge, 2006), *Seeking the Truth of Things* (ACTA, 2010), *The Ethics of Business* with Alexei Marcoux (Rowan & Littlefield, 2012), and *10 Virtues of Outstanding Leaders* (Wiley & Blackwell, 2013).

RONALD M. GREEN is Professor for the Study of Ethics and Human Values, Dartmouth College. A member of Dartmouth's Religion Department since 1969, Professor Green served from 1992 to 2011 as the director of Dartmouth's Ethics Institute. He is a *summa cum laude* graduate of Brown University and received his PhD in religious ethics from Harvard in 1973. In 1996 and 1997, Professor Green served as Director of the Office of Genome Ethics at the National Institutes of Health. He is the author of eight books and co-author or editor of four, and has published over 150 articles in theoretical and applied ethics. In 2005, he was named a Guggenheim Fellow. His most recent book is *10 Virtues of Outstanding Leaders: Leadership and Character*, co-authored with Al Gini.

EDWIN P. HOLLANDER, CUNY Distinguished Professor of Psychology at Baruch College and the Graduate Center since 1989, is now Emeritus. He has written three books on leadership and three on social psychology, and taught at Carnegie-Mellon (CMU), Washington (St. Louis), American (DC), and SUNY-Buffalo, once Provost of Social Sciences there. A visiting professor at Istanbul, Wisconsin, Oxford, and Harvard, he began studying leadership in 1951 as a Naval Aviation Psychologist at Pensacola, applying psychometrics and social psychology to research on aviation cadets. With this, he earned his PhD at Columbia in 1952, on active duty, and then joined CMU's faculty in 1954.

MICHAEL KEELEY was Chairperson and Professor of Management at Loyola University of Chicago prior to his retirement. He has degrees in engineering and business, and a PhD in Organization Behavior from Northwestern University. He is the author of *A Social-Contract Theory of Organizations, Labor Supply and Public Policy, Population, Public Policy, and Economic Development* as well as numerous articles in management and applied philosophy journals.

NANNERL O. KEOHANE is Senior Scholar at Princeton University. She served as the president and professor of political science at Wellesley College and then Duke University. Her publications include *Thinking about Leadership, Higher Ground: Ethics and Leadership in the Modern University, Philosophy and the State in France: The Renaissance to the Enlightenment,* and *Feminist Theory: A Critique of Ideology.* Professor Keohane has taught at Swarthmore College, the University of Pennsylvania, and Stanford University, as well as at Wellesley, Duke, and Princeton. She is a member of the Harvard Corporation, the Board of Trustees of the Doris Duke Charitable Foundation, the Social Science Research Council advisory committee, and the Board of Directors of the American Academy of Arts and Sciences. She received her BA at Wellesley College; MA from St. Anne's College, Oxford (as a Marshall Scholar, class of 1961); and PhD on a Sterling Fellowship from Yale University.

JOSEPH S. NYE, JR., is University Distinguished Service Professor and former Dean of Harvard's Kennedy School of Government. He received his bachelor's degree *summa cum laude* from Princeton University, won a Rhodes Scholarship to Oxford, and earned a PhD in political science from Harvard. He has served as Assistant Secretary of Defense for International Security Affairs, Chair of the National Intelligence Council, and Deputy Under Secretary of State. His most recent books include *Soft Power, The Powers to Lead,* and *The Future of Power.* He is a fellow of the American Academy of Arts and Sciences, the British Academy, and the American Academy of Diplomacy. In a recent survey of international relations scholars, he was ranked as the most influential scholar on American foreign policy, and in 2011, *Foreign Policy* named him one of the top 100 Global Thinkers.

TERRY L. PRICE is Professor and Senior Associate Dean for Academic Affairs at the Jepson School of Leadership Studies at the University of Richmond, Virginia. He currently serves on the editorial board of *Leadership Quarterly* and the *Journal of Business Ethics,* as well as a series editor of *Jepson Studies in Leadership.* Price is co-editor of *The International Library of Leadership, The Quest for Moral Leaders, The Values of Presidential Leadership,* and *Executive Power in Theory and Practice.* He is the author of *Understanding Ethical Failures in Leadership* and *Leadership Ethics: An Introduction,* both published by the Cambridge University Press.

ROBERT C. SOLOMON is Quincy Lee Centennial Professor of Business and Philosophy and Distinguished Teaching Professor at the University of Texas at Austin. He is the author of over 37 books, including *Above the Bottom Line, It's Good Business, Ethics and Excellence,* and *New World of Business,* as well as *The Passions, In the Spirit of Hegel, About Love, A Passion for Justice, Up the University, A Short History of Philosophy, The Joy of Philosophy,* and *Building Trust* with Chilean Senator Fernando Flores.